CLASSIC BAPTISM

ΒΑΠΤΙΖΩ

CLASSIC BAPTISM

ΒΑΠΤΙΖΩ

AN INQUIRY INTO THE MEANING OF THE WORD AS DETERMINED BY THE USAGE OF CLASSICAL GREEK WRITERS

BY

James W. Dale

NEW FOREWORD BY

Jay E. Adams

NEW INTRODUCTION BY

Robert H. Countess

Bolchazy–Carducci Publishers
and
Presbyterian and Reformed Publishing Co.

Cover by:
Cynthia Henderson

Reprint of
1867 Edition, Boston, Draper & Halliday

©Copyright 1989
Robert H. Countess, Introduction
Jay E. Adams, Foreword

Published by:

BOLCHAZY–CARDUCCI	PRESBYTERIAN & REFORMED
PUBLISHERS	PUBLISHING CO.
1000 Brown St.	Box 817
Wauconda, IL 60084	Phillipsburg, NJ 08865
ISBN 0-86516-224-7	ISBN 0-87552-230-0

Printed in the United States of America
Library of Congress Catalog Number
88-92850

Library of Congress Cataloging-in-Publication Data

Dale, James W. (James Wilkinson), 1812–1881.
   Classic baptism : baptizō : an inquiry into the meaning of the word as
determined by the usage of classical Greek writers / by James W. Dale : new
foreword by Jay E. Adams : new introduction by Robert H. Countess.
374 p.   15.25 x 23 cm.
   Reprint : Originally published : Boston : Draper & Halliday, 1867.
   ISBN 0-86516-224-7 : $25.00
   1. Baptism. 2. Baptizein (The Greek word) I. Title. II. Title:
Baptizō.
BV811.D3   1989   89-6959
234'. 161—dc20   CIP

Foreword

No other work on baptism begins to approximate James Wilkinson Dale's four-volume set: *Classic Baptism*, *Judaic Baptism*, *Johannic Baptism*, and *Christic and Patristic Baptism*. Four comprehensive volumes on the use of the word βαπτίζω—think of it!

Sometimes the work of the Baptist T. J. Conant is presented as a *tour de force* by those who do not know better. But Dale utterly destroys every one of Conant's arguments. Indeed, Conant's work pales in significance when contrasted with the deep scholarship of this Presbyterian pastor. There is nothing like Dale's work in all of Christian literature—four volumes on the use of one word!

In his comprehensive treatise on βαπτίζω, Dale examines every occurrence of the word in the Bible and all of the extra-biblical examples that were known in his day. His analyses of the uses of βαπτίζω demonstrate beyond reasonable doubt that the word does not mean "immersion," contrary to the views of Conant and others. Dale shows that βάπτω means "to dip" (i.e., "to put into and to remove from") but that βαπτίζω means "to put together so as to remain together."

Dale's understanding of βαπτίζω has significant theological implications. According to Paul, Christians have been "baptized into one body" by God's Spirit (1 Cor. 12:13). Christians are not *dipped* into the body and removed; they are permanently *united* with it. Elsewhere, Paul says that all the Israelites were "baptized" into Moses, the cloud, and the sea (1 Cor. 10:2). The Israelites were *united* with Moses in these events. Water baptism is the outer ritual that refers to the inner reality of Spirit baptism. Thus water baptism is an appropriate "uniting ordinance" that permanently intro-

1

duces Christians to the visible Church, just as Spirit baptism permanently unites Christians with the invisible Church.

I do not want to elaborate on the many themes that Dale treats so convincingly. Let me simply say "Hurrah!" for the reappearance of this work, which is being republished thanks to the persistence of Dr. Robert Countess.

I congratulate you on your wise purchase of this volume and hope that it will not be long before the remaining volumes will be available once again.

Jay E. Adams
Director of Advanced Studies
Westminster Theological Seminary
Escondido, California
February 1989

Introduction

Robert H. Countess

Dale's monumental four-volume work on βαπτίζω is a masterpiece of lexicographical scholarship. Although written in part as a response to mid-nineteenth century dogmatism, Dale's conclusions are directed neither at Baptists nor at Presbyterians but should be of interest to both. For according to Dale, the literal and metaphorical senses of βαπτίζω refer to general, not specific, actions. Thus it is as incorrect for Presbyterians to assert that βαπτίζω means "sprinkle" or "pour" as it is for Baptists to assert that it means "immerse" or "dip."

Dale appealed for a contextual understanding of the meaning of βαπτίζω. He insisted that churches should ground their teachings about the mode of Christian baptism on specific biblical passages and their contexts, not on the alleged meaning of a single term. Thus Baptists might appeal to Romans 6:1-9 and argue that immersion symbolizes the full significance of Jesus' death, burial, and resurrection. Presbyterians, Methodists, Catholics, and Episcopalians might appeal to Acts 2:16-18, 38 and argue that pouring symbolizes the outpouring of the Holy Spirit. Similarly, one might appeal to Hebrews 9–10 to support sprinkling. Dale left the issue of paedobaptism to students of biblical and systematic theology.[1] Thus Dale's views should help Christians "agree to disagree" about

---

1. In keeping with his covenant theology, Dale baptized children of believing parents.

3

the mode of baptism and to avoid the opprobrium that frequently has colored this discussion.

REASONS FOR REPRINTING DALE'S WORK

There are eight reasons for reprinting Dale's work, which has been out of print for decades.

(1) *Classic Baptism* is a scholarly work that contains all the references to βαπτίζω in classical Greek literature that were known in Dale's day. The remaining three volumes strove for the same goal of completeness.

(2) *Classic Baptism* provides the context for each use of βαπτίζω, and this helps us understand how various writers used the word.

(3) Dale argued that dictionaries show how words *are* used, not how they *should be* used. Lexicons are the descriptive results of lexicographical investigation and interpretation, not normative authorities for usage.

(4) Dale had a firm grasp of what has come to be called lexical semantics, though he wrote before the "neogrammarians" of the 1870s.[2] Dale understood the difference between diachrony (the change in the meaning of a word over time) and synchrony (the meaning of a word during a given period). Additionally, Dale distinguished between the intent of the author and the understanding of the audience. All of this has enormous import for understanding the meanings of βάπτω and βαπτίζω.

(5) Dale interacted with Alexander Carson's *Baptism: Its Mode and Its Subjects,* a work by a capable Irish Baptist that still is widely regarded as *the* authoritative treatise on this topic. Even those who agree with Carson concerning the mode of baptism have not added appreciably to his conclusions.

---

2. E.g., Ferdinand de Saussure. *Classic Baptism* was published in 1867, after twenty years of investigation.

(6) In Dale's day, *Classic Baptism* and the succeeding volumes in the series received the sort of favorable scholarly reviews that justified his twenty-year study. Those who have ridiculed Dale's work often have done so out of ignorance or because of an inability or unwillingness to lay aside their dogmatism.

(7) Because it focuses on lexical issues, Dale's work can facilitate the peaceful discussion of what often is a controversial topic.

(8) Dale's work can stimulate interest in the Greek language and in classical Greek literature. The recent resurgence of Latin and Greek studies cannot help but profit from this reprint of *Classic Baptism*.

BIOGRAPHICAL SKETCH OF JAMES WILKINSON DALE

In 1886 the Rev. James Roberts, D.D., circulated a private biography of Dale.[3] According to Roberts:

> Not long after Dr. Dale's death, a warm friend and former parishioner of his, with the sanction of the family of the deceased, requested the writer to prepare a suitable Memorial of his life and labors. . . .
> In the prosecution of the work, the conspicuous absence of such material as usually falls in the hands of a biographer soon became apparent. Marked and influential as the life had been, the written records from which to construct an adequate Memorial are almost wholly lacking. No diary was kept. No memoranda of personal experience remained. Only occasional dates of events, and a few letters to his family and friends, had been casually preserved. Dr. Dale was a very reticent man and seldom spoke of himself or his personal affairs, except to his most intimate friends, and even to them with a lingering flavor of reserve. For instance, he carried on his remarkable researches on the subject of Baptism, by day and by night, for twenty long years, without ever saying to a human being that he was

3. James Roberts, *A Memorial of the Rev. James W. Dale, D. D.* (Philadelphia: Watson and McManus, 1886).

making a book, until he had gone over the whole ground of the Inquiry, and his first volume was ready for the press.[4]

Dale was born in what is now Odessa, Delaware, on October 16, 1812, and he died on April 19, 1881, at Media, Pennsylvania. On his father's side, Dale's ancestors were English Episcopalians who settled in Maryland. Dale's father, Dr. Richard C. Dale, served as a surgeon during the War of 1812 under a General Wilkinson, for whom James Wilkinson Dale was named. On his mother's side, Dale's forebears were Roman Catholics who lived in Philadelphia.

Dale became a Christian during his second year at the University of Pennsylvania and joined the Arch Street Presbyterian Church. At age nineteen he graduated with an A.B. degree from the university as the valedictorian of his class. Later he received the A.M. and M.D. degrees from the University of Pennsylvania. To prepare for the ministry, Dale enrolled at the theological seminary in Andover, Massachusetts, spent his second year at Princeton Seminary, and returned to Andover to complete his course of studies. Dale was ordained as an Evangelist by the Andover Congregational Association of Massachusetts on August 29, 1837.

Dale studied medicine and the Rajpoot language in order to serve as a missionary in India, though he was not sent out by the Presbyterian board because he lacked a missionary companion. As a result of his study of law, medicine, and theology, Dale became quite adept at Greek, Latin, Hebrew, German, and French. His medical thesis, "The Connection Between Medical Science and Revealed Religion," was printed by the medical faculty of the University of Pennsylvania.

Dale spent seven years representing the Philadelphia Bible Society and in this capacity traveled to all the cities and principal towns of Pennsylvania, as well as throughout much of Delaware and Maryland. In 1844 Dale married Mary Goldsborough Gray. During the course of their marriage, they had six children. In 1846 Dale was installed in the pastorates of two struggling Presbyterian churches in Ridley and Middletown, Pennsylvania,[5] whose mem-

4. Ibid., iii.
5. Both of these towns are in Delaware County.

bers were scattered over one hundred square miles. By 1855 Dale
had helped to erect a building for the Media Presbyterian Church.
His third pastorate was in Wayne, Pennsylvania, a prominent Philadelphia suburb. Because of his wife's long illness, Dale commuted
to Wayne from his home in Media. In 1876 Dale was stricken with
a softening of the brain, a disease that finally took his life several
years later. After his diagnosis, Dale resigned from the church at
Wayne and sought to improve his health at Clifton Springs, New
York.

Sometime around 1847, the year after his installation in the
Delaware County pastorates, Dale began to study the sources for
βαπτίζω. At this time he may have had Baptist tendencies regarding
the mode of baptism.[6] Dale wrote his brother, Dr. Thomas F. Dale,
who was traveling to Paris, to solicit his help in securing the rele-
vant works on baptism.

> My special object is to investigate a theological question which
> turns on certain points of usage in the Greek language. The Greek
> of the New Testament is, I think, very explicit; but some think that
> "the Fathers" are opposed to the interpretation derived from the
> New Testament usage and would, hence, throw doubt on such in-
> terpretation. My impression is that there will be found an agree-
> ment between the New Testament and patristic usage, on a proper
> examination. This can only be made by an extended search through
> the Greek writers of the first centuries. I think that the result will
> vindicate the expense and labor; besides there will be great inciden-
> tal advantage in the study of these earliest writers upon the great
> themes of Christianity. I have, therefore, concluded to order the set
> of the Greek Fathers as they stand in the catalogue for the first four
> centuries; and to select some of the Latin Fathers.[7]

Roberts describes how Dale delighted in the sixty-five volumes
of the Greek Fathers and in the thirty-six volumes of the Latin Fathers. "Sometimes he would tell his wife, in the morning, that if it
could possibly be avoided, he would rather not be disturbed all day,
no, not so much as to eat." There were times when he studied all

6. Ibid., 84n.
7. Ibid., 86.

night long,[8] as gradually over a period of twenty years he compiled the data for his books.

In the spring of 1862, as a student on vacation from college,[9] Roberts spent a few hours socializing with Dale in his study. When Dale learned of Roberts' enthusiasm for Professor F. A. March—a highly regarded comparative philologist at Lafayette—Dale said:[10]

> I wish that I could get Professor March to read a book for me. I have a book. There, you are the first and only person to whom I have ever said that I had a book. It is a book on Baptism. For years I have worked away at the subject, without consulting anybody with regard to my labors or their results, except the works of the authors which I have read and studied. I am now at a point where I feel that I need counsel. A part of my labor is now ready for the printer, if what I have written is at all worth printing. I think that there is something in my book, and that I have reached results in a way that will prove valuable to the cause of truth; but I cannot tell how much my work and the conclusions which I have reached will impress other minds. My own mind is perfectly clear as to the correctness of the result and the scientific accuracy of the method by which it has been reached; but I want someone to read the book who is competent to do so, and who will give to me his honest opinion in regard to its merits. *It is not the opinion of a theologian that I want just now.* [Emphasis added by editor.] I want the judgment of a linguist and philologist. From what you say of Professor March, I believe that he is just the man to read it. He seems to have all the essential qualifications. That part of the book about which I am most concerned is in his line. *Then he has never seen me and knows nothing about me, so that he is not likely to be prejudiced in favor of my book by any feelings of personal friendship.* [Emphasis added.][11]

Roberts took Dale's manuscript to Dr. March, who read it, and then returned it to Dale with March's response: "It is the most elaborate discussion of a single word that I have ever seen. . . . It is full of subtle analysis; but it is all so perspicuous and earnest that it

---

8. As did John Calvin as a student.
9. Perhaps Lafayette College, in Easton, Penn.
10. The following quotation is Roberts' reconstruction of Dale's remarks.
11. Ibid., 87–88.

holds the attention throughout." Dr. March expressed his desire that the manuscript would soon be published. [12]

Roberts also mentions the lexicographer J. H. Thayer, another contemporary of Dale's. Thayer's unrestrained praise for *Classic Baptism* seems anomalous when compared with his entry under βαπτίζω in his *Greek-English Lexicon of the New Testament* (Grand Rapids: Zondervan Publishing House, 1962). On page 423 of *Johannic Baptism* (Dale's third volume), Thayer is quoted as saying:

> If I were to utter my first impressions, I should break out in unfeigned admiration. That one, occupied with the ordinary duties of the pastorate, should have the leisure, patience, and mental energy for an inquiry seldom surpassed as respects thorough research, is to me a marvel. I can give emphatic testimony to the analytic power and acuteness which the treatise exhibits, as well as to its marked perspicuity and directness of statement.... The theory that βαπτίζω expresses a definite act—"mode and nothing but mode"—is shown to be pitiably helpless when applied to "all Greek literature."

Curiously, however, on page 94 of his lexicon Thayer defined βαπτίζω as "I. 1. to dip repeatedly, to immerge and submerge" etc. Thayer appears to have equated βάπτω with βαπτίζω in the generally confused manner that goes back at least as far as Calvin, if not farther. [13]

Two schools—Hampden Sidney College and the University of Pennsylvania—recognized Dale's publications by awarding him the degree of Doctor of Divinity. Dale did not profit financially from his books, whose publication was underwritten by his generous brother-in-law, Gustavus S. Benson. According to Roberts, Dale wrote a popular volume that incorporated the highly technical content of *Classic Baptism*. [14]

---

12. Ibid., 89.

13. Thayer's lexicon appeared in or about 1885 and was revised in 1889. His remarks about Dale's *Classic Baptism* appeared in 1871. There was ample time and opportunity to incorporate his understanding of Dale's analysis in his lexicon.

14. Roberts, 94, 100. I have not been able to learn if this manuscript is in the archives of the Presbyterian Historical Society in Philadelphia.

After Dale's death, numerous printed citations in the Media Presbyterian Church and many monuments in the Middletown cemetery honored his memory.[15]

DALE'S METHOD

Dale described the prevailing understanding of βαπτίζω as "dogmatic" and those who held it as "dogmatists." In his writings he refers to their position as "the theory." According to "the theory," βαπτίζω has a single, univocal meaning. It signifies one particular act. In *Classic Baptism*, Dale explained what different authorities had declared this univocal meaning to be. Dale also examined and explained the various ways βαπτίζω is used by the ancient writers.

First, Dale cited Roger Williams, A. Barber, A. Booth, Dr. Gale, Alexander Carson, Fuller, Dagg, Stovel, and Jewett, all of whom held to a univocal understanding of βαπτίζω. According to Dale, their position can be described as follows.

(1) Βαπτίζω, through all Greek literature, has but one meaning; which meaning is definite, clear, precise, and easy of translation.
(2) Βαπτίζω and βάπτω have precisely the same meaning, dyeing excepted, and, in all respects, whether as to form or force, or effect, they differ nothing.
(3) Βαπτίζω expresses an act, a definite act; mode, and nothing but mode—to dip. Βάπτω primarily expresses an act, a definite act; mode, and nothing but mode—to dip.
(4) Βαπτίζω has the same meaning in figurative as in literal use, always referring to the act of dipping.[16]

A casual reading of the works of the "dogmatists" may not reveal any contradictions among them. Conant, however, listed seven meanings for βαπτίζω—"immerse," "im-merge," "submerge," "dip," "plunge," "whelm," and "im-bathe." This broad and diverse definition indicates disagreement with other "dogmatists" and is an equivocal, not univocal, way of defining

15. Ibid., 133–35.
16. *Classic Baptism*, v.

βαπτίζω. If βαπτίζω has seven meanings, what is the *one* act to which it always refers? What has happened to "the theory"?

There were further disagreements among the "dogmatists." Cox, Morell, and Fuller argued that "immersion may be by pouring," and according to Conant, βαπτίζω refers to a condition that is the result of an act, not to an act itself. The earlier, precise definition of βαπτίζω as "dip" had given way to the more ambiguous "immerse." Dale examined the evolution of the "dogmatic" definition of βαπτίζω and the appropriateness of translating a non-compound source word by an English compound word, which would be the equivalent of accepting "develop" and "over-develop" as English synonyms. (*A Greek-English Lexicon*[17] lists ἀνα-, ἐπι-, κατα-, and παρα- as compounds of βαπτίζω.)

Second, in his "Inquiry Entered Upon Independently" Dale wrote:

> If this is to be done with any degree of thoroughness, it will require patience to traverse the whole ground, knowledge of well-settled principles of interpretation, candor and competency in their just application, and common sense to know that a universal conclusion cannot, safely, rest on a single particular, nor on many, but only upon what remains after a matured consideration of the action and reaction of all cases of usage upon each other.

Additionally, Dale argued that the "closely related, yet essentially different word . . . βάπτω" and the Latin words *mergo* and *tingo* and the English words *immerse* and *dip* should be examined.[18]

Figure 1 illustrates the results of Dale's investigations of types of verbs, actions, and resultant conditions.

---

17. Henry George Liddell and Robert Scott, *A Greek-English Lexicon*, rev. ed. (Oxford: Clarendon Press, 1940).
18. Dale, 104.

FIGURE ONE

GREEK	ENGLISH	MODE: KIND OF VERB	ACTION: SPEED DURATION	ACTION: DURATION	RESULTANT CONDITION
Baptō[1] [βάπτω]	dip	Very specific	May range from the gradual and the gentle to the very fast	Momentary	Probably some degree of cleanliness
Baptō[2] [βάπτω]	dye	Specific at first; then dependent on context	Originally by dipping; eventually by staining, sprinkling, pouring, soaking (which is an immersed condition and thus not a dipping)	Momentary to some long continuance	Different color
Baptizō[1] [βαπτίζω]	merse[lit.]	Non-specific (but a physical envelopment of a subject or object)	Gradual to violent (and of a destructive nature)	Continuance (but depends on the context)	Literally, a destructive resultant condition (as in "death by drowning" is an example of Baptizō[1])

Subdivisions of B.[1]

1. With influence: Example: "We all, therefore, changed our position to the higher parts of the ship, so that we might raise up the *baptized* part of the ship." (Achilles Tatius, iii, 1.)
ὅπως τὸ μὲν βαπτιζόμενον τῆς νηὸς ἀνακουφίσαιμεν

2. Without influence: Example: "Alexander, falling upon the stormy season, and trusting, commonly, to fortune, pressed on before the flood went out, and through the entire day the army marched *baptized* up to the waist." (Strabo, xiv, 3, 9.)
μέχρι ὀμφαλοῦ βαπτιζομένον

3. For the express purpose of influence: Example: "And the dolphin, displeased at such a falsehood, *baptizing*, killed him." (Aesop)
βαπτίζων αὐτὸν ἀπέκτεινεν

(Resultant condition for the above subdivisions: Various shades of literally destructive result)

English examples of Greek verb forms: drowning, destroying, ruining, plunging, sinking (=submerging), intoxicating, stupefying (=narcotizing)

GREEK	ENGLISH	MODE: KIND OF VERB	ACTION: SPEED DURATION	ACTION: DURATION	RESULTANT CONDITION
Baptizō[2] [βαπτίζω]	merse[fig.]	Non-specific (fig./metaphorical envelopment of subject/object)	Not noted or not relevant	Continuance (but dependent on context)	Continuance in the "element" *into* (eis) which one is said to have been baptized.

The following figure shows how βάπτω may have evolved into βαπτίζω. Readers may add synchronous and diachronous information as their study of βάπτω and βαπτίζω progresses.

FIGURE TWO: LINEAGE OF βαπτίζω

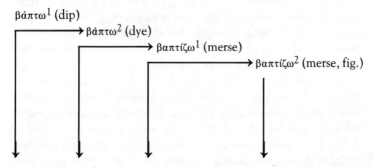

βάπτω[1] (dip)

→ βάπτω[2] (dye)

→ βαπτίζω[1] (merse)

→ βαπτίζω[2] (merse, fig.)

(The horizontal line represents diachronic movement and the vertical the synchronous.)

The meanings of βάπτω and βαπτίζω[1] may have developed in this manner. Initially, βάπτω[1] simply meant "dip." Then it came to refer to *dyeing* by dipping, which led to the meaning "dye" (βάπτω[2]). Over time, as items were dyed in one or more ways, βάπτω[2] came to mean "stain." At this point in its evolution, βάπτω[2] had lost all reference to dipping and simply referred to any mode that was required to change an object's color.

Βαπτίζω[1] grew out of βάπτω[2]. The suffix -ιζω introduced a causative notion to βάπτω[2], so that βάπτ+ιζω refers to that which literally could cause a thoroughly changed condition. Thus βαπτίζω[1] (which at first meant "merse," according to Dale) refers to an object's thoroughly changed condition that has been brought about by the object being introduced into some new circumstance.[19] At this point in its development, βαπτίζω[1] referred to placing an object in any fluid that could change the object's condition (without respect to time). After the object's condition has been changed, the enveloping fluid has no further power to effect additional change

---

19. Βαπτίζω[1] never means "dye" and so never refers to a dyed condition.

on the object. [20] In antiquity there were many liquids (e.g., vinegar, oil, melted wax, and milk) that lacked the ability to *color* objects but that could impart characteristics to objects that were placed in them. Other fluids, such as wines and opiates, might not color an object but could nevertheless influence objects that were placed in them or into which they were placed (i.e., the human body).

Βάπτω[2] progressed from referring to dyeing-by-dipping to referring to dyeing-by-sprinkling, dyeing-by-pouring, and dyeing-by-beaming (of sun rays). Similarly, βαπτίζω[1] grew out of βάπτω[2] (not βάπτω[1]) and came to refer to many kinds of conditions that were brought about by a wide range of actions.

Βαπτίζω[2] developed from βαπτίζω[1] and was used to refer to Christian baptism as a baptism εἰς (into) the receiving element that could effect a thoroughly changed condition without regard to time. Thus to be baptized εἰς Χριστόν or εἰς τὸ ὄνομα τοῦ πατρὸς καὶ τοῦ υἱοῦ καὶ τοῦ ἁγίου πνεύματος takes on a distinctive significance. Neither dipping nor destructive immersion (as with βαπτίζω[1]) are in view.

If this reconstruction of the history and meanings of βάπτω and βαπτίζω accurately reflects Dale's work and the actual development of these words, then this more accurate understanding of these words may help to resolve the impasse over mode.

CONCLUSION

Forty different English verbs are used to translate the classical uses of βαπτίζω. Thus it is difficult not to agree with Dale's conclusion that Carson's dictum— "ΒΑΠΤΙΖΩ in the whole history of the Greek language has but one [meaning]. . . . It not only signifies to dip or immerse, but it never has any other meaning"[21]—is incorrect.

20. By analogy, *dip* refers to a momentary action, and the power of the fluid into which an object is dipped has only a moment to affect the object. This changed with *dye* by the time dipping was no longer the primary or only mode to accomplish a dyeing.

21. Alexander Carson, *Baptism, Its Mode and Its Subjects* (Evansville, Indiana: The National Foundation for Christian Education, 1969), 19.

In the writers he cites, Dale clearly demonstrates that βάπτω and βαπτίζω are not synonymous in their physical or figurative senses. He shows that the physical sense of βαπτίζω refers to that which is destructive for persons and for things. And he shows that the figurative, or metaphorical, use of βαπτίζω refers to a condition that results from baptism and to the cause of that condition, regardless of the way (i.e., mode) in which the condition is effected. This latter use of βαπτίζω (i.e., βαπτίζω[2]) will most interest those who are studying the theological and ecclesiastical aspects of Christian baptism.

Although Dale neither advocates nor assaults a particular mode of baptism, readers may find their dogmatisms challenged by *Classic Baptism*!

SYNOPSIS.

BAPTIST WRITERS.

THEIR VIEWS PRESENTED AND DIFFICULTIES SUGGESTED.

A. R., A. Barber, Booth, Carson, Conant, Cox, Confession of Faith, Curtis, Dagg, Fuller, Gale, Jewett, Morell, Ripley, Stovel, Roger Williams, Wayland.

GREEK WRITERS.

Using βάπτω.—Achilles Tatius, Ælian, Æsop, Æschylus, Antoninus, Aratus, Arrian, Aristophanes, Aristotle, Barker's Classical Recreations, Bentleii Epigr. Collect., Constantine, Dionysius, Euripides, Eustathius, Epictetus, Eupolis, Herodotus, Helladius, Hippocrates, Homer, Iamblichus, Julius Pollux, Lucian, Lycophron, Menander, Plato, Plutarch, Sophocles, Strabo, Suidas, Theocritus.

LATIN WRITERS.

Using Tingo.—Calpurnius, Celsus, Cicero, Horace, Juvenal, Martial, Ovid, Perseus, Pliny, Propertius, Seneca, Virgil.
Using Mergo.—Catullus, Curtius, Horace, Juvenal, Livy, Lucan, Lucretius, Martial, Ovid, Perseus, Plautus, Pliny, Quintillian, Seneca, Statius, Virgil, Valerius Flaccus.

ENGLISH WRITERS.

Using Dip and Immerse.—Booth, Bonheur, Chalmers, Sir A. Clarke, Coleridge, Cowper, Current Literature, Dryden, Col. Gardiner, Glover, Hanna, Judge Brackenridge, Kane, L'Es-

trange, Leyburn, Judge Kelley, Milton, Sir Thomas More,
Pope, Sir Walter Scott, Spenser, Mrs. Sherwood, Shakspeare,
Rev. Dr. Thornwell, Warburton, Young.

GREEK WRITERS.

Using βαπτίζω.—Achilles Tatius, Æsop, Alcibiades, Alciphron,
Alexander Aphrodisias, Archias, Aristotle, Arrian, Athenæus,
Chariton Aphrodisias, Conon, Demetrius, Demosthenes, Dio-
dorus Siculus, Dion Cassius, Epictetus, Eubulus, Evenus,
Heliodorus, Hippocrates, Heimerius, Homer, Julian. Egypt.,
Libanius, Lucian, Nicander, Orpheus, Pindar, Plato, Plotinus,
Plutarch, Polyænus, Polybius, Porphyry, Proclus, Strabo,
Suidas, Themistius.

OTHER WRITERS.

Addison, Bauer, Blair, Elizabeth Carter, De Wette, Ency-
clop. Americana, Prof. Ewing, President Halley, Houghton,
Rev. J. H. Orbison, Robinson, Prof. Stuart, Valla, Prof.
Wilson, Quintillian, Horne Tooke, Sir William Hamilton,
Chaucer, Fabian, Mortimer.

I.

COURSE OF INQUIRY.

INTRODUCTORY.

DISCUSSION has continued through centuries. Baptists claim to have reached demonstrated and absolute truth. Truth, unmixed with error, when presented, has power to compel conviction. If already discovered, no apology for rejecting or neglecting, and originating renewed inquiry. Obligation to examine and determine the value of Baptist results.

BAPTIST WRITERS.

Their principles. Their translations. Their practice.

BAPTIST POSTULATES.

1. *Βαπτίζω*, through all Greek literature, has but one meaning; which meaning is definite, clear, precise, and easy of translation.

2. *Βαπτίζω* and *βάπτω* have precisely the same meaning, dyeing excepted, and, in all other respects, whether as to form, or force, or effect, they differ nothing.

3. *Βαπτίζω* expresses an act, a definite act; mode, and nothing but mode,—*to dip*. *Βάπτω*, primary, expresses an act, a definite act; mode, and nothing but mode,—*to dip*.

4. *Βαπτίζω* has the same meaning in figurative as in literal use, always referring to the act of dipping.

COUNTER PROPOSITIONS.

1. *Βάπτω*, in primary use, expresses a definite act, characterized by various and essential limitations,—*to dip*.

(v)

2. *Βάπτω*, dip, in secondary use, expresses a limited force, with a correspondingly limited effect.

3. *Βαπτίζω*, in primary use, expresses condition, intusposition, without limitations.

4. *Βαπτίζω*, in secondary use, expresses condition effected by controlling influence, without limitation of intusposition, or otherwise.

MEANING OF THE WORD.

BAPTIST VIEWS EXPRESSED BY ROGER WILLIAMS AND "A. R.," A. BARBER, GALE, BOOTH, COX, CARSON, FULLER, DAGG, STOVEL, JEWETT.

Dip, Plunge, Immerse, used, at will, as convertible and equivalent terms. Is this true? Can it be tolerated in assigning a definite, critical, and controversial meaning to a word?

Booth says, No. "The substitution of these words for one another makes sentiment and practice ridiculous." *Dagg* says, No. And sharply discriminates between dip and immerse in a long list of definitions; after which he turns his pen and blots the distinction made. *Fuller* says, No. And by his negation makes a way of escape from difficulty; but soon denies his denial, in order to escape from equal difficulty on the other side.

IMMERSE, A REFUGE FROM THE DIFFICULTIES OF MODAL ACTION.

Modal action the *sine qua non,* heretofore, of the Baptist theory.

Dr. Fuller, A. R., Baptist Confession of Faith.

Doubt arising about "the definite act" theory. Parties among the Baptists.

1. Some affirm the theory absolutely (Carson). 2. Some doubt (Gale). 3. Some deny (Fuller). 4. Some *non liquet* (Conant).

Carson earnestly condemns Gale and Cox as abandoning the point at issue. Morell, dissatisfied with Carson's defence, frankly declares that he does give up the point. "Immersion may be by pouring" (Cox, Morell, Fuller).

Dr. Conant.

His labors great and valuable; but do not meet the severe demands of the Baptist system. Do not sustain modal meaning,—to dip, to plunge. Introduce submersion, condition. Affirms act of passing from one element into another. Seacoast baptism. No such act of passing in it. Carson says there is such act expressed. Gale and Fuller deny. The one contradicts common sense; the others contradict Baptist principles.

Dr. Conant's Definition: *Act* is made a vanishing quantity; *condition* is brought into high relief. Secondary or analogous meaning,—*state* of life. Cannot be founded on the form of an *act*.

Second Definition.—Seven defining words. Inconsistent with Baptist principles. Bound to define by a term of absolute unity. Carson acknowledges the obligation; attempts to meet it; and presents *dip*, and stumbles at the threshold against "*or.*" Conant rejects dip almost as utterly, as Carson maintains it exclusively. Makes it one of seven defining words, yet excludes it from more than six-sevenths of the cases. Objections to the seven defining words,—*to immerse, to im-merge, to sub-merge, to dip, to plunge, to whelm, to imbathe.* Form of act abandoned. Words compounded with prepositions should not, unnecessarily, translate uncompounded words. Never means dip. Confounded with βάπτω.

Metaphorical Use.—Not based on act, but condition. Wine-cup, perplexing questions, opiate drop, and such like, familiar agencies of baptism. If Dr. Conant will accept condition without " the image of the act," he will agree with us, and differ from Baptists.

Immerse as a Latin Derivative.

Growing disposition to use *immerse* as a shield against the difficulties of argument, while *dip* is held in reserve as a necessity for practice. No confession of past error.

Duplex Use.—1. The Latin preposition *in* expresses, sometimes movement, sometimes position. In im-mergo it expresses position and not movement. Under the plea of Latinism, movement is, erroneously, introduced, and the translation, to dip, to plunge, grounded on it, and applied to cases of baptism in which the object is moved.

2. Im-merse, in English, does not express movement; hence, in other cases of baptism, where no movement of the object takes place, and dip or plunge will not answer to the facts, this word can be slipped in.

Bury, and such like words, do not express movement. "Bury *into*" does not give power of movement to bury. The duplicity of use which characterizes Baptist usage in employing immerse must be guarded against.

FAILURE.

Baptist writers fail to show: 1. One clear, precise, definite, easily translatable meaning. 2. That βάπτω and βαπτίζω have the same meaning, form, and force. 3. That βαπτίζω expresses act, definite act, mode and nothing but mode—to dip. 4. That βαπτίζω, in secondary use, pictures the act of dipping. 5. That any English word daguerreotypes the Greek word.

ADMINISTRATION OF THE RITE.

How is the rite of baptism to be administered? Baptist Confession of Faith says: "Dipping or plunging the whole body." "Immersing the subject in water" (Booth). Candidate placed under the water (Ripley). "Immersing of the body in water" (Wayland). "Immersion or burial of the body in water" (Curtis). "Immersion of the subject in water is essential;" "commanded to perform the act represented by the word baptize" (Jewett). "Not sprinkling or pouring; the motion takes place in the man, and ceases when the man in baptized in water" (Stovel).

THE ACT.

"Commanded to perform *the act*." What act? "The act of immersing the subject." What is *the act* of immersing? "The act which we are commanded to perform by the word *baptize*." Very clear and very precise! "The act is to move a man until he is baptized." And "to move" expresses an act so clear, so precise, and so definite as to need no elucidation! The Confession of Faith uses no enigmatical terms; with frankness and perfect explicitness it declares,—"the act is dipping or plunging." With such statement, nothing is left but to inquire, Does God command us to perform one or the other of those well-defined *acts*,—to dip, to plunge? If so, which? They differ essentially; dipping is not plunging, plunging is not dipping.

The Object.

What is the object of the act? "The man" (Stovel). "The subject" (Booth, Jewett). "The body" (Wayland, Curtis). "The whole body" (Conf. of Faith). No discord in the utterance of this element of Baptist sentiment. Practice, however, antagonizes sentiment. "Baptism does not take place until after the greater part of the body has been put under water by the act of *walking*" (Ripley). This is practice. What, now, becomes of the sentiment which announces "the act of dipping," as specifically the divine command, and "the whole body" as the object of that act?

The End.

What is the end of the act? "The act ceases when the man is baptized in the water" (Stovel). "In plunging the whole body under water" (Conf. of Faith). "Emersion is not in the word, simply puts into or under the water" (Conant).

Remarkable confessions. 1. Abandons the definition, to dip. 2. Puts a living man under water, with, confessedly, no provision to take him out. Beyond all credibility that any such act should have been commanded. To substitute $\beta\acute{a}\pi\tau\omega$ for $\beta\alpha\pi\tau\acute{\iota}\zeta\omega$, overtly, none dare to do; to retain, verbally, $\beta\alpha\pi\tau\acute{\iota}\zeta\omega$, and give to it the meaning of $\beta\acute{a}\pi\tau\omega$, is to do covertly what none venture to do overtly.

Validity.

What are the requisites to valid baptism? 1. Immersion of the subject. 2. Immersion of the subject in water. 3. Immersion of the subject in water by the act commanded in baptize.

1. "Immersion." In immersion there is no limitation of time. Is this a divine injunction? 2. "The subject." As the subject is never immersed by Baptists in their ritual service, but the head and shoulders, only, they hereby destroy their own baptism. 3. "The act commanded." The act, universally, performed in practice is *dipping;* but men high in Baptist authority now admit that the word does not always mean to dip. How do they know that it means to dip here? Besides, to dip is, now, rarely found in any Baptist translation of the word; its appearance is becoming more and more rare; how do they know that βαπτίζω *ever* means to dip?

The foundations of Baptist baptism, in its validity, are shaken by its friends.

RESULTS.

We gather from Baptist records:

1. *As to the Word.* The disagreement between one writer and another, and the disagreement of every writer with himself, shows either an imperfect understanding of the word, or a failure to find any word in the English language to expound their conception.

2. *As to Ritual Administration.* Sentiment and practice are in irreconcilable contradiction.

3. *As to Validity of the Rite.* Honesty in stating the elements which are essential to valid baptism is unquestionable, inasmuch as they destroy their own, no less than that of all others.

4. *As to the Propriety of Renewed Investigation.* Want of accord with principles, and want of agreement between writers, show some radical error, and require a new investigation.

II.

RENEWED INVESTIGATION.

BAΠTIZΩ—What is its Meaning.

Advantage of a simultaneous and comparative examination of the usage of *βάπτω* and *βαπτίζω*—tingo and mergo—dip and immerse.

Verbs demanding Condition for their Object.

bury. drown. whelm.

Bury demands covered condition for its object, without limitation in the form of the act by which such condition may be effected.

Drown demands: 1. Covered condition. 2. Condition resulting from such covered condition—suffocation. 3. Condition resulting from controlling influence *without any covering*.

Whelm demands: 1. Covered condition. 2. Irresistible influence *without covering*.

Form of act is demanded by none of these words.

plunge.

Plunge demands the execution of an act of definite characteristics. This word belongs to a class widely separated, in nature, from the preceding.

Βάπτω belongs to the same class with *plunge; βαπτίζω* to that class represented by *bury, drown,* and *whelm.*

Farther Explanation.

1. Form of act does not belong to *βαπτίζω*. 2. Intusposition, within a closely investing medium, essential to the primary use. 3. Indefinite continuance in such condition equally essential to the word. 4. Feeble influence, the result of superficial entrance and momentary continuance, excluded. Carson insists, unqualifiedly, on a definite act. Gale doubts. Conant leans to Gale. President Halley, of England, and Professor

Wilson, of Ireland, adopt *state, condition*, in opposition to *act*. Form of act, whether in primary or metaphorical use, must be abandoned.

Intusposition. Condition of intusposition carries with it the idea of completeness. 1. Complete investiture, simply, as of a rock. 2. Complete influence resulting from such investiture, as in a ship sunk. 3. Complete influence induced by other causes than an investing element. Exigencies of language require such modification. 4. Frequent and perpetuated use expressive of a definite influence begets a specific meaning; as in the case of water, *to drown*, and in the case of wine, *to make drunk*.

As βαπτίζω has for its starting-point *a condition of intusposition*, complete as to extent and indefinite as to duration; while βάπτω sets out from *a trivial act* of superficial entrance and of evanescent continuance in an element; these words may be well expected to have a development broadly divergent.

Representative Word.

Baptists have failed to present a representative word. Now, they offer one, now another, and now a third, each differing in form and in force.

No English word, in its radical thought and development, squarely correspondent with the Greek word.

To drown, to whelm, to merse, to steep, to inn, each may present some specialty of claim. The Greek word having but one form throughout its usage, it is desirable that there should be, if possible, but one English word used in its translation. In a controverted issue, *it is especially desirable to avoid the shifting from one word to another*, even at the expense of using, sometimes, unfamiliar forms of phraseology. We choose, from among other imperfect terms, Merse.

Definition.

1. To intuspose, to merse; specifically, *to drown*.
2. To influence controllingly; specifically, *to make drunk*.

The facts of usage must sustain this definition, or it is erroneous. Every known case of classical usage adduced. The period covered by the quotations is about a thousand years.

ΒΑΠΤΩ—ITS MEANING.

To Dip.

To dip expresses a gentle, downward movement, entering slightly into some diverse element, with immediate return.

Dip and plunge are evidently separated in nature. Plunge expresses movement characterized by rapidity and force, entering into some element without return. To dip passes on from its special, primary use, to express *to wet, to moisten, to wash,* without involving the form of the act.

Ælian, Aristophanes, Aristotle, Constantine, Dionysius Halicarnassus, Euripides, Iamblichus, Lycophron, Theocritus, Aratus, Herodotus, Plutarch, Suidas.

To Dye.

Gale says, this word is used in the art of dyeing, but always implying the act to dip. Carson denies that the act is preserved in dyeing; and all Baptists, now, adopt his doctrine, and admit that *dipping* (retaining one word throughout the modifications of meaning, as does the Greek) may be by *sprinkling*.

To dye, in the progress of usage, becomes *to stain, to smear, to gild, to temper, to imbue,* or *tincture*.

Achilles Tatius, Æsop, Aristophanes, Eustathius, Hippocrates, Iamblichus, Julius Pollux, Menander, Plato, Antoninus, Æschylus, Aristotle, Epictetus, Eupolis, Helladius, Homer, Sophocles, Strabo.

Βάπτω : 1. *Dips,* putting momentarily into a fluid.
" 2. *Dips,* by dipping into a coloring fluid,—*dyes*.
" 3. *Dips,* without dipping, by means of coloring matter,—*stains*.
" 4. *Dips,* without dipping, without dyeing, without staining, by communicating uncolored quality, —*tinctures*.

Βάπτω, dips, without the modal act of dipping.
" dyes, without imparting the quality of color.

Βάπτω, to dip, takes as its syntax εἰς, with the accusative; βάπτω, to dye, takes as its syntax the coloring matter in the dative, usually, without a preposition.

TINGO—TO DIP.

The meaning of this word is uncontroverted. It is in remarkable harmony with βάπτω in all its phases.

It means, *to dip, to wet, to moisten, to wash, to anoint.*

Celsus, Juvenal, Ovid, Perseus, Propertius, Virgil.

TINGO—TO DYE.

It means, *to dye, to stain, to paint, to temper, to imbue,* or *tincture.*

Cicero, Horace, Juvenal, Martial, Ovid, Perseus, Pliny, Virgil, Seneca.

Tingo: 1. *Dips,* putting momentarily into a fluid.
   "   2. *Dips,* by putting into a coloring fluid,—*dyes.*
   "   3. *Dips,* without dipping, by means of coloring matter,—*stains.*
   "   4. *Dips,* without dipping, without dyeing, without staining, by communicating uncolored quality, —*tinctures.*

DIP.

The English *dip* corresponds, in all radical features, with βάπτω and *tingo.* It means to put in superficially and momentarily, *to dip, to wet, to bathe slightly, to examine superficially, to engage in limitedly, to mortgage, to take out a small quantity.*

Booth, Chalmers, Dryden, Sir A. Clarke, Glover, Milton, Sir Thomas Moore, Pope, Sir Walter Scott, Shakspeare.

DIP = DYE.

It means *to dye, to stain, to imbue* or *tincture.*

Coleridge, Cowper, Milton, Pope, Scott, Spenser, Warburton, Young.

CONCLUSION.—*Βάπτω, tingo, dip*, each represents a form of act characterized by limitations as to—1. Force. 2. Extent of penetration into an element. 3. Duration of continuance in it. 4. Magnitude of its objects. 5. Degree of influence.

In using one word to translate *βαπτίζω*, it should be borne in mind, that the Greeks and Latins used but one word to express the modal act of dipping, and the quality of color by dyeing, as well as all the subordinate modifications of each of these terms. Were we to translate in these cases, throughout, by the one word expressive of the primary meaning, we should have to use such phrases as—*Dip* the pastures *with dew; Dip* the face *with tears; Dip* the grass by *sprinkling* blood upon it.

Such breadth of usage, and such widely divergent, not to say contradictory, meaning in the use of these terms, affords but a poor basis whereon to ground the anticipation of finding in *βαπτίζω* "a definite act, mode and nothing but mode, one meaning through all Greek literature."

But the facts of usage, only, have authority; let us hear them.

First, let us inquire into the testimony of the corresponding English and Latin words, Immerse and Mergo.

III.

IMMERSE.

IMMERSE and *dip* are confounded together by Baptist writers, and interchanged at will. There is no authority for so doing.

MEANING: *To cause to be in a state of intusposition without limitation of depth, or time, or force, or object, or mode of accomplishment.*

In all of these particulars it is in irreconcilable contrast with *dip*. Dip performs an act upon its object transitory and limited in all directions. It does not put its object in a new state or condition.

Immerse makes no demand for the performance of any definite act. It does demand state, condition, intusposition. This state is of indefinite continuance; it may be changed by the intervention of foreign influence, but it is never changed by *immerse*. In mersion, brevity of continuance is an accident, not belonging to the state; in dipping, brevity of continuance is of the essence of the act, and is always present. The accidental feature of brevity, cannot convert a state of mersion into an act of dipping. The compounding preposition "*in*" denotes position only, and not movement. *Immerse* is used to express thorough influence of any kind.

Booth, Chalmers, Cowper, Current Literature, Dr. Kane, Pope, Sir Walter Scott, Young.

Βάπτω, *tingo*, *dip*, touch at all points; *immerse* is separated from each at all points.

MERGO.

1. MERGO expresses no form of act. 2. It is alike indifferent to the movement of the object or the element. 3. Its object may be a grain of sand or a world. 4. The time of its mersion is without limit. 5. The force it may call into action has no bound. 6. It demands intusposition for its object, and with this is satisfied.

SECONDARY USE.—1. It expresses a condition resultant from

some controlling influence. 2. Absolutely, it expresses (generally) destructive influence. 3. Specifically, it means *to drown, to make drunk.*

Catullus, Curtius, Horace, Juvenal, Livy, Lucan, Lucretius, Martial, Ovid, Pliny, Statius, Quintillian, Valerius Flaccus, Virgil.

Mergo and *immerse*, with some specialties of use, are in perfect harmony. *Mergo* is in broad contrast, throughout all its usage, with βάπτω, *tingo*, and *dip.*

ΒΑΠΤΙΖΩ.

WHAT IS ITS USAGE?

USE is of supreme authority, and the rule in the language.

1.

Βαπτίζω expresses intusposition without influence.

Aristotle, Archias, Julian the Egyptian, Lucian, Orpheus, Plutarch, Polybius, Porphyry, Strabo.

1. *Βαπτίζω* is without limitation as to power, object, duration, and form of action.

2. Expressing no form of act, it accepts of all forms of act competent to effect its demand.

3. The confusion of βάπτω and βαπτίζω is a grave error and without excuse.

4. The corner-stone of the Baptist system—"Baptizing is Dipping, and Dipping is Baptizing"—is pure error.

5. While some objects are uninfluenced by intusposition within a fluid, most objects will be thoroughly influenced by being placed in such a condition.

2.

It expresses intusposition with influence.

1. Vessels sunk by storm. 2. Vessels and persons sunk by weight. 3. Animals, &c., mersed by the flowing or uprising of water and of blood. 4. "Drowned" or "drunk" by mersion continued four days. 5. Mersion of the soul.

Achilles Tatius, Æsop, Alexander Aphrodisias, Diodorus

Siculus, Dion Cassius, Epictetus, Eubulus, Heliodorus, Hippocrates, Homer, Plotinus, Plutarch, Polybius, Strabo, Suidas.

3.

Intusposition for influence.

1. To drown.   2. To saturate.   3. To incrust.   4. To destroy vessels.

Æsop, Achilles Tatius, Alcibiades, Dion Cassius, Heliodorus, Heimerius, Hippocrates, Lucian, Nicander, Polyænus, Plutarch, Polybius, Strabo, Themistius.

4.

Influence with rhetorical figure.

1. Overflowing wave.   2. Tempest.
Chariton Aphrodisias, Dion Cassius, Libanius, Pindar.

5.

Figurative language.

FIGURE becomes worn out by constant use. Any word which, originally metaphorical in its use, has secured for itself a well-defined meaning, diverse from literal use, lays aside the character of figure and takes its place among literal words.

Βαπτίζω, through daily and long-continued use, has secured a secondary use, conveying an idea derived, but dissociated, from the primary use, which gives it a *status* of its own without recurring to the source whence it sprang.

Carson, Blair, Quintillian.

SECONDARY USE.

CONTROLLING INFLUENCE—GENERAL.

1.

Without Intusposition.

Achilles Tatius, Æsop, Alciphron, Alexander Aphrodisias, Demosthenes, Demetrius, Diodorus Siculus, Heliodorus, Heimerius, Libanius, Plotinus, Plutarch, Proclus, Themistius.

The changes now shown to have taken place in βαπτίζω—viz., 1. Intusposition without influence; 2. Intusposition with influence; 3. Intusposition for influence; and 4. *Influence without intusposition*—find a complete parallel and vindication in those changes which have been shown to take place in the usage of βάπτω, viz., 1. Dipping without dyeing; 2. Dipping for dyeing; 3. *Dyeing without dipping*.

Βάπτω—1. Dips without dyeing. 2. Dips for dyeing. 3. *Dyes without dipping*.

Βαπτίζω—1. Merses without influence. 2. Merses for influence. 3. *Influences without mersing*.

So, STEEP—1. Intusposes. 2. Intusposes for influence. 3. Influences without intusposing.

Βαπτίζω, used absolutely, or with appropriate case, in unphysical relations, expresses, directly and not figuratively, controlling influence. The modality of position, out of which this idea grows, has disappeared.

2.

CONTROLLING INFLUENCE—SPECIFIC.

Without Intusposition.

Some things exert over certain objects a definite and unvarying influence. Water exerts over all human beings, mersed in it, the specific influence of suffocation—*drowning*.

Wine freely drunk, *makes drunk*. An opiate swallowed, *stupefies*. When βαπτίζω is used to express the condition resulting from these influences (as it very frequently is), it no longer expresses controlling influence generally; but expresses, from the necessity of the case, that specific influence which belongs to water—*to drown*; or to wine—*to make drunk*; or to an opiate—*to stupefy*.

Whatever breadth of meaning any word may be possessed of, if it be persistently used to denote a condition, such as results from wine drinking and kindred influences, deeply marked and of unvarying uniformity, it cannot but be, that the idea of such condition becomes incorporated in the word. *To drink* has a very broad application; but persistently used to express the drinking of intoxicating liquors, " a drinking

2

man" comes to express *a drunken* man. The Greek word has great breadth of application; but used familiarly, and long, to express the condition induced by wine-influence, it comes to express directly *the state of drunkenness.*

Some of the specific conditions expressed by this word, and which render its translation by an appropriate term justifiable, if not compulsory, are as follows:

1. To bring into a condition of stupor—*to stupefy;* by swallowing an opiate.

2. To bring into a state of drunkenness—*to make drunk;* by drinking wine.

3. To bring into a state of coldness—*to make cold;* by pouring water on hot iron.

4. To bring into a state of bewilderment—*to bewilder;* by asking sophistical questions.

5. To bring into an unintoxicating state—*to temper wine;* by pouring water through it.

6. To bring into a state of pureness—*to purify;* by using sea-water in any way.

Achilles Tatius, Athenæus, Conon, Evenus, Homer. Alleg., Lucian, Plato, Plutarch.

From such usage, figure (*dipping!*) has irrecoverably disappeared.

PARABAPTISTS.

A CLASS OF PERSONS OF DEFECTIVE CHARACTER.

Implied contrast with persons who are *Baptists*—persons of decided character, who are under some controlling influence.

Arrian.

GENERAL RESULTS.

1. Certain old and long-cherished errors have been corrected and abandoned.

2. Other errors yet remain to be corrected.

3. USAGE has spoken freely, and been, I trust, reported truly.

Usage declares:

1. *Βάπτω, tingo,* and *dip* to be equivalent terms in their original import, and, also, that they run parallel, in a remarkable degree, in all the variations of their development.

2. *Usage* bears the same testimony to the common nature and kindred development of *βαπτίζω, mergo,* and *merse.*

3. As the former class of terms agrees, essentially, in all its members, so it is in essential disagreement with all the members of the latter class.

Βάπτω.

1. Puts its object into a simple fluid element, and *withdraws it promptly.*

2. Changes the state or quality of its object, as to color, *by putting into coloring* liquid.

3. Changes the state or quality of its object, as to color, by *pressure, sprinkling,* or otherwise.

4. Changes the state or quality of its object where *color is not involved.*

Βαπτίζω.

1. Intusposes its object within a fluid element *without providing for its removal.*

2. Influences, controllingly, its object *by* intusposition.

3. Influences, controllingly, its object *without* intusposition.

4. It *drowns.* It *makes drunk.*

Βαπτίζω expresses *any complete change of condition by whatsoever agency effected, or in whatsoever way applied.*

TEST OF TRUTH.

A master key proves its character by throwing back the bolts of every lock to which it is applied.

The meaning assigned to *βαπτίζω* gives proof that it is such a master key. Applied to every passage of classical Greek in which the word is used, a clear and adequate solution is at once revealed.

Try the opposing meaning—*a definite act*—and fashion a key after that principle (of what model you will), *dip, plunge, sink, overflow,* or what not, and each must, in turn, be thrown aside in utter disappointment. The usage of βαπτίζω cannot be "mastered" by any effort in that direction.

Abandon all such endeavor, and apply the meaning—CON-DITION :

(1.) Condition of complete intusposition ;

(2.) Condition of complete influence ;

And we have a key which opens every passage, "as on golden hinges turning."

The meaning assigned throws light upon the origin of the conflicting views so long maintained, and their relations to the truth.

1. On the one side we have *dip*. The origin of this meaning is traceable, most unmistakably, to βάπτω. It is an intruder within the domain of βαπτίζω, and, as such, should be unceremoniously dismissed.

2. *Plunge, sink, overflow,* are traceable to βαπτίζω as among the accidents of form through which it secures its essential demand of condition ; while the attributing of such accidents to the essence of the word, involves the absurdity of making the same word express many definite acts diverse and contradictory in form.

3. On the other side we have *pour* and *sprinkle*. These forms of action are not the most natural servitors of βαπτίζω. And yet their competency to fulfil this duty, under favorable circumstances, is admitted by some of the ablest Baptist writers. But it is in baptisms of influence where these words have their just and appropriate use.

To say that baptism may be by such acts, is to declare a truth; but to make βαπτίζω *mean* to pour or to sprinkle, is an error similar to that into which those of the other side have fallen.

The explanation of the protracted conflict would seem to be a repetition of the history of the struggle beneath "the shield with its *golden* and *silver* side."

All the truth has not been in view.

CLASSIC BAPTISM,

WITH A VIEW TO ITS BEARING ON

CHRISTIAN BAPTISM.

PART I.

THREE centuries have witnessed the continued discussion of the meaning of the word βαπτίζω, and the proper manner of administering the rite of Christian Baptism.

One hundredth part of this time would seem to have been sufficient to gather together all the materials involved in such discussion, and to have issued a judgment, based upon them, from which there could have been no hopeful appeal. And if this has not been done most exhaustively, the fact is marvellous; but if it has been done, it is no less marvellous that the judgment reached has not compelled universal acceptance.

The mind is not at liberty to accept or to reject the truth when presented distinctly before it, with its evidences; it must accept it.

In examining this subject, with exclusive reference to personal instruction, it has appeared to me that the investigation has not been, adequately, carried out in certain directions. This has arisen, doubtless, from the little promise which seemed to be held out of valuable results from such inquiry. Sometimes, however, our anticipations receive favorable disappointment. It may be so in

(21)

this case. And I submit the results gathered up, not only along the main route of inquiry, but in some of its less fully explored collateral branches, in the hope of assisting to a final and generally acceptable judgment. If I shall fail to make the best use of the materials furnished, more skilful hands may take them and find their labors crowned with greater success.

There is a large and respectable class of persons who will consider this whole inquiry a work of supererogation. They say that the work has been done, well done; all the truth has been evolved, and that now " it is not so much light that is needed as honesty."

So fully convinced are we of the "honesty" of these persons, that we accept it, at once, with or without their affirmation; and because we do, gladly place ourselves within the clear shining of their "light," hoping that no "lack of honesty" will either cloud our perception or silence our confession. Wisdom and duty alike demand that we should pursue this course. If absolute truth has been already reached through the labors of others, it will be less laborious to pass over a path already trodden, and to examine results already wrought out; and if these results are luminous with uncolored truth, as they are said to be, then it is a privilege and a duty cordially to accept them.

This course I propose to adopt. If the course of investigation and results reached, by our Baptist brethren, are beyond impeachment, after due examination, then our task will be ended; but if otherwise, then even they will confess that "light" may be sought at some other source without necessarily abandoning "religious honesty."

BAPTIST POSTULATES.

Baptist writers demand the acceptance as verities, by all lovers of truth, of certain general results reached by them in their investigations.

Among these are the following :

I. Βαπτίζω, *throughout the entire course of Greek literature, has but one meaning, which is definite, clear, precise, and easy of translation.*

This proposition is not self-luminous with truth. The demand for its acceptance, therefore, cannot reasonably be expected to follow on its mere enunciation. Apology for this hesitancy may be found in the fact, that if this proposition embodies a truth, it is a very unusual one. Few things are more rare in the history of language than to find a word used by a cultivated people for ages in the same absolute sense. In farther vindication of this hesitancy, allow me to present the following quotation from Sir William Hamilton:

"And here it is expedient to take into account two circumstances, which mutually affect each other. The first is that the vocabulary of every language is necessarily finite, it is necessarily disproportioned to the multiplicity, not to say infinity, of thought; and the second, that the complement of words in any given language has been always filled up with terms significant of objects and relations of the external world, before the want was experienced of words to express the objects and relations of the internal."

"Either words of a language must each designate only a single notion—a single fasciculus of thought—the multitude of notions not designated being allowed to perish; or the words of a language must each be employed to denote a plurality of concepts. . . . Of these alternatives, the latter is the one which has been universally preferred; and, accordingly, all languages by the same word express a multitude of thoughts, more or less differing from each other."—*Logic*, p. 436.

My object, now, is not to disprove the above postulate, but merely to look at it as the fruit of Baptist labors, and see whether it carries on the face of it justification for the bold demand which it makes for acceptance. The impression made is, that farther evidence, and a good deal of it, is needed to make good such a point.

II. *Βαπτίζω and βάπτω have precisely the same meaning, dyeing excepted; in all other respects, whether as to form, or force, or effect, they differ neither more nor less.*

This proposition constitutes another demand for acceptance on the ground of unquestionable truth. We are compelled, however, again to hesitate. And in apology we offer this query: Is it usual for language to repeat itself?

If it be true that all nations have been compelled, through the paucity of words, to use "each one to denote a plurality of concepts," is it not something for wonder that the Greeks should employ *two* words to express the same identical conception?

2. We remember, also, that we have been asked, heretofore, to adopt this same proposition without any exception. It may be that complete truth has not been yet reached, and that the list of exceptions will go on to increase until these words shall be found to be in harmony with that broad law of language—one word for many concepts, but not two words for one.

3. We are not sure that all possible differences between these words have been well considered. Points of resemblance may, through prepossession for a certain conclusion, have claimed an attention which induced unconsciousness of existent differences. "Words are often employed with a plurality of meaning, several of which may quadrate, or be supposed to quadrate, with the general tenor of the discourse. Error is thus possible; and it is also probable, if we have any prepossession in favor of one interpretation rather than another."—*Sir W. H. Logic*, 437.

Baptist writers are not the only ones who may be supposed to "have a prepossession in favor of one interpretation rather than another" in the case before us; but I suppose they can hardly claim exemption from this disturbing influence.

III. *Βαπτίζω expresses an act, a definite act; mode, and nothing but mode;* TO DIP. *Βάπτω (primary) expresses an act, a definite act; mode, and nothing but mode;* TO DIP.

Before giving in adhesion to the demand for an acknowledgment of the identity of these words as expressed in
this concrete form, I would like to know whether the
various phases assumed by the class of verbs to which
they belong have been maturely considered in their bear-
ings upon both, separately and jointly.

Active transitive verbs admit of numerous subdivisions
possessed of characteristics by no means unimportant.
Among the divisions will be found, 1. Words which, directly, express *action*. 2. Words which, directly, express
condition.

Baptist writers say that the two words under consideration belong to the former of these classes and not to the
latter. Has this ever been proved? Has it ever been
attempted? Possibly; but if so, it has never come under
my notice. And as there is no self-evidencing power in
the statement, I must hesitate in my faith.

Words which, directly, express action are still farther
divided into, 1. Words which express action, generally.
2. Words which express action, particularly. To the
former of these classes belong such words as *to do, to work,
to move*, &c. To the second class belong *to dig, to roll, to
speak*, and the like.

To this latter class, it is said, βάπτω and βαπτίζω must both
be attached. But has this ever been, distinctively, proved?
Suppose that we should be willing to admit that one of
them, βάπτω, for example, did belong here, but felt some
embarrassment in making such admission as to the other;
is it unreasonable to ask to be relieved from pressure on
this point until some proof shall be adduced?

Farther; among words which express action in some
definite form, there are, 1. Those which express action
characterized by rapidity and force. 2. Those which are
marked by comparative slowness and gentleness. To the
former belongs *plunge*. To the latter belongs *dip*. When
Baptist writers say that βάπτω and βαπτίζω mean " *to dip*,"
do they mean, understandingly, to say that they belong to
a class of verbs characterized by a movement " slow and

gentle," and not to that class which has the elements of "rapidity and power?" They cannot belong to both classes. If Baptist writers have failed to mark this discrimination, and have failed to test, by usage, the true classification of each of these words, they must not be astonished if there is questioning, instead of unqualified acceptance, of their conclusions.

But what shall be said of that very large class of words which does not express, immediately, action either definitely or indefinitely, and therefore neither powerfully nor feebly, but which expresses, directly, *result, state, condition?* Such as *to put, to set, to lay,* expressive of condition as to place; *to pen, to surround, to inclose,* expressive of condition characterized by some encircling material; and *to cover, to bury, to whelm,* expressing condition marked by envelopment on all sides?

As verbs which embody an act represent power, greater or less, through the act which they indicate; so verbs which shadow forth condition denote influence, greater or less, through the nature of such condition.

To place an object momentarily within a fluid, is to place it in a condition where the influence exerted upon it will be of the feeblest character. To place an object within a fluid element, indefinitely, is to place it in a condition where the influence exerted upon it will be of the strongest possible character.

To dip is an act by which the former condition is effected; *to merse* is a condition of the latter kind effected by any competent act, the nature and form of which are undefined and of absolute indifference.

These classes of words are separated from each other by a great gulf, so that there is no passage from the one side to the other without an essential change in the nature of the word.

Have Baptist writers maturely considered these distinctions, and come to a critical judgment, in view of a full induction of facts, that βάπτω and βαπτίζω do neither both nor either belong to verbs of condition, but do both belong to verbs expressive of action, and more limitedly to verbs expressive of definite action ?

If they have so done, I know not where they have hidden the fruit of their labors, and until these shall be revealed I plead against the demand to accept a conclusion which ignores the existence of a class of words which are in nature and development radically different from " an act, a definite act; mode and nothing but mode; *to dip*."

IV. *Baπτίζω has the same meaning in figurative as in literal use, always referring to the act of dipping.*

Subscription to this demand, as truth, may be given or withheld according to the idea attached to the "figurative" use of language. Words are sometimes used in connections where literality of meaning is impossible, and yet where it is no less manifest that it is designed to place the literal use vividly before the mind for greater effect. In such cases of transference of words from physical to metaphysical relations, in order to awaken the intellect by unwonted combination, and thus produce a profounder effect; the word carries its meaning with it, and produces its awakening effect only because it does convey such meaning.

But where words once used in material relations are now used in immaterial, and that every day, and without design on the part of the speaker to utter figure, and by reason of familiarity incapable of producing any such impression on the mind of the hearer,—in a word, the simple, necessary, universal tropical use of words should not be considered as figure.

If, however, Baptist writers insist that such prosaic use of language must be dignified by the title of figure, we must wholly decline the acceptance of their proposition. Its contradictory proposition, *βαπτίζω, never* carries into secondary or tropical use, unmodified, its primary or literal use, is nearer the truth. This must be so in the nature of things. Words in trope and metaphor make meanings for themselves, and the same word is variously modified in meaning, to fit in the various relations in which from time to time it finds itself. And when the special friends of βαπτίζω run for a solution of every tropical and metaphorical use to the water, they will find that such course will be suggestive largely, to others, of the ridiculous and the absurd, as well as the impossible.

The tropical or secondary use of words is of great value as reflecting light back upon the primary use. And as it is true in language, as well as in everything else, that an original divergence is made increasingly manifest the farther progress is made from the starting-point, words whose divergence was not so manifest in primary, literal use, will reveal it more strikingly as they pass on to metaphor, trope, and secondary use.

In general, words which literally are directly expressive of *action* will be employed in metaphor to denote *force*, not physical but mental and moral; and words which literally are directly expressive of *condition*, find their use in metaphor to denote *influence*.

Some words, while expressing a definite act, carry with them some result inseparable from that act. The secondary use will develop sometimes one, sometimes another aspect of such words. To this class belongs *dip*. Its secondary use gives prominence sometimes to the act, sometimes to the effect of the act, always characterized by feebleness and limitation. If at any time it appears to pass beyond these boundaries, the explanation will be found in some adventitious circumstance, in the nature of the object or the character of the element; not, therefore, inherent in the word.

The secondary use of *merse* never stands related to any form of act, but is always used to express the development of influence in the fullest measure of which the case will admit.

The contrast between *dip* and *merse* is absolute.

As we shall have largely to do with the secondary use of βαπτίζω, it seemed desirable, at once, to bring it into prominent view, with distinct intimation of the different

value attached to it, compared with that maintained by
Baptist writers.

It is admitted, on all hands, that words once used figuratively may cease to have a figurative use ascribed to
them. The ground of this change is to be found in frequency of use, and the attainment thereby of power to
express a modified thought of their own. Horne Tooke
and others have shown that all of our prepositions, con-
junctions, adverbs, adjectives, and abstract substantives,
are referable to nouns or verbs, describing sensible ideas.
These words, in their first use, had all the vividness and
force of figure; but they have so no longer.

Whenever a word or phrase becomes so familiar in form
or application as no longer to be suggestive, to speaker or
hearer, of physical ideas, but conveys, on enunciation, an
idea of its own, it ceases, in fact, to be figurative, and we
should cease to treat it as such.

There are cases in which we may feel embarrassment
whether to assign a secondary or a figurative meaning to
a word or phrase.

Take an example which happens to be, this moment,
under my eye.

" Had Mr. Harris and others, instead of diving deeper
than they had occasion into Aristotelian mysteries, con-
tented themselves with observing plain facts, they would
soon have perceived, ... Whereas, in the way they
proceeded, their labor was immense, and " . . . —*Divers.
of Purley*, xiii.

Now, the form of the phraseology, "diving into Aristotelian mysteries," is fully figurative, and if its words be
considered disjunctly, "dive" can only be regarded in its
literal sense, and "Aristotelian mysteries" as an element
into which "Mr. Harris" plunges head foremost. And
some might say that this must be and is the only way in
which it can be treated. Let us see. Consider, 1. That
such phraseological combinations are exceedingly common. 2. Such familiarity of use educates the mind to
put aside the physical picturing, and to see only the

thought which is the outgrowth of that picturing. 3. Such phrases come to have the force of compound words, in which its several parts are no longer to be treated as distinct words, but only as syllabic parts of one whole, conveying a new idea. 4. It is extremely doubtful whether any physical picture of " Mr. Harris entering head foremost into Aristotelianism," was for a moment before the mind of the writer, or intended to be conveyed to the mind of his reader. There is every reason to suppose that the conception before his mind was identical with that which he subsequently expresses by saying " *their labor was immense,*" and this should govern the interpretation. The origin of the phrase is another matter. Any one who chooses to treat such language as figure will find in it all the materials necessary for his purpose; and, on the other hand, any one who prefers to regard it as a familiar and organic combination, possessed of unity and self-expression, will have no lack of material for his vindication. It is wholly immaterial which view is adopted, so far as sentiment is concerned. The sentiment reached is the same.

Before leaving this subject, it may be well to remark that, while "diving into Aristotelian mysteries" may and does well express "immense labor," *dipping* into them neither does nor can, by any possibility, express any such idea, but directly the opposite. On the other hand, *mersion* in those mysteries would express, not the idea of " immense *labor,*" but of *complete influence* proceeding from this form of Aristotleism, and affecting ".Mr. Harris and others" by its controlling power.

As already remarked, *dive*, primarily, expressing action characterized by rapidity and force executed head foremost, passes, secondarily, to express mental *activity*, " immense *labor;*" while *merse*, expressing, primarily, no form of force, but pointing to condition of intusposition, comes to denote, secondarily, not *activity* of mind, but the reception by it of controlling *influence*. I cannot accept the Baptist position that " βαπτίζω has no secondary meaning;

but is exclusively employed in a primary, literal, and in a figurative sense, without any modification of import; always meaning, literally and figuratively, to dip, and nothing but dip." On the contrary, I cannot but regard such statement as error, and nothing but error.

PROPOSITIONS TO BE SUSTAINED BY PROOF.

Over against these four postulates, nakedly assumed, or assumed without adequate proof, I would place four other propositions, for which no other acceptance is asked than that which may be secured by satisfactory proof.

The statement of these propositions is now made briefly and incompletely, to be filled up hereafter, that the mind may have something definite to rest upon as the inquiry progresses.

They are as follows:

I. *Βάπτω, in primary use, expresses a definite act characterized by limitations*—TO DIP.

II. *In secondary use, " Dip" expresses a limited mental force, and a limited effect.*

The Greek language does not furnish us, so far as I am aware, with exemplifications of this secondary (metaphorical) use; but it is found in connection with the corresponding words in the Latin and English languages.

III. *Βαπτίζω, in primary use, expresses condition characterized by complete intusposition, without expressing, and with absolute indifference to the form of the act by which such intusposition may be effected, as, also, without other limitations*—TO MERSE.

IV. *In secondary use it expresses condition the result of complete influence effected by any possible means and in any conceivable way.*

If any one should be disposed to imagine that between those postulates and these propositions there can be no such difference as to revolutionize results, let such idea be held in abeyance until we patiently trace these differences to their ultimate conclusions. The mathematician who found in his calculations a steadily diminishing element, and concluded that it might safely be assumed as ultimately disappearing, and, therefore, might safely be neglected, was disappointed in the result reached. No error being visible, and the verity of figures being proverbial, the difficulty was inexplicable. At length he determined to take up that supposed vanishing quantity, and follow it on until it should, in very deed, *merge* into nothingness. In so doing, however, he found, to his great surprise, that as it *dipped* into the outer rim of zero, it refused to go farther; but returned upon its path, becoming a steadily increasing quantity, with power adequate to control the mathematical result.

Assumption is dangerous, whether in logic or mathematics.

Let us assume nothing in this inquiry as too unimportant to be investigated; and we may find that even the difference between "dip" and "merse," when faithfully followed out, becomes no vanishing quantity, but a growing increment, with power to control, happily and satisfactorily, our investigation.

BAPTIST WRITERS.

As preliminary to a direct investigation of the subject before us, it seems to be desirable, on many accounts, to institute an examination of Baptist writings, to see how far they illuminate and sustain their favorite postulates.

If they do squarely and harmoniously maintain them not only *in thesi*, but do unfalteringly bear them, challenging criticism, "through all Greek literature," then they will, at least, win the not ignoble award of consistency and courage; but if, on the other hand, it shall be found, that between postulates and writings there is no harmony; that between writer and writer there is as little harmony; that the pages of the same writer compared with each other perpetuate this disharmony; that there never has been an attempt by any one writer, through these three hundred

years, to carry these postulates " through all Greek literature;" that the burden which they would bind upon others
they utterly refuse to bear themselves; then we may hope
that such facts will be deemed a fair apology for declining
this Baptist postulation, and a sufficient justification for a
direct inquiry after that great desideratum—a meaning
of βαπτίζω, which may be carried, without fear and without
reproach, through all Greek literature.

In examining Baptist writings there must be some limitation. It is not practicable to go over all such writings,
nor is it necessary to go back indefinitely as to time; I will,
therefore, limit myself to writers of representative and
generally accredited character, and to that period which
has elapsed since Baptist views were introduced into this
country.

WHAT DOES ΒΑΠΤΙΖΩ MEAN?

"It means to dip, and nothing but dip."

ROGER WILLIAMS AND TRACTATE OF A. R., 1644.

Roger Williams has not left us, so far as I am aware,
any formal writings of his own on this subject; but while
he was on a visit to England, there was a treatise published, which he brought back with him and introduced
into this country, and which, therefore, may be accepted
as embodying his own views.

This work was designated as a "Tractate by A. R.,
London, 1644." The title which it bore was, "Dipping is
Baptizing, and Baptizing is Dipping." Whether the definition thus given by this tractate be true or not, all must
admit that it is "definite, clear, and precise," and thus
harmonizes with the postulate. We are not merely told
baptize and dip are equivalents, nor yet that they are
counterparts, duplicates, but that the one is the other, and
the other is the one; that they are identical. The attire
differs, in the one case Grecian, in the other case English;
but under that attire, in either case, appears the self-same
personage.

3

Beyond this, for definiteness, clearness, and precision, definition cannot go. These words do, respectively, expound each other in the most universal and absolute manner. Whatever differs from dip, differs, in like manner, from baptize; and whatever differs from, or agrees with, baptize, does, in like manner, differ from and agree with dip. There is neither deficiency nor excess in the one compared with the other. As a foot is twelve inches and twelve inches are a foot, so baptize is dip and dip is baptize.

Now, so far from objecting to this sharpness of definition, we feel unfeignedly grateful for it; definition and postulate do most admirably echo each other, and thus our task is simplified and assisted.

The friends of the Baptist scheme claim it as a glory that its doctrines are unambiguous, its definitions are precise, and that its ritual service demands an act which is definite and absolute. Such characteristics, apart from the question of the truth of the scheme to which they belong, are highly meritorious. If they belong to a system of truth, they will, thus, best abide assault; and if with what is erroneous, the error will receive most speedy and patent revelation.

While Baptist writers give a testimony one and unambiguous, we will give them full meed of praise. Now, we thank " A. R." for his " definite, clear, and precise" utterance, announcing that " Dipping is Baptizing, and Baptizing is Dipping."

" A. BARBER, HIS TREATISE OF DIPPING."

This was another publication issued at London in the same year with the preceding. Its title is less full and perspicuous, but has nothing inconsistent with the other. They were both, doubtless, intended to present the same front as to one single, exclusive, and universal meaning.

That this identification of Dipping and Baptizing was fully recognized at the time by opponents, will appear from a publication issued in London, 1645. The author

of this work was Dr. Featly.   It was avowedly an answer
to " A. R."   An extract will show that the issue made,—
" Dipping is Baptizing, and Baptizing is Dipping,"—was
controversially accepted.

Dr. Featly thus writes : " But the question is, whether
no other baptizing is lawful; or whether dipping in rivers
is so necessary to Baptism, that none are accounted baptized but those who are *dipped* after such a manner?   This,
we say, is false; neither do any of the texts alleged prove
it.   It is true, *dipping* is a kind of baptizing; but all baptizing is not *dipping.*   The apostles were baptized by fire,
yet were they not dipped into it.   Tables and beds are
said to be baptized; that is, washed, yet not *dipt.*   The
Israelites in the wilderness were baptized with the cloud,
yet not *dipt* into it.   The children of Zebedee were to be
baptized with the baptism of blood wherewith our Saviour
was baptized, yet neither he nor they were *dipt* into blood.
Lastly, all the Fathers speak of the baptism of tears wherewith all penitents are washed, yet there is no dipping in
such baptism." (pp. 45, 50.)

This quotation is made, not for the sake of its argument
(that is not our business now); but to show that the assault,
whether successfully or unsuccessfully, is fairly delivered
against the position—" Baptizing is Dipping, and Dipping
is Baptizing."

Whether, then, we look at the language itself, or at the
interpretation given to it on its enunciation, all must admit
that the Baptist position in London, in 1644, and thence
transferred to Rhode Island by Roger Williams, was most
unequivocal.

DR. GALE.   LONDON, 1711.

' Dipping only is Baptism."

More than half a century after A. R., Dr. Gale thus
writes : " We cannot believe that it is so doubtful in sacred
Scripture as many pretend, whether dipping only be baptism." (p. 93.)

" To baptize, *i. e.* dip 'em by affusion or sprinkling."

This phraseology is used by Gale to show an absurd use of terms. He says, " It is absurd to speak of baptizing by sprinkling, because baptizing is dipping."

" The word baptize *necessarily includes in its signification dipping*, and that Christ by *commanding to baptize has commanded to dip only.*" (p. 94.)

" The primary meaning is simply to dip." (p. 95.)

" I don't remember one passage where all other senses are not excluded besides dipping." (p. 96.)

" Though the genius of our language may oblige us sometimes to render βαπτίζω to wet, or wash, or dye, &c., it is most absurd to infer that it, therefore, signifies anything else besides or different from *to dip.*" (p. 186.)

Whatever of bluntness or of blunder there may be in this language, it is largely redeemed by its heartiness of faith.

" Christ, by commanding to baptize, has commanded to dip only." All other senses are excluded. To doubt whether the Scriptures so teach is to be guilty of false pretence. To conclude that a word which we are obliged to translate *wet, wash, dye,* &c., can mean anything else than *dip,* is most absurd (!).

Such language shows, unmistakably, that it was by faith that Dr. Gale proclaimed that " only" meaning, while deeply enveloped in clouds and darkness. With manful courage he holds on to dip while sorely (it may be " absurdly") struggling with " *wet, and wash, and dye, &c.*"

As coming events cast their shadows before, we may, herein, also find a foreshadowing of unity entangled amid diversity, to be a future and fruitful source of perplexity to our Baptist friends.

Whether " wet, wash, dye, &c.," are meanings of this word, I do not now inquire; but whether or not, the question is equally pertinent—What must be the ideas of language entertained by that man who feels " obliged" to translate a word by these terms, while he believes that it has no such meaning at all?

ABRAHAM BOOTH. LONDON, 1711.

"The primary sense of the term is to dip."

The "venerable Booth" appears as a writer somewhat more than three-fourths of a century after the learned Dr. Gale.

He thus writes: "When our Lord says, 'go, baptize,' he speaks the language of legislation; he delivers Divine law. Does Jehovah make use of a term which properly signifies *dipping?* He means as he speaks, and requires immersion. That dipping, pouring, and sprinkling denote three different acts, we have many examples in the writings of Moses." (pp. 81, 82.)

"While Pœdobaptists maintain that our great Lawgiver intended anything less than *dipping.*" (p. 95.)

"I do not, indeed, recollect so much as one learned writer, in the whole course of my reading, who denies that the primary sense of the term is to dip." (p. 125.)

Mr. Booth is confident and precise in these utterances, and generally harmonious with himself and his predecessors. The exception to this harmony is found in the statement, that when "Jehovah uses a term that signifies *dipping*" (and "He means as He speaks," yet) "He requires *immersion.*"

Now, this new word introduces a note of discord. Mr. Booth has not proved that "dipping is immersion, and immersion is dipping." The proposition is not self-evidently true. On the contrary it is most evidently untrue. These terms are not only devoid of identity, but they do not belong to the same class of words. This, however, is not the time to enter into a full examination of the points of difference. I only, therefore, remark that "dipping" is characterized, essentially, by limitations in all directions, while "immersion" is as essentially destitute of them. The position of Booth, then, is that when Jehovah commands a result full of limitations, he requires a result destitute of all limitations! This jar, by reason of the

introduction of "immersion," added to "wet, wash, dye,
&c.," induces the feeling that the "one only meaning"
holds its position by but a precarious tenure. However,
we must content ourselves, for the present, by simply attaching to this notable passage an N.B.

"F. A. COX. LONDON, 1824."

"The idea of dipping is in every instance."

After the lapse of a third of a century we meet with
Dr. Cox.

This writer, in common with his predecessors, believed
that βάπτω and βαπτίζω not only had some elements in common, but that they were most absolutely equivalents;
indeed, that the greatest difference between them was that
the one word was spelled with two, and the other with
three syllables. He interchanges them at will, and quotes,
indifferently, passages where the one word or the other is
found as equally to the purpose.

Dr. Cox informs us, that "the idea of dipping is in every
instance conveyed; and no less so by all the classical current uses of the terms (βάπτω and βαπτίζω) in question."
(p. 46.)

Having quoted a number of passages in which *dip* is
given as the translation, he adds: "Numberless other
passages of the same kind might easily be introduced,
were it at all needful; let these, however, suffice as speci-
mens of the undoubted use and current acceptation of the
contested terms."

This utter confusion of these words, so long persisted in
by Baptist writers, notwithstanding all the evidence to the
contrary, is now, I believe, universally abandoned so far as
relates to *dyeing*. The acknowledgment of this error, so
long and so earnestly maintained, might lead, one would
suppose, to some reserve in maintaining that these diverse
words are in all other respects identical. But this still
remains as an acquisition of truth to be attained in the
future. Let us hope, not in the far distant future.

It is very evident that Dr. Cox gives his clear testimony to the undoubted use, " in every instance," scriptural and classical, of βάπτω and βαπτίζω, as conveying the meaning, *to dip.*

How much this conclusion may have been affected by the confounding of these words with each other, and by the transference of the meaning of βάπτω to βαπτίζω, I do not inquire. To point the finger toward so weak a point is sufficiently suggestive, and will prevent any thoughtful person from embracing conclusions which are founded on it.

ALEXANDER CARSON, LL.D., BAPTIST BOARD OF PUBLICATION. PHILADELPHIA. 1853.

" My position is that it always signifies *to dip;* never expressing anything but mode." " To dip *or immerse.*" " It never means *to dye.*"

Dr. Carson thus quotes from Dr. Gale: " I think it is plain from the instances already mentioned, that they (βάπτω and βαπτίζω) are exactly the same as to signification;" and then expresses his own opinion thus: " As far as respects an increase or diminution of the action of the verb, I perfectly agree with the writer. That the one is more or less than the other, as to mode or frequency, is a perfectly groundless conceit. *Βάπτω* has two meanings, the primary to dip, the secondary to dye: βαπτίζω, in the whole history of the Greek language, has but one. It not only signifies to dip or immerse, but it never has any other meaning." (p. 19.) " If we dip an object in any way, we cause it to dip or sink." (p. 20.) " The mode essentially denoted by it." " Baptism means to lay under water." " This was a large object that was not supposed to be taken up and dipped, but to be caused to dip, as it were, by sinking." (p. 21.) " It is strictly univocal." (p. 23.) " The proof is equally strong with reference to βαπτίζω. My position is that it always signifies to dip; never expressing anything but mode." (p. 55.)

Dr. Carson's writings mark an era among Baptist authors

as to the accepted meaning of βαπτίζω. They had, heretofore, refused to acknowledge any difference whatever between this word and βάπτω; but from the time of Dr. Carson's enunciation, that the one word presided over the mysteries of dyeing, while the other was excluded from all participation in them, the doctrine was promptly and universally accepted. Dr. Carson does not attempt to show why the work of dyeing fell to the lot of one word rather than another; on the contrary, he would have us believe that the distinction was wholly without reason; because "it is a perfectly groundless conceit to suppose that the one is more or less than the other."

Such ratiocination makes another severe demand on our faith. It was hard to believe that two words, native born, existed in the same language without any difference, "either more or less;" but this we were asked to believe. We are now asked to believe, that of two such words one secures a secondary meaning while the other utterly fails, without reason assigned or assignable, seeing that the two are identical in "mode," and "force," and "frequency," &c., &c.

Now, we do not say that both or either of these statements present an impossibility; but there is so much of incredibility about them that, in the absence of reason, there should be the most conclusive evidence of fact.

There has been, absolutely, no evidence to prove that βάπτω and βαπτίζω "differ neither more nor less" in their primary meaning; and consequently there has been no evidence to show that βάπτω has secured its secondary meaning, without reason and in a purely arbitrary manner. We can accept of neither of these positions, and the necessity for their assumption brings down a double and damaging blow against the Baptist system.

But not only is this admission of Dr. Carson of a difference as to secondary meaning, like the letting out of water which threatens to sweep away his scheme; but it is no less matter for sinister foreboding that he feels the necessity of introducing into the severely simple definition of his predecessors a pregnant "OR," qualifying, also, the primary meaning. It is, indeed, most true that there is no acknowledgment of valuable service rendered by this particle, while the whole book is made to rest upon it. Whatever Dr. C. may think, others will not consent to his slipping away from the "definite, clear, and precise" definition, "baptizing is dipping, and dipping is baptizing," into "dip *or immerse*," "or" something else. If it be affirmed that to dip is to immerse, and to immerse is to dip, we reply, with a quiet smile, then this redundant "or immerse" will only be an incumbrance, therefore indulge us with its dismissal. But if "or immerse" be admitted to be anything "more or less" than *dip*, what becomes of the postulate—"*one* meaning through all Greek literature"?

So long as Dr. Carson declares that "βαπτίζω has but one meaning in the whole history of the Greek language, that it is strictly univocal, that mode is essentially denoted by it, that increase or diminution of action of the verb compared with βάπτω is a groundless conceit, that it always signifies to dip;" this is all clear and self-harmonious, and mingles with, without clouding, the earlier pellucid Baptist testimony. But when he goes on to say: "It not only signifies to dip *or immerse;*" "if we dip an object *in any way,* we cause it to dip *or sink;*" "caused to dip *as it were by sinking;*" "baptism means *to lay under water,*" &c., &c., we are fairly bewildered, and cannot imagine what Dr. Carson can be thinking of.

What conceivable unifying bond subsists between "dip and nothing but dip," and "dip *in any way,*" "dip *or immerse,*" "dip *or sink,*" "dip *or lay under water*"? So long as the utterance is—baptizing is dipping, and dipping is baptizing, consistency is maintained; when this takes the multiform shape, "dipping, *or immersing, or sinking, or laying under water*—is baptizing," the one meaning has vanished.

R. Fuller, D.D., Charleston, Southern Baptist Board of
Publication. 1859.

Dip, sink, plunge, immerse.

Dr. Fuller, in entering on his work, makes loud and
earnest proclamation, like his predecessors, of *the act* of
baptism and one definite meaning; which act and which
meaning is to be found nowhere save in such verbal
iteration.

He says: "In all translations of classical works βαπτίζω
is rendered dip, immerse. In short, the translators of our
Bibles have themselves exposed the pretext, that there is
any difficulty as to the word. In the case of Naaman, the
Septuagint uses βαπτίζω, and the translation renders it dip."
(pp. 10, 11.)

"In Greek, the addition of *zo* rather enforces than
diminishes the primitive word. And just so βάπτω, to dip;
βαπτίζω, to make one dip, that is, to immerse.

"Where the ordinance is mentioned, βαπτίζω is always
the word; and never was there a word whose meaning
was more clear and precise." (pp. 12, 13.)

"From these examples it is manifest that βαπτίζω means
to immerse. If any one attempts to contradict this argument, let him meet it fairly and honestly." (p. 17.)

Dr. Fuller gives as a caption to his book—"the act of
Baptism"—showing that he set out to advocate some definite and exclusive act as belonging to ritual baptism.
This he supposed, at the outset, to be very clear and
precise, as is manifest, from his saying, on the second
page, "Jesus says, he that believeth and is baptized shall
be saved. To charge him with wrapping up his meaning
in obscure phraseology is impious; it is to accuse him of
the enormous guilt of the Roman tyrant," &c. For a while
it seemed as though this definite act was to be represented
by *dip* (inasmuch as the Doctor approves of the rendering by
"our translators" from the Septuagint!); but, like others
of his friends, he finds it for some reason convenient to
say one thing and do another. He gives fourteen classical

quotations to establish the meaning of βαπτίζω, announcing that it is manifest that it means, not dip, but immerse. But what is strangest of all is, that this manifest meaning (in which there is no definite act at all), he never gives as the translation of any one of his fourteen quotations, but introduces dip, sink, and plunge. Are these four terms the same in " form and force," " neither more nor less," representing each, alike and equally, the one, definite, modal act of baptism? If not, why put shame on an inquiry which purports to make proof of such act by the use of such contrariant terms?

If we turn from this confusion to seek " the act of baptism" in that meaning indicated by Dr. Fuller's philology —baptize, to make dip—our search is all fruitless. This discovery having been made by the help of zo, it would seem to be regarded as too precious to be used, for never again does it appear throughout the book.

Notwithstanding, therefore, " there never was a word the meaning of which was more clear and precise," Dr. Fuller seems to be at a loss which to choose amid dip, and make to dip, and sink, and plunge, and immerse, in order to mark " the act of baptism," which, as appears from the title of his book, he was anxious to accomplish.

PROF. RIPLEY, NEWTON THEOLOGICAL INSTITUTE. 1833.

To dip, its radical, proper meaning.

Professor Ripley pays deferential regard, in definition, to the traditional meaning, to dip.

He translates; " the sword was so *dipped* as even to become heated," remarking, "Should the reader stop to think *dipped into what?* How instantaneous and how irresistible the reply, *into the blood.*" The meaning, dipped, is not forced or inappropriate. (p. 19.)

My business, now, is not to question interpretations, but to let Baptist writers speak and make out, if they can, a *primâ facie* case for themselves, indicating, as they pass along, only such difficulties as appear on the surface.

Again he remarks: " One of which sorts was performed by the dipping of the hands into water, and this was properly expressed by the peculiar term (βάπτίζω) which he has employed. If so, this word is here used in its radical, proper meaning." (p. 42.)

This " radical and proper meaning" is announced only to be rejected on the succeeding page.

It would, surely, take the seven wise men of Greece to render a reason justly defensive of such procedure.

Others, less wise, will be tempted to think that theory suggests one course, while the exigencies of truth constrain to the other.

J. L. DAGG, CHURCH ORDER, SOUTHERN BAPTIST PUBLICATION,
CHARLESTON. 1859.

" To immerse."

Professor Dagg quotes some fifty passages containing the word βάπτω, each of which he translates by *dip*. He also quotes a still larger number containing the word βαπτίζω, each of which he translates by *immerse*.

Unless the Professor is charged with acting very unreasonably, while he acts very systematically, we must conclude that these persistent differences in translation are intended to denote real differences in the words translated. And this conclusion is well founded; although the difference appears to be imperfectly apprehended and inadequately stated.

We are told, " the termination *ιζω* is, with greater probability, supposed by others to add to the primitive word the signification of *to cause* or *to make*, like the termination *ize* in *legalize*, to make legal. According to this hypothesis, if βάπτω signifies *to immerse*, βαπτίζω signifies *to cause to be immersed*. This makes the two words nearly or quite synonymous."

Not "nearly or quite," but absolutely, according to Professor Dagg's explanation of this causality. *Βάπτω* causes its object "to be immersed," and βαπτίζω, according to the explanation, does precisely the same thing. The explanation is faulty. It makes βαπτίζω causative not of βάπτω but of the immersion, over which βάπτω is itself already causative; and so only repeats that word. To be truly causative of βάπτω, it must reach the cause which puts βάπτω into operation; that is, it must cause some person to dip.

Of more value is the statement—"βάπτω more frequently denotes slight or temporary immersion than βαπτίζω. Hence the English word *dip*, which properly denotes slight or temporary immersion, is more frequently its appropriate rendering. In nearly one-half of the examples in which βαπτίζω occurs in the literal sense, it signifies the immersion which attends drowning and the sinking of ships." (p. 33.)

The Professor here fairly touches the nerve of truth without fully laying it bare; yet sufficiently so to send a shock through all the Baptist system. If βάπτω signifies "*an immersion which is slight and temporary;*" and if βαπτίζω signifies "an immersion which is profound and enduring;"' what becomes of the *dicta*, "baptizing is dipping, and dipping is baptizing"—" one meaning, dip *or immerse*"—"that the one is more or less than the other is a groundless conceit"?

If Professor Dagg is right, the postulate which demands equality "in form, and force, and effect," for these words, is all wrong.

C. STOVEL. LONDON, 1846.

"It means, caused the people to dip."

"Βαπτίζω, is causal of βάπτω. The baptizing of John, might have been performed entirely by other hands under John's direction. The sense of the original must be retained in the causal form of the verb; and if it be right to say, let Lazarus dip the tip of his finger in water, it cannot be wrong to say, John caused the people to dip, or to be dipped in water."

Whether Mr. Stovel's philological principles be right

or not, he seems disposed to apply them right honestly. While Drs. Carson, Fuller, and Dagg all unite in making βαπτίζω causative of βάπτω, they all unite, also, in declining to apply the principle. They still represent the one as the *alter ego* of the other. They were aware that if made really causative, it could find no exemplification in Scripture facts. I dip, expresses an act which I perform. I baptize, if causative of to dip, would make the act expressed by that word to be done by some other person. Now, this Mr. Stovel acknowledges, very justly, for good reasoning, but very awkwardly for the history of ritual baptism. He should, however, have gone a step farther, and said, not only that John *might* have stood by while he baptized, *to wit*, caused the people to dip themselves or one another, but that he must have so done. "For it cannot be wrong to say, John caused the people to dip (themselves), or to be dipped (by one another), in water," seeing that it is said, "let Lazarus dip the tip of his finger in water"!

Novelties in this controversy are rare; but Mr. Stovel seems disposed to treat us to such an exhibition. Whether it will tend to the gratification of his friends; or whether they will think that his philology carried out elucidates that one, definite, precise, clear, and only meaning of βαπτίζω is doubtful.

M. P. JEWETT, A.M.   BOSTON, 1854.

"To dip, or immerse, and never has any other meaning."

"βαπτίζω, in the whole history of the Greek language, has but one meaning. It signifies to dip or immerse, and never has any other meaning." (p. 13.)

"In baptism, we are commanded to perform the act represented by the word baptize."

In the first of these quotations, Prof. Jewett repeats the language of Dr. Carson. In the second, he reiterates a declaration handed down from mouth to mouth, without apparent consciousness of its import, or that its utterers were under obligation to conform to it.

To affirm, in the critical discussion of a word which is declared to be the most precise of all words, and whose value has been determined to a hair, that it means dip OR immerse, is of all extraordinary things the most extraordinary.

If it be, indeed, true that Baptizo, in the whole history of the Greek language, has but one meaning; and if it be, indeed, true that Jewett and friends have found out what is that meaning; then, why not tell us what it is? Why give us such Delphic utterance as—it means *this;* OR if it does not mean this, then it means *that;* but if it does not mean that, then certainly it does mean *something else!*

Will an attempt be made to rebut this condemnation by the assertion that dip and immerse have but one meaning in the whole history of the *English* language? Such a line of defence would be bold, hazardous, desperate, but the exigency is great; let it be tried.

While waiting the issue of such effort, we will venture to say that such clay-iron definition, persisted in through long years, repeated by unnumbered authors, and in contradiction to cherished and fundamental postulates, cannot proceed either from defective knowledge or through oversight; but must proceed from some unrevealed and dire necessity.

DIP—PLUNGE—IMMERSE.

It may be worth while to ask and obtain an answer to the question—Are Baptist writers, while using these terms avowedly to express a meaning which is " one, definite, precise, clear," aware that these terms do not and cannot express any such meaning?

Let them answer for themselves. First, hear "the venerable Booth."

" The reader needs only *to dip* into a Hebrew or Greek Lexicon, into Ainsworth's Latin, or Johnson's English Dictionary, to be convinced of this. I have just dipped into the works of such an author. Now this, far from signifying that I feel my mind, as it were, immersed in the author's writings, only means, as Johnson tells us, that I have entered slightly into them."—*Pædobaptism,* vol. i, pp. 115, 123.

Surely Booth was aware that dip and immerse could not express one and the same meaning, whatever may be the fact with regard to others. But he did not stand alone. We have but to call to mind the language of Professor Dagg to see distinctly stated that primary, literal use of dip, in which this figurative use of Booth is grounded.

"*Βάπτω* more frequently denotes *slight* or *temporary* immersion." Here, in the trivial effect which must follow upon "a slight and temporary immersion" in any physical element, we see the most satisfactory foundation laid for the expression of an extremely limited knowledge of an author, by saying, "I have merely *dipped* into his writings."

On the other hand, Dagg says: "*βαπτίζω* signifies the immersion which attends drowning or the sinking of ships." And he might have added: "In the whole history of Greek literature" *βάπτω* is never once employed to denote such immersion. By such characteristics as attend on immersion unlimited (unlimited as to the depth to which it penetrates, and unlimited as to the time of its continuance), immerse becomes perfectly adapted to express, as is done by Booth in figure, the extreme opposite of dip, namely, thorough engagedness in the study of an author.

Who could imagine that writers so conversant with these differences would ever venture to ask any one, in a critical controversy, to adopt, as the meaning of a word, a word which they affirm has but one meaning, *dip* or *immerse?*

But what do Baptists think of *plunge?* Is there authoritative sanction for making it co-ordinate with dip and immerse in expounding *βαπτίζω?* And if so, do they regard all these terms of "the same form and force"?

In regard to the first of these inquiries, an answer is

found in "the 40th article of the Confession of Faith of those churches which are commonly, though falsely, called Anabaptist," which says: "The way and manner of dispensing of this ordinance the Scriptures hold out to be dipping *or* plunging." This testimony is two centuries old. It has, however, received constant reaffirmation during all this interval. A single exemplification of which, representative of all, may be found in the following language of Dr. Cox: "Dipping, *plunging*, or immersing, is the unquestionable, settled, and universally admitted primitive signification."

Hear, now, Booth, as to the fitness of these three terms to express with equal absoluteness one precise meaning: "Dr. Williams uniformly contrasts his chosen verb *purify*, with the term *plunge;* as if that had been the expression most commonly used by us. But this, notwithstanding his boasted candor, is very unfair. For he knows that it is not the verb to plunge, but the word immerse, that is usually adopted by us on this occasion. He, also, knows that the term plunge does not signify, merely, to immerse; but suddenly and violently to immerse; for which reason we do not think it the most eligible word by which to render the enacting term baptize. On the verb active, to plunge, Dr. Johnson says: ' This word, to what action soever it be applied, commonly expresses either violence or suddenness in the agent, or distress in the patient.' Now, it should seem that, for this very reason, Dr. Williams made choice of the term plunge, rather than immerse or dip, in order to give a ridiculous air to our sentiments and practice."—*Animad. on Ed. Williams.* London, 1792, p. 316.

Most strange complaint on the part of this venerable man! Dr. Williams "uniformly" employs plunge to express the meaning. And is this to be urged as a ground of complaint by those who postulate uniformity of meaning "through the whole history of Greek literature"? It signifies, "suddenly and violently to immerse;" therefore "we do not think it the most eligible word by which to

4

render baptize." But who selected this word? Was it not the Baptist " Confession of Faith," which said, "plunging is the way and manner of dispensing this ordinance taught in the Scriptures"? Was it not Dr. Cox, representing a host of others, who said, " plunging is the unquestionable, settled, and universally admitted primitive signification"? And now shall it be said, to use this word as the exponent of baptize is " very unfair," and is done " in order to give a ridiculous air to our sentiments and practice"! Surely the charge of unfairness, and of purpose to ridicule, rests not on Dr. Williams; but on those who for generations have insisted that plunge was the meaning of that word which is declared to be of unresolvable simplicity, and without the shadow of a change through a thousand years.

If harsh complaint is to be preferred because an " opponent made choice" of an alternative meaning, why is such alternative meaning held forth, page after page, by Booth himself, as well as by others? Why say dip, or immerse, or plunge, or—, if an opponent to whom such language is addressed is "very unfair" to notice it? Would that Baptist writers, instead of employing defining terms "most commonly," or speaking of such as are " usually adopted," and finding fault with a " uniform" use for a declared univocal word, might be found aiming at consistency by settling down on some word which they would venture to carry through all Greek literature. But while we have been told through hundreds of years that βαπτίζω has but one meaning; that that meaning is clear and precise; that difficulty in translating is pretence; still it remains an ominous fact, that no Baptist writer has ever ventured to give us the exponential translating word, vindicating his judgment by a uniform application to all cases of use. We must have, sooner or later, a long procession of terms whose only uniformity is their interlinking vinculum " or."

But while plunge, thus tried, is found wanting, Booth thinks, " our sentiment and practice" would not be put to shame by the use of " dip or immerse." Unhappily for this conclusion, " dip," since Booth's day, has fallen into no little disrepute among its once ardent admirers. And the plea might again be presented—"not usually adopted;" and the complaint made of " unfairness," and of a purpose to make the subject " ridiculous;" if an opponent should " uniformly" use this *petite* and undignified word.

It is important to bear in distinct remembrance that plunge was discarded because of its essential and distinguishing characteristics; " effecting an immersion *suddenly and violently*." Is dip to be discarded on similar grounds, to wit, because of its essential and distinguishing characteristics, which are, as Dagg informs us, " *superficial* and *temporary* immersion?" It would seem to be even so. And, thus, while Booth repudiated plunge, because it made both " our sentiments and practice ridiculous," while his successors have discovered that dip must be thrown into the background, because uniformly applied to " the sentiment" it would make classic Greek " ridiculous;" still it must be kept at hand for " practice," as otherwise Baptist baptism cannot be administered. Thus we have a word which, *e confesso*, cannot be applied to the usage of βαπτίζω, made the sole, sovereign arbiter in administrative baptism.

I say that this hopeless break down of dip is a matter of confession. Without multiplying testimony, one or two instances may suffice as representatives of many.

Prof. Dagg gives as the uniform translation of βάπτω, to dip. He does not give this word as the translation of βαπτίζω in a single instance. Why is this? It was not of accident; for he tells us that it was of design. It was not because he regarded the different words employed as of the same value; for he expressly tells us that they were of widely different value. It was not because it was a matter of indifference to the system which he advocates; for the Baptist system lives or dies as dip does or does not represent βαπτίζω. Why, then, such translation? The only answer that can be given is—Prof. Dagg thus confesses that " the sentiment" that dip expounds βαπτίζω, must, in the face of Greek usage, be utterly abandoned; while in the face of Baptist "practice" claimed to be founded on βαπτίζω, it must, imperatively, be retained.

Hear, also, Dr. Fuller. Dr. Carson had said of this word, "It is strictly univocal. My position is, that it always signifies to dip." And in a sea-coast baptism, by the rising tide, he declared with unflinching courage, that the word in such a case had the meaning to dip just as much as in any other. But Dr. Fuller, on the same passage, with fainter heart, remarks: "A fourth passage is produced to show that βαπτίζω does not always denote the act of plunging (or dipping). My position is that βαπτίζω means to immerse." (p. 29.) Thus these doctors flatly antagonize each other. The one affirming, "My position is that βαπτίζω always signifies to dip," and manfully protecting his *protégé* under difficulties; while the other, alarmed at the inrolling billows, exclaims, "My position is that βαπτίζω means to immerse," and abandons dip to a hopeless sea immersion. Thus dip perishes amid the conflict of its friends.

"THE ACT OF BAPTISM—THE ACT IS IMMERSION."

While Dr. Fuller discards "the act of plunging," and with it the act of dipping, he fondly imagines that immerse will more than make up this double loss, and furnish to him "the act of Baptism," which will never "make ridiculous our sentiments or our practice."

This welcome and much-needed auxiliary he finds, and with exultation announces thus: "It is as plain as the sun in the heavens that the act is immersion."

It must have been a remarkably cloudy day, and the solar position singularly uncertain, when Dr. Fuller made this comparison. Mathematical calculation can locate "the sun in the heavens," even amid clouds and darkness; but how the ingenuity of Dr. Fuller can locate act in "immersion," so as to give it definiteness, clearness, precision, modality, remains to be seen.

When the Doctor speaks of "the act of immersion"

bathed in solar effulgence, he must mean to designate some definite act, if he meant to speak anything to the purpose. He is engaged in rebutting an argument addressed against the Baptist position—βαπτίζω expresses a definite act—and in doing so assails those definite acts, plunging, dipping, which are selected by the advocates of the system. Dr. Fuller finds the argument against these acts unanswerable, and he seeks escape from absolute defeat by abandoning these long-cherished representatives, and falling back upon the support of a new auxiliary—"the act of immersion." In doing this there is no avowal of abandonment of the principle of the system, namely, *definite act*, but only of the specific acts, plunging and dipping, in the place of which he offers the definite act which is exhibited in "immersion." We are, therefore, compelled to suppose that Dr. Fuller wishes to be understood as still maintaining, while in fact abandoning, the theory that βαπτίζω expresses a definite act. Such holding on and letting go of a vital point in argument cannot be allowed. Plunging expresses a definite act; but Dr. Fuller frankly says that will not answer as the one definite act of all Greek literature. Dipping expresses a definite act; but this too, (we may believe with profound regret,) he declines to adopt. "Immersion" no more expresses a definite act than does "point no point" express a sharply defined headland. It expresses definite condition, not definite action. And Dr. Fuller, in saying "the act is immersion," imitates "the Roman tyrant," whom he condemns for "wrapping up his meaning in obscure phraseology."

IMMERSE—A REFUGE FROM THE DIFFICULTIES OF MODAL ACTION.

Dr. Fuller is not singular among Baptist writers in seeking refuge in "the act of immersion" from the inextricable difficulties which invest the definite act theory. It is of primary importance that we should understand the fact and the necessity for such retreat, as, also, the true nature of that place of refuge to whose protection they have made appeal.

That "immersion" is a shelter into which the friends of the definite act system have been driven from other untenable positions, is made most certain by a glance at the history of this controversy.

A. R., the friend of Roger Williams, says nothing about "immersion." With him, "Baptizing is Dipping, and Dipping is Baptizing."

The Baptist Confession of Faith, two centuries old, does not speak of "immersion." It says: "The way or manner of dispensing this ordinance the Scriptures hold out to be dipping or plunging."

But Dr. Cox began to awake to a consciousness that these definite acts, unaided, could not bear the burden laid upon them. He, accordingly, without discarding them, associates with them *immerse.* He declares that "dipping, plunging *or immersing,* is the unquestionable, settled, and universally admitted primitive signification."

Booth, under controversial pressure, is more outspoken, complaining that "plunge gives a ridiculous air to our sentiment and practice; immerse is usually adopted by us."

Dr. Conant says: "The Bible Society for which I have the honor to labor, has adopted as its fundamental principle the faithful translation of every word; the literal meaning of this word, its true and only import, is *to immerse.*" And yet, notwithstanding the lifting up of so just and noble a standard; and notwithstanding all the breadth and sharpness of this language, Dr. Cox does formally define that word whose "true and only import is to immerse" by dip and plunge. What can be that inexorable necessity which thus constrains Baptist writers to write down such univocal definitions only to turn the stylus and blot them out?

BAPTIST DOUBTS AS TO "THE DEFINITE ACT" THEORY.

The embarrassment of our Baptist friends is strongly

exhibited by the doubt suggested by some of their best writers, whether, after all, they have got hold of the true meaning of βαπτίζω, and by the earnest antagonism with which such suggestion has been repelled.

Dr. Gale uses this language: "Besides, the word βαπτίζω, perhaps, does not so necessarily express the action of putting under water, as in general a thing's being in that condition, no matter how it comes so, whether it is put into the water, or the water comes over it, though, indeed, to put it into the water is the most natural way, and the most common, and is, therefore, usually and pretty constantly, but it may be not necessarily implied."

It is obvious that this view, suggested, hesitatingly, by Dr. Gale, revolutionizes the Baptist view as to the meaning of βαπτίζω. A word which "expresses *the action* of putting under water," and a word which "expresses a thing's *being in that condition*," are separated from each other by essential difference of nature. They belong to different classes of verbs. The one designates an act, the other a condition. If any one should be disposed to say, that this difference is of no moment as to this investigation, I would answer: 1. No such judgment should be pronounced until the distinction has been thoroughly traced to its results. 2. That whether it should be found changing results or not, it is a confession that the Baptist view of the character of the word was essentially erroneous. 3. Dr. Carson did not regard the difference as unimportant, but lifts up an earnest cry of "treason!" immediately upon its enunciation. He feels that the setting up, thus, of condition against act is to pierce the heart principle of the system —" act, and nothing but an act"—in the house of its friends. He thus comes to the rescue; "Dr. Gale was induced to suppose that it does not so necessarily express the *action* of *putting* under water, as that the object is *in that state*. But this is evidently inconsistent with the meaning of the word." (p. 20.)

" When this word is applied to an object lying under water, but not actually dipped, the mode essentially denoted by it is as truly expressed as in any other instance of its occurrence." (p. 11.)

Dr. Carson's courage is admirable. He unflinchingly affirms mode, while admitting that there is none.

The courage of Dr. Cox is not so heroic. He yields to that strong pressure which drew from Dr. Gale a qualified confession of error as to the meaning of the word, and with far less reserve concedes the untenableness of the position that βαπτίζω expresses modal action or act at all, in contradistinction from condition. This writer always proceeds on the assumption that βάπτω and βαπτίζω are absolute equivalents. In his interpretation of Daniel 4 : 33, he attaches no importance to the fact that it is the former and not the latter word which is used; but remarks: "The verb does not imply *the manner* in which the effect was produced, but *the effect* itself; not *the mode* by which the body of the king was wetted, but its *condition*."

This exposition is enforced by an appeal to other words, *e. g., to hurt, to burn, to drown*, none of which expresses modal action, but condition only. He then continues: "*The state* of the body is intended as having been drenched with dew; signifying *the condition* of having been drenched; as being burnt with lightning, or in a conflagration, would mean *the state* of being burnt, which resulted from the accident or visitation of fire."

Such views, casting utterly away the "perhaps" of Dr. Gale, appeared to Dr. Carson so grievous, that he determined "to settle the question though it should occupy some pages." (p. 36.) He will not tolerate any departure from modality—"If all the water in the ocean had *fallen on* him it would not have been a literal immersion. The mode would still be wanting." On this passage in Daniel, Dr. Gale having remarked, "Hence it appears very clear, that both Daniel and his translators designed to express the very great dew Nebuchadnezzar should be exposed to," Dr. Carson pronounces what is so "very clear" to Dr. G. to be, in fact, "very absurd;" thus, "Dr. Gale absurdly supposes βάπτω means to cover with water without reference to mode, and

at the same time metaphorically alludes to dipping." Let
all who revere the name of Carson take notice, that to
make a word which expresses condition, also to express
action, is to act "*absurdly.*" His opposition to Cox is no
less uncompromising. To his remark—"a body exposed
to Eastern dews would be as wet *as if* plunged into water,"
he replies: "This leaves the mode unaccounted for. Without doubt the verb here expresses mode as well as anywhere else. To suppose the contrary gives up the point
at issue, as far as mode is concerned." Again let it be
noted that, Carson being judge, to abandon the idea of
modal act in βαπτίζω, is to abandon the Baptist system,
which is founded in modality.

Farther, in reply to the argument of Cox from the word
hurt he says: "Nothing of manner is here expressed, and
for an obvious reason; nothing of manner is expressed in
the verb. But will Dr. Cox grant that this is the case with
the verb βάπτω? If he does, about what is he contending?
Βάπτω not only necessarily *implies* mode, but literally expresses nothing but mode. Mode is as much expressed
here as it is in the commission of our Lord to his apostles."

Dr. Carson clearly and boldly hazards his system on the
merits of modalism in action, rebuking the fainthearted-
ness and disloyalty of his associates.

With what consistency the Doctor binds βάπτω down, with
iron clamps, to modalism in Daniel, and yet refuses, on
other occasions, to allow it to be restrained by so much as
a gossamer thread, others may determine; I exhibit the
facts. Dr. Gale had taken the ground in relation to dyeing with coloring matter, which Carson takes respecting
wetting with dew; to wit, that the modal act of dipping
was necessarily involved. This position is thus sharply
criticized by his friend: "What does the learned writer
mean when he expresses a doubt of the propriety of this
usage (*i. e.* βάπτω dropping mode)? Does he mean that
such an extension of the meaning of words is in some
degree a trespass against the laws of language? But such
a usage is in strict accordance with the laws of language;

and the history of a thousand words sanctions the practice. Use is the sole arbiter of language; and whatever is agreeable to this authority stands justified beyond impeachment. *Βάπτω* signifies *to dye by sprinkling*, as properly as by dipping, though originally it was confined to the latter."

Dr. Carson is a study! When his friend Gale trembles at the consequences of admitting that *βάπτω* may signify *to dye*, still more that it may signify to dye *by sprinkling*, and stoutly affirms that it has no such meaning, "but always implies and refers only to its true, natural signification, *to dip;*" then, Carson interposes, declaring that *βάπτω* can mean, and does mean, *to dye*, nay, "to dye by *sprinkling* as properly as by dipping;" but when it is said that *βάπτω* may mean to wet (to wet by sprinkled dew-drops), without dipping, then *βάπτω* not only "necessarily implies mode, but literally expresses nothing but mode." How a word which "expresses nothing but mode"—*to dip*—can yet mean *to dye by sprinkling*, while it cannot mean (by reason of its modalism) *to wet by sprinkling*, is a mystery left unsolved. "Use stands justified beyond impeachment," except a bill of indictment be drawn by Dr. Carson!

But notwithstanding Dr. Carson's positiveness, and his declared purpose "to settle the question though it should occupy some pages," he has failed to carry conviction to the minds of some of the ardent friends of the Baptist system.

Morell abandons Carson and goes over to the side of Gale and Cox, thus: "That the word *βαπτίζω* uniformly signifies to dip I will not venture to assert, or undertake to prove. I believe, however, that it is pretty generally admitted, on both sides, that the word does mean to dip; that this is its generic meaning, and its most usual meaning. But it appears quite evident that the word also bears the sense of *covering by superfusion*. This is admitted by Dr. Cox, who says, 'A person may be immersed by pouring; but immersion is the being plunged into water, or overwhelmed by it. Was the water to ascend from the earth, it would still be baptism were the person wholly covered by it.' Thus far we surrender the question of immersion, and in doing so feel no small pleasure in finding ourselves in such good company as that of Dr. Cox." (p. 167.)

Will our Baptist friends turn the edge of their ridicule from others, and try its edge upon their friend Morell, as he now affirms that "a person may be baptized, immersed, by *pouring*"? Is "dipping by pouring" (so long made the butt of ridicule) any more facile of execution in the hand of a friend than of an opponent? Or, having accepted from Carson, what was so long rejected when proffered by others, that βάπτω does not merely mean to dip, but to dye by *sprinkling;* will they accept from Morell, as simple verity, what was so ridiculously false when stated by opponents, to wit, that baptism is *not* dipping, that immersion is *not* dipping, and that baptism by pouring, or immersion by pouring, is *not* "obscure phraseology employed for the purpose of covering up the absurdity of *dipping* by *pouring*"? Whether or no, we have a house divided against itself; a general "surrender thus far of the question of immersion."

Morell is one of the fairest of opponents, and we will not abuse his candor by perverting his surrender. He does not give up immersion, but he does give up dipping as necessary to it. But on sober second thought he will, no doubt, find that, having "surrendered" so much, he has not surrendered enough. The admission that βαπτίζω does sometimes mean, not to dip, nor to put into an element, but to immerse (that is, to secure intusposition without regard to act), does necessitate the conclusion that βαπτίζω does *never* mean a modal act—*to dip.* "Dipping by sprinkling," the performance of one modal act by a diverse modal act, is not more patently absurd than that the same word should express a modal act and an immodal act; or a modal act and a result, without designating any form of act by which that result was effected.

But let us pass on to a farther development of Baptist

testimony to the "one, clear, precise, and definite meaning" of this word.

Dr. Fuller thus testifies: "A fourth case is presented
by Pœdobaptist authors from Aristotle. It is produced to
show that βαπτίζω does not always denote *the act* of plunging. My position is that βαπτίζω means to immerse. It
matters not how the immersion is effected." (p. 29.)

"Suppose a man should lie in the baptistery while it is
filling. The pouring of the water would not be immersion, yet an immersion would take place, if he remained
long enough." (p. 31.)

Again we have the use of the word "immersion," as
expressing a thought wholly dissevered from the form of
the act inducing it, whether that form be pouring, or
plunging, or *sprinkling;* for "if a man should lie in the
baptistery long enough," under the act of sprinkling, "an
immersion would take place." And yet it is the same
writer who speaks of "the act of baptism being the act
of immersion," which act of immersion is said to be "as
plain as the sun in the heavens"!

Well, then, in the light of this *dictum* we must even
believe that "the act of baptism" is the act of immersion,
which act is that of plunging, or pouring, or sprinkling,
either of which will "baptize the man who lies in the
baptistery long enough"!

Whether Dr. Fuller has added to the clearness, the
simplicity, and the precision of the one definite act of baptism by his "plain as the sun" position is quite doubtful.

One word as to the incongruous use of immerse and
immersion by Drs. Fuller and Carson. The latter says,
βαπτίζω has but one meaning; that meaning is one of mode,
and nothing but mode, which mode is definitely expressed
by *dip*—"dip *or immerse.*" Now, these words must be
used as the absolute equivalents of each other, or shame is
poured over all the pages wherein they appear. But Dr.
Fuller does most expressly antagonize to dip and to plunge,
by to immerse. He argumentatively rejects the definite
act as not expressing the meaning of βαπτίζω, and takes,

instead, *to immerse*, as destitute of all expression of definite act, proclaiming as his position, "It matters not how the immersion is effected." "Immersion may be by pouring," but pouring never produces dipping or plunging.

That such use of these terms is in utter contradiction, the one of the other, I need not say "is as plain as the sun in the heavens;" but it is important to say that no notice is ever given by Baptist writers of such contradictory usage; while the use, now in one sense and now in another, is met with everywhere, not only in different writers, but in the pages of the same writer.

To these writers—Gale, Cox, Morell, Fuller, all in the front rank of Baptist scholars—who have been constrained by the stress of testimony to abandon the long-cherished definite act theory, "mode and nothing but mode," must be added the certainly not less eminent name of Conant.

Dr. Conant presents for embalmment, in the "new version" of the holy Scriptures, neither the definite act *to dip*, nor the modal act *to plunge*, but the same word, "to immerse," in which Fuller and friends seek refuge when compelled "thus far to surrender the question of immersion." The foreign origin of this word and its composite character throws around it an indefinite penumbral character, which is its qualifying merit as a retreat from the long-honored, but no longer tenable, position of "one clear, precise, definite act through all Greek literature."

Henceforth, our business is to dissipate this penumbra, and to show that when its outlines are sharply lighted up, there is no more within it a place of refuge for the Baptist theory, than has been found in the abandoned *dip* and *plunge*.

But the views of Dr. Conant—the latest, the most elaborate, as well as every way qualified investigator of this subject—demand special consideration.

"THE MEANING OF ΒΑΠΤΙΖΩ."

T. J. CONANT, D.D., AMERICAN BIBLE UNION. NEW YORK, 1860.

Too much praise cannot be accorded to Prof. Conant for the exhaustive labor which he has bestowed upon the collection and accurate exhibition of all passages in which βαπτίζω is found. It gives me great pleasure to acknowledge my indebtedness to him for quite a number of passages, after having devoted the leisure intervals of some years to securing such a collection; as, also, for the correction of some errors of quotation. Indeed, so well satisfied have I been of the accuracy of Dr. Conant, and oftentimes of the greater accessibility of the editions referred to by him, that I have, throughout, conformed my quotations and references to his, on a review; this inquiry having been, substantially, completed before meeting with his treatise.

Dr. Conant has not been satisfied with the mere collection of materials, but has made them the subject of very elaborate study. He has felt that a large responsibility was resting upon him, and he spared no pains to acquit himself well under it. And he has done so. None will question the honesty of his purpose, the fulness of his labor, or the adequacy of his scholarship, however much they may differ from him in some of his views.

The results reached generally by Prof. Conant may be accepted as sufficiently correct for all ordinary purposes of language, while, with a special application to the Baptist system and its sharp demands, their accuracy may be questioned and their essential modification be demanded.

HIS ACCORD WITH THE BAPTIST THEORY.

The orthodox Baptist view of the meaning of βαπτίζω, undoubtedly, is that it expresses a clear, precise, and definite act; which act has been expressed in a thousand treatises, and in every ritual service, by the word *dip*, through more than two hundred years.

Dr. Conant seems to adopt the theory that this word has but one meaning, and that that meaning is an act, a definite act. This is his language :

" This word is rendered into English—the translation expresses its true and only import." " The word βαπτίζω, during the whole existence of the Greek as a spoken language, had a perfectly defined and unvarying import." " The constant usage of Greek writers, and the only recognized meaning of the word." " The simple, distinct, and corporeal sense to which the word was appropriated by unvarying usage."

This is explicit. The language employed designating this meaning as an act, a definite act, would seem to be not less so. Take the following :

" The Greek word βαπτίζειν expresses nothing more than *the act* of immersion." " *This act* is performed on the assenting believer—and this distinguishes it from all other acts of life—*the act* expressed by the same word is a superstitious Pharisaic ceremony—*the act* designated by the word in all these cases is the same." " *The act* which it describes was chosen for its adaptation to set forth by lively symbolism the ground thought of Christianity." " The name of the element in which *the act it expresses* took place." " *The other acts* with which it is compared in the New Testament." " The daily and hourly repetition of *the act* in common life which it described."

Can language like this be read with any other feeling than that Dr. Conant casts in his lot with those who declare that, " one meaning, a clear, precise, and *definite act* reigns through all Greek literature ?" This conclusion is confirmed by more full and explanatory statement;—" with the preposition into before the name of the element into which an object is plunged or immersed expressing fully *the act* of *passing* from one element into another." " The verb βαπτίζω, *immergo*, has, in fact, but one sole acceptation. It signifies literally and always *to plunge*." This last passage is a quotation (with approval) from another writer.

We are, then, taught by Dr. Conant that βαπτίζω has but

one meaning, that that meaning is an expressed act, a definite act characterized by passing from one medium into another, and it is distinctively represented by *plunge.*

This is all clear and consistent, whether correct or not. It has not merely the merit of self-consistence, but is in perfect harmony with the ancient and severe definition, " Baptizing is dipping, and dipping is baptizing." It accords, also, with the more modern exposition of Dr. Carson, " dip, and nothing but dip," maintained, theoretically, with cast-iron inflexibility; as, also, with the general stream of Baptist utterance.

But this is not all which Dr. Conant says as to the meaning of this word, and what he says more mars this beautiful simplicity of definition, and introduces a note of irreconcilable discord. Like every other Baptist writer who has attempted to maintain modal action in the face of the facts of usage, Prof. Conant fails to be self-consistent in his statements.

He does not distinctly avow a purpose to carry a definite act through every case of usage, and therefore recognize the obligation, with Dr. Carson, by some catechrestical distortion to shape facts after such model; but apparently feels at liberty to speak, as circumstances require, in conformity with the modal action of Carson, or the state and condition of Cox; all in the name of one, clear, definite, and unchanging meaning.

The evidence of this is found in language like the following:

HIS WANT OF ACCORD.

" The word βαπτίζειν, which, by constant usage, expressed an entire submersion of the object." " A sense founded on the idea of total submergence, as in floods of sorrow." " Among the several words, all agreeing in the essential idea of total submergence, by which βαπτίζειν may be expressed in English, the word immerse has been selected for use in this revision." " We speak of a man as immersed in calamities, &c., always with the idea of totality, of being wholly under the dominion of these states or influences . . . it suggests the clear image of the act on which all are founded."

These statements represent the meaning of βαπτίζω as turning wholly upon a *state* or *condition*, namely, of " entire submersion," while we were previously told that this meaning was concentred in an *act*. These two views do not coincide in one clear and precise meaning, but are essentially diverse and irreconcilable. The same word cannot express both act and condition, although act and condition may be inseparably united in one word. But in such case, act or condition must immediately control the word, and hold the other in subordination; both cannot be equally expressed. To plunge expresses directly the nature of the act which may carry its object into and under water; while to swamp expresses nothing, directly, of the nature of the act which carries its object under water, but gives expression to the condition effected, whatever may have been the nature of the act.

It is of the first importance that these differences should not be lost sight of in determining with critical accuracy the meaning of a word, and above all in tracing out the development of a word. It would be a forlorn hope to expect any just issue in the investigation of the usage of a word expressive of condition by a person whose mind was full of the idea that it was a word expressive of some action. Plunge has a development growing out of its peculiarities as an act; swamp, one which is based on condition. " I plunge into misfortune;" " I am swamped by misfortune;" express ideas essentially diverse. The structure of language is controlled by such differences. "I plunge into misfortune;" "misfortune swamps me;" are diversities of phraseology not accidental, but growing out of the essential diversity of the terms. Plunge expresses the course of action by which misfortune is reached. Swamp says nothing of this. As plunge and swamp should not be confounded, so, for like reason, act and condition should never be confounded; nor should one word be treated as though it expressed both act and condition, or at one time act, and at another time condition. This confusion vitiates Dr. Conant's treatise.

Some Baptist writers have felt, and confessed the impracticability of carrying βαπτίζω through its usage as expressing an act; but in making this confession they still doubly failed of the truth: 1. In not abandoning the idea that βαπτίζω ever expresses a definite act; and, 2. In not prosecuting the inquiry into the meaning of this word under the acknowledgment that its meaning centred in condition.

A portion of these writers met the difficulty by allowing the word at one time to mean act, and at another time to mean condition, a mending of their error quite inadmissible; while others chose a word, sufficiently vague, to slur over the difficulty. Dr. Conant appears to combine the various views and policies of those who have gone before him. He adopts the one meaning, the act, condition, and immerse, which is of such facile use now, to express an act, and now, to express condition.

Dr. Conant endeavors to lay a basis for appeal both to act and condition, by making both prominent in the meaning which he assigns to the word. Thus he says: " The ground idea expressed by the word, is, to put into or under water (or other penetrable substance), so as to immerse or submerge."

By this language, βαπτίζω is represented as expressing both an act and a condition resulting from that act. No objection can be made to the idea of an act which results in effecting a condition; but it is objectionable to make a word to distinctively represent both act and condition.

It may be noted that immerse and submerge, in this passage, are both used to express, distinctively, condition and not act. The same is true of the use of the same words in the following passage: "The object immersed or submerged is represented as being plunged, or as sinking down into the ingulfing fluid, or the immersing element overflowing, and thus ingulfing the object." "Immersed," "submerged," "immersing," represent condition; it is impossible to substitute for them words expressive of action; the act is performed by "plunging" and "sinking," or "overflowing." But if βαπτίζω does, by its proper force, express the act which belongs to plunge, or to sink, or to overflow, then, unless one and the same thing can be another and a diverse thing, it cannot express the condition which belongs to immerse and submerge, or "*ingulf*," here used as the equivalent of immerse.

But these words are used, very unallowably, to express act as well as condition. Βαπτίζω, "with the preposition *into* before the name of the element into which an object is plunged or immersed, expresses fully the act of passing from one element into another." Here "immerse" is used to express, coequally with plunge, "*the act of passing* from one element into another;" while before it was used to express condition resultant from the act of plunging.

Dr. Conant never makes such double and impossible use of *plunge;* why does he seek to make such, equally unallowable, use of *immerse?*

While freely acknowledging that "into," used as suggested, does indicate "an act passing from one element into another;" it is by no means admitted that such use with βαπτίζω shows that such act is to be found in that word. Words which of themselves express no movement may, still, be found with *into*, the word necessary to the movement being supplied. Such usage is not infrequent; and the explanation given meets with general acceptance.

That βαπτίζω does not express any definite movement, nor any independent movement whatever, "causing its object to pass from one medium into another," is conclusively shown by the use of this word in cases where no movement of any kind in the object takes place.

The sea-coast is baptized by the rising tide; but there is no act exercised upon it inducing a movement of the coast, "causing it to pass from one medium into another."

Such usage shook the faith of Gale in the notion of movement as inherent in this word, and wholly overthrew

that of Cox, while all the billows of the sea could not
move that of Carson a hair's breadth. He boldly affirmed
that movement was as much expressed by the word in such
cases, when no movement took place, as when movement
did take place; and to admit otherwise was to give up the
issue. He chided his friends sharply for their defection,
and endeavored to encourage them and sustain himself by
an appeal to some figure of speech. Dr. Carson, no doubt,
fully convinced himself that when an object was baptized
without being moved, that still it was said to be moved
because it was said to be baptized; and baptized "has but
one meaning through all Greek literature," "expressing
an act, clear, precise, definite," making its object "to pass
from one medium into another." His reasoning, however,
has failed to convince, I will not say his opponents, but
his friends; for no Baptist writer, following him, has ventured to stand upon the sea-coast and bid the inrolling
billow to cease its movement until "the coast" should
come to it and be lawfully baptized; "*passing* out of one
medium into another."

Dr. Carson, however, is right when he takes the ground
that βαπτίζω, if it ever expresses an act of movement must
always express such act; and if such meaning be abandoned in one case, it must be abandoned in all. Morell
cannot say: "It means, most usually, to dip, while it
appears quite evident that it, also, means to cover by
superfusion." No word can express "usually to dip," and
unusually "to superfuse." If it expresses the one, it never
does or can express the other; and if, in the usage of any
word, these and like terms meet together, they must stand
on the same basis; namely, that the word means one as
much as the other, in fact, means neither. The fact of
baptism by superfusion is admitted by Baptist writers.
Some saying that baptism by *superfusion* means baptism
by *dipping;* while others admit the fact, but decline to
work it out to its conclusions, and hold on to a position
which the admission subverts, namely, "one meaning, a
definite act, through all Greek literature."

Dr. Conant is involved in this inextricable embarrassment when he attempts to sustain "one meaning, expressing fully the act of *passing* from one element into another," while he also says: "The object is represented as being *plunged* or as *sinking down* into the ingulfing fluid, *or* the immersing element overflows, and thus ingulfs the object."

If βαπτίζω, of its own proper force, ever plunges or sinks its object, then it never overflows it; and if it ever overflows it, then it never plunges or sinks it; if it does, of its own proper force, distinctively plunge and sink and overflow its object, then it embodies a power which can work philological miracles; but if plunge, and sink, and overflow meet on equal terms in expounding the usage of this word, then Dr. Conant errs when he describes this word as representing an "act passing from one element into another," for such act cannot be represented by these several and diverse terms.

HIS FORMAL DEFINITION.

"The word BAPTIZEIN, during the whole existence of the Greek as a spoken language, had a perfectly defined and unvarying import. In its literal use it meant, as has been shown, to put entirely into or under a liquid, or other penetrable substance, generally water, so that the object was wholly covered by the inclosing element. By analogy, it expressed the *coming into a new state of life or experience,* in which one was, as it were, inclosed and swallowed up, so that, temporarily or permanently, he belonged wholly to it."

In this definition it is noteworthy that act, which has, heretofore, in Baptist writings, reigned with such supremacy, becomes, as to form, an absolutely vanishing quantity; and in its undefined obscurity exhausts itself in effecting a well-defined condition, which is placed in high relief in the foreground as the grand idea. In this, Dr. Conant has made decided advance on his predecessors.

It, also, claims especial attention as a novelty from a

Baptist writer, that a second very remarkable meaning is assigned to this word, which, as we have been so long told, possessed a solitary grandeur, in that, through ages, it never swerved from the idea of putting into water. It is none the less remarkable, because it appears, now, for the first time, as the meaning of this word, and is only introduced to our notice to be withdrawn without again reappearing.

It may, however, be made the occasion of again remarking how absolutely act is discarded as an element of value in determining the meaning of βαπτίζω. We are told that this secondary meaning comes "by analogy." Well, there are but two elements, act and condition, whereon the analogy can rest. On which does it rest? "Coming into a new state of life or experience, so as to be inclosed and swallowed up, and belong wholly to it." Where is the analogy to act, definite or indefinite, plunge, dip, or put into? Where is the likeness to plunging, or dipping, or putting, in "coming into a new *state*"? Are we to make a point of "coming into" a moral state with *putting into* water? Well, let us know what is this *quo modo*, and let us see what is the admirable tracery of the analogy. Until this is done, we shall rest content with such analogy as may be found between the *condition* of envelopment by a physical element and the condition of that moral *state*, wherein those who enter it are wholly subject to its control. Others may fill up the picture, at leisure, showing the analogy between the act of putting into and the *modus operandi* of moral influence in inducing this "new state of life."

In this definition by the use of "put"—"put into or under"—Dr. Conant gives a greater breadth and freedom to βαπτίζω than any of his friends who have preceded him. They have insisted that it meant to dip, to plunge, and nothing else. Dr. Conant says, it no more means to dip, to plunge, than does "to put;" that is, it means no such thing. These, and a host of other words, may act as servitors fulfilling the behests of βαπτίζω, while they no

more, in their individuality, represent the meaning of that
word than does the swelling frog the stately ox. Βαπτίζω
exercises a sovereignty over a multitude of words expressive of action; but no one of its subjects can, by any
amount of puffing, be made meet to fill the place of its
sovereign. Indeed, there is no light thrown by this word,
of itself, upon the act by which, in any given case, its demand may be met. You might as well attempt to learn
from it the name of the man in the moon, as to seek to
learn from it the style and title of the act which performs
a baptism. If any one doubts this, let him tell me, when
I inform him that a certain Greek was *baptized* in the days
of Plato, what was the act by which the baptism was
effected? When a truthful answer, gathered from βαπτίζω,
shall be returned to this question, the respondent may
boldly approach the sphynx sure of resolving every
enigma.

HIS SECOND DEFINITION.

A more fully developed definition is furnished, elsewhere, as follows :

"From the preceding examples, it appears that the
ground idea expressed by this word is, *to put into or under
water* (or other penetrable substance) so as entirely to *immerse* or *submerge;* that this act is always expressed in the
literal application of the word, and is the basis of its
metaphorical use. This ground idea is expressed in English, in the various connections where the word occurs, by
the terms (synonymous in this ground element), *to immerse,
immerge, submerge, to dip, to plunge, to imbathe, to whelm.*"

And on another page we have the meaning more briefly
and formally stated. "BAPTIZEIN: To immerse, immerge,
submerge, to dip, to plunge, to imbathe, to whelm."

A first thought which occurs, on reading such exposition, is this: The translation of βαπτίζω, after all, does not
appear to be so very easy. It has been said that the suggestion that there was any difficulty in the translation of
this word in the English Bible was nothing more than a

"pretence." "The meaning of the word was clear, definite, always the same, and one of the easiest words ·to translate." Now for the proof. Dr. Conant has spent years in the study of this word. What translation does he give us of it? Why, on Baptist principles, just none at all. Our Baptist friends are bound, by all their unmeasured reproof of us, and by all their equally unmeasured claims of most certain knowledge for themselves, to give us an English word which shall sharply, squarely, and "on all fours" represent this Greek term. Now, what Baptist writer furnishes us with such a word? Does Dr. Conant? Does he profess to do it? Is it possible for him, on his own showing, to do it? These questions must be answered in the negative.

We are told that this word "expresses putting into or putting under, immersing or submerging." Does Dr. Conant mean by this language that the word means either to put *into* or to put *under?* but he cannot tell which. Or, that sometimes it means the one and sometimes the other; not being fixed in its meaning? Or, that it means both; there being no difference between "into" and "under"? Or, that it means, exactly, neither; but some third thing? Surely we are left quite in the dark as to any definite idea of the action expressed by this word. "To put," gives no definite information, for it has sixty-seven variations of usage according to Webster, and sixty-seven more, perhaps, might be added. No valuable aid is found in "put *into*," "put *under*," for these terms are very far from agreeing in one. It is just because they differ that they are used. If the "one, clear, definite" idea is not found in this part of the definition, is it found in those seven defining terms which are added?

If so, is it equally in each? This cannot be. If one word can be found in English the absolute equivalent of βαπτίζω, there can hardly be found seven! If there is one such word in this collection, which is it? Is it the first, "immerse"? If so, then why the other six? If the second, "immerge" differs from "immerse," and this is the representative word; then, so far, "immerse" fails, and must be rejected. The third ("*sub*merge") cannot bear scrutiny if the first is the standard. The same is true of the fourth, "to dip;" and the fifth, "to plunge;" and the sixth, "to imbathe;" and the seventh, "to whelm;" each of which has its own peculiarities of character distinguishing it from "immerse," and, therefore, rendering it incapable of representing the Greek word, if such representation is made by IMMERSE. The Baptist world has demanded the philological "pound of flesh," and has pledged itself, without fail, to dissect it from the English language. We have nothing to say against the rightfulness of the demand; but, remember, when weighed over against βαπτίζω, it must be nothing more, nothing less.

But Dr. Conant admits that each of these terms differs from its fellows. Why, then, use them? Why, because they agree in some "common ground idea." What is the nature of that "ground idea"? Is it an act or a condition? Not an act, because, manifestly, immerse and submerge, plunge and whelm, have no such bond of union. And the character of the act becomes a matter of supreme indifference.

Is the "ground idea" found in condition — "entirely covered"? Then, 1. Dr. Conant repudiates Baptist argumentation of two centuries, which has labored to prove that the idea involved was an act, absolutely modal, to change which was to subvert the truth. 2. What is the English word which represents this "ground idea" without expressing any modal action?

We have a description of the idea of βαπτίζω, as Dr. Conant understands it, in which description all special form and force of act is rejected, and power to effect condition, only is demanded; which idea is not translated into any one word, but is distributed among seven, not one of which exhibits, simply and only, this idea.

But while Dr. Conant is compelled to abandon, on examination of his exposition, all idea of a form of act entering into and controlling the idea of βαπτίζω, still he clings to the idea, so long cherished, of an act, a movement, a force, as belonging to and controlling the usage of this word. Thus he says: "This *act* is always expressed in the literal application of the word, and is the basis of its metaphorical use."

It is an error, and a very serious one, to say that "act is always expressed" by this word, in contradistinction from condition. It cannot be said, properly, ever thus to express an act. This is manifest from the seven words already quoted, which express diversity and contrariety of action, but which are given as expositors of the same word. Of course they cannot be exponential of that in which they differ. Therefore, they cannot expound the action in βαπ-τίζω. Dip and plunge do, strictly, express acts, and their usage turns, wholly, on the character of those acts; but this is in nowise true of the word under consideration. The acts by which baptism may be effected are almost endless, both as to form and force. The same reason which gives the seven words, referred to, as the meaning sought for, would justify the addition of seven more- -to duck, to souse, to steep, to sink, to swamp, to ingulf, to swallow up; or seven times seven, which could be readily furnished, each putting its object "into or under" the water. Dr. Conant gives, in his translations, two score acts by which baptism was effected. 1, To assault; 2, to let fall; 3, to flow; 4, to weigh down; 5, to walk; 6, to pierce; 7, to hurl down; 8, to march; 9, to rush down; 10, to surround; 11, to press down; 12, to rise above; 13, to dip; 14, to submerge; 15, to thrust; 16, to blow; 17, to rush down; 18, to strike; 19, to proceed; 20, to sink; 21, to immerge; 22, to imbathe; 23, to plunge; 24, to lower down; 25, to immerse; 26, to come on; 27, to over-turn; 28, to boil up; 29, to flood; 30, to whelm; 31, to let down; 32, to enter in; 33, to pour; 34, to souse; 35, to bring down; 36, to depress; 37, to steep; 38, to drench; 39, to play the dipping match; 40, to duck. Is each act, severally expressed by these forty words, a *fac-simile* of βαπτίζω? According to the definition, "put into, under, its object, entirely," it does so; but if so, then it must, among words of action, stand forth a Briarean monster, or a Protean prodigy. Certainly no act of forty fold form "is always expressed in the literal application of the word."

Other objections lie against the words selected (without good reason from a host of others), as the representative words. We are told that

" Βαπτίζω means—To immerse, immerge, submerge, to dip, to plunge, to imbathe, to whelm."

We object to the employment of words compounded with prepositions, to represent words which have no such composition.

As the Greeks use both εμ-βαπτίζω, and κατα-βαπτίζω, the translation of which would, properly, be with a compound word (but with which we have nothing to do), why introduce the distinctive peculiarity of these words into the translation of βαπτίζω? The composite character of these defining words must be rejected as inconsiderately, I would by no means say surreptitiously, introduced.

We would, then, have: merse, merge, dip, plunge, bathe, whelm.

Of these terms, "merge" must be set aside as having an almost exclusive, and somewhat peculiar, metaphorical use in our language.

"Dip" must be rejected on its merits. The statement of Carson, that "dip is the meaning, and the only meaning, of this word through all Greek literature," is met by the equally broad and contradictory statement, that it never, through all Greek literature, has the meaning to dip.

The notion that βαπτίζω means to dip was never derived from a study of the usage of this word, but was borrowed from βάπτω, with which it was long absolutely identified, and with which it is still identified by Baptist writers, so far as the primary meaning is concerned. For such identification there never was the semblance of a reason. In usage, these words are as nearly opposites of each other as they well could be. I do not now enter upon any justification of this position. My business, now, is to hear what

Baptist writers have to say, and to suggest difficulties which appear on the surface of things. Hereafter I will endeavor to make good the position that *dip*, the primary meaning of βάπτω, no more belongs to βαπτίζω than does *dye*, its secondary meaning.

We strike out *dip*, then, from Dr. Conant's list of representative words, as having no right to be there.

"Plunge," also, must be rejected on its merits. Its lack of merit, however, is quite different, in important respects, from *dip*. This latter word has a defect of nature which renders it essentially unfit to fulfil the demands of βαπτίζω. This is not the case with the former word. It is entirely competent to fulfil the demands of the Greek word; but it is not the more, on that account, an exposition, in its individuality, of the value of βαπτίζω. It might as well be said that *to hinder* means, to tie a hundred weight to a man's foot. Most assuredly this would prove a hindrance; but though the demand of "hinder" may be thus met, shall we say that *to hinder* means, "to tie a hundred weight to a man's foot"? To do so would be just as rational as to say that βαπτίζω means to *plunge*, because it can, under certain circumstances, meet its demands. To plunge expresses a distinctive act, with strongly marked characteristics, which has no expression whatever in the Greek word. And since to attribute to it such a meaning tends to foster the erroneous idea that it belongs to that class of verbs, we exclude plunge from the seven defining words.

"To bathe" has no claim whatever to be used to express the meaning of the Greek word, either as to act or condition. And as it is employed but once by Dr. Conant, if I remember rightly, and in its compound form—*im*-bathe— he will not feel that its erasure brings much loss with it.

"To whelm" does not express any specific form of act any more than does *to cover*, and, in so far, is calculated to act as a representative word. But it does express the idea of the whelming element coming over its object, and in this fails to find any correspondence in the Greek word. That word cordially accepts such mode of fulfilling its

behests, but neither enjoins nor expresses it. Its breadth
is greater. It has no regard to form of action. It contemplates, exclusively, condition — intusposition — and whatever act will accomplish this it accepts as a true and loyal
servitor, one as truly as the other, whatever may be their
diversities. It refuses, with absolute denial, to be bound
to any, whether labelled with "into," or "under," or
"over."

Whelm, in certain respects, serves very admirably as an
interpretative word. I would, therefore, allow the first,
(stripped of its preposition,) and the last of "the seven"
to stand as valuable helps, with proper explanation, to
expound the Greek word.

METAPHORICAL USE.

The metaphorical or secondary use of βαπτίζω claims our
special attention. It is all-essential to a proper understanding of the word. Some call this use figurative. I
do not like the term. It is suggestive to most persons of
something unreal, shadowy, fanciful. This is far from
being the case in the present instance. Nor is it so dependent on the literal physical use as some would have us
believe. This usage is as frequent, well-nigh if not quite,
in classic writings as is the primary. And while freely
confessing that the secondary use does proceed from and
draw its meaning from the primary use, we do emphatically deny that that meaning is merely an allusive one; we
claim that it has, and does directly suggest a meaning of
its own, which excludes the idea of physical investiture.
Dr. Conant traces this usage to an act. Thus, again,
showing the control held by the idea that the word expressed an act, as does dip or plunge, which idea is a constant source of misconception and improper use of language.

He says: "This act is always expressed in the literal
application of the word, and is the basis of its metaphorical uses." (p. 59.)

" In the metaphorical application of the word, both cases" (plunging and overflowing) "are recognized as the ground of this usage." (p. 60.)

" The ground idea is preserved in the several metaphorical uses of the word." " The idea of a total submergence lies at the basis of these metaphorical uses." (p. 61.)

" In the metaphorical sense it is often used absolutely, meaning *to whelm in* (or *with*) *ruin, troubles*, &c." (p. 61.)

" We speak of a man as immersed in calamities, &c., always with the idea of totality, of being wholly under the dominion of these states or influence; it suggests the clear image of the act on which they all are founded." (p. 107.)

The metaphorical use of this word is dependent in nowise on any form of act. It is no more dependent on dipping, plunging, sinking, as forms of acts, than it is dependent on walking, throwing, falling.

Nor does this usage turn on the picturing of an object as in a state of physical immersion, submersion, or envelopment. Cases of such picturing may, doubtless, be found; but they are not properly arranged under this head of metaphorical use; they belong to what is more properly designated as figure-picturing. The secondary or metaphorical use of words does not draw pictures of primary use, but takes some leading thought pertaining to it, and makes an application of it as the case plainly indicates. Such, at least, we claim for fact in this case. In every case of physical envelopment there is an opportunity for the investing element to exercise its influence over the object in the highest degree; what the nature of that influence will be depends upon the element and the object.

There is nothing more obviously natural than that the word which is expressive of such envelopment should be taken, not merely to draw physical pictures, but to represent, directly, that constantly needed thought of *controlling* influence. This, we say, has been done in the case of this word, and that such is its true metaphorical or secondary use. Hence a baptism can be effected by anything, of whatever dimensions, or of whatever nature, physical or unphysical, which is capable of exercising a controlling influence over its object, thus bringing it into a new condition.

It was on this ground that the Greeks represented a baptism to be effected by a cup of wine, by perplexing questions, and by a few drops of an opiate. Whether these, or such like things, baptize by dipping, or plunging, or sinking, or overflowing, may be safely left to the determination of common sense. It will tax the powers of a very lively imagination to show, how an embarrassing question lets loose a water-flood into which the bewildered respondent is plunged, or by which he is overflowed.

But give what explanation you will, the stubborn fact, the truly important thing, remains; that the Greeks daily effected baptisms by a draught of wine, by a bewildering question, and by droppings from an opiate. Accumulate around these baptisms metaphor, figure, picture, and what not, I make my argument with finger pointed to the cup, the question, and the opiate drop, and say, *the old Greeks baptized, through a thousand years, by such things as these!*

Dr. Conant pronounces a just critical judgment when he says of this class of baptisms, they exhibit those receiving them as "wholly under the dominion of these states or influences;" but when he proceeds to add, "they suggest the clear image of the act on which they all are founded," we take exception: 1. To the introduction of "the image of the act." No such suggestion can be made, for the very good reason that there is no such "the act" to be "imaged." The acts by which these, and all other baptisms, are effected are endlessly diverse, and, therefore, cannot have "the image" reflected in any one word. The image of the act of dipping is one thing; the image of the act of plunging is another thing; the image of the act of sinking is yet another; and the image of the act of flowing is still another. Each of these words has a metaphorical or secondary use peculiar to itself and incapable of interchange; such use may, in each several case, suggest "the image of the act" appropriate to itself, but no word

can suggest at the same time, or equally, or at all, the
several distinctive acts of dipping, plunging, sinking, flowing.   But while these modes have "the image of an act"
to suggest, βαπτίζω has none; for the reason that neither in
primary nor in secondary use has it anything whatever, as
to its meaning, to do with the form of an act.   This word
demands for its object condition, and condition solely; it
says nothing, and it cares nothing for dipping, plunging,
sinking, flowing, pouring, provided only that it is competent to fulfil the demanded condition.   This it insists
upon.

If Dr. Conant will erase " the image of the act" (abandoning the idea that βαπτίζω expresses the form of an act,
and accepting the idea of condition), and will say that the
metaphorical or secondary use indicates and expresses that
the baptized person is " wholly under the dominion of the
state or influence" appropriate to the case; which meaning
(not image) is clearly traceable to the primary use, wherein
an object is encompassed by a physical element, and thus
wholly subject to its influence, then, my objection is at an
end, and Baptist argumentation, as to the character of this
word, is abandoned by Dr. Conant.

It remains to be seen whether such abandonment of the
character so long attributed to this word, will necessitate
the abandonment of their entire system or not.   They
must, at least, look over the field from a new stand-point,
to see whether their conclusions can be adjusted to the
new aspect of things.

I only observe, now, that this meaning does, on the face
of it, extinguish all idea of βαπτίζω having anything to do
with dipping; dipping never brought any object " wholly
under the dominion" of anything.   And by the same inexorable necessity must be abandoned the long-affirmed
unity between this word and βάπτω.   How much of logically
affiliating error these changes will sweep away with them
farther inquiry will show.

We conclude: 1. This examination of the leading points
in Dr. Conant's treatise does not encourage us to adopt the

Baptist postulates: (1.) One clear, precise, definite meaning. (2.) Identity between βάπτω and βαπτίζω. (3.) βαπτίζω expresses a definite, modal act. (4.) Metaphorical use is a mere picture of the primary use.

2. It shows that Dr. Conant is not in accord with previous Baptist writers in his exposition of the word, particularly with Dr. Carson, who insists, in the most absolute manner, on modal action. Thus the most powerful controversialist furnished from the Baptist ranks, and the latest and ablest philological expositor of their views, cannot agree as to the essential value of that word "which has but one meaning," and to understand which "needs not light, but honesty."

3. The exposition, translation, and current phraseology lack self-harmony.

IMMERSE AS A LATIN DERIVATIVE.

The record taken from Baptist writers, as now presented, shows a growing disposition to present, and to rely upon *immerse* as a shield to protect their system against controversial blows, which otherwise could not be endured.

This course has been adopted, not under a frank confession of essential error in past views; but for the sake of covering the temporary retreat of their forces, that they may be preserved for use under happier auspices. Dip and plunge are still claimed as the meanings of a word "which never has but one meaning;" while immerse is introduced as another meaning, to shield them under confessed incompetency to meet the demands of actual usage.

Two questions here arise: 1. Why is it that, thus, with patent inconsistency, dip and plunge are held on to so tenaciously? 2. And how is it that immerse becomes so valuable a covering force in these times of disaster?

In answer to the first inquiry it may be said: The deeply fixed notion that βαπτίζω means to dip, sprang out of the error which regarded this word and βάπτω as substantially the same word, "the one in a long coat and the other in

6

a short one;" or, as a translator of the Baptist Bible Union says, "the one in a modern dress, the other in more ancient attire." This conception is an entire mistake, as will, hereafter, be shown; but it has served to fasten what is the undoubted meaning of βάπτω upon its associate word, notwithstanding its protest from every case of usage. Unprepared to give up this imaginary relationship between these words, they have held on to the meaning, "dip," in the face of facts, now at last admitted, which render such meaning impossible.

But why perpetuate this inconsistency which affirms that a word has but one meaning, and yet confesses, in an exigency, that it has another? The only appropriate and adequate answer seems to be found in the vital connection of the act of dipping with the Baptist system. The rite of baptism is performed, under this system, only by dipping, and we are told that it cannot be performed in any other way, because the word means specifically "to dip, expressing mode, and nothing but mode;" and this word expresses a divine command, which can only be obeyed by the performance of this specific act. Now, to admit that βαπτίζω *never* means to dip (for to that must come the admission, that *sometimes* it does not), is to admit that God has not commanded a dipping; and to admit this, is to dissipate that excellent glory which has been so passionately claimed for ritual dipping. All this, human nature will be slow to do.

But how is it that immerse becomes "a friend indeed," under these circumstances? The explanation is found in a little duplicity (pardon the word to point the argument, I use it *Latinice*) of use. This facile, duplex use is due to its Latin origin and composition, together with an essentially less pointed character than many other words.

Without entering into details, it seems desirable, now, to refer to the Latin original of our English word immerse, and point out its meaning in that language.

MERGO—IM-MERGO.

Mergo (from which *im*-mergo is formed by composition with the preposition *in*, and from which *im*-merse is derived), does not mean to dip or to plunge; nor does it express any definite act; nor yet act or movement undefined in character; but it expresses condition characterized by inness of position, commonly within a fluid element, which condition may be effected by any act competent thereunto. Mergo expresses none.

That this word does not signify to dip, to plunge, is evident from the prepositions with which it enters into composition.

Sub-mergo, De-mergo, E-mergo, exhibit a cast of composition which could not be intelligently associated with a word having the character of action which belongs to plunge. But may not *in* be associated with such form of act? Undoubtedly it may; but it does not follow that every word which is compounded with this preposition does originally or compositely express movement. As *in* does, of itself, express simply inness of position; so it does, also, in composition. And the contrary must not be assumed in any case. We deny that, as appearing in im-mergo, it expresses of itself movement, or that it indicates that mergo has such character. On the contrary, we say that it expresses merely position, and serves to express with emphasis the idea of inness, which is the leading characteristic of the word with which it is associated.

Proof of this position is found in the following facts: 1. Ovid speaks of a house as mersed, and boats sailing over it. This house was not plunged into the water, but was mersed by the water rising up above it. 2. Pliny speaks of one river being mersed into another. This was not by the act of plunging into, but by the act of flowing. Will it be said that mergo means to flow? The act of flowing, by which the mersion was effected, is wholly distinct from mergo, although no distinct word is employed

to express that action.   The mersion follows on the flowing.   3. While it is more usual to leave unexpressed the
word by which the act effecting the mersion would be
designated, still there are instances in which the phraseology, in this respect, is made complete.

"Spargite me in fluctus, vastoque immergite ponto."

"*Cast me into the waves and immerse me in the deep sea.*"
(Æ. iii, 605.)

Here the act by which the mersion is effected is stated
to be "casting;" the mersion follows as a consequence.
Had "immergite" been used alone, it would not have
meant to cast, to plunge; but the condition would be expressed, which would, of necessity, carry with it some adequate form of act left unexpressed.

"Ab Jove mersa suo Stygias penetrârit in undas."

"*Mersed by her Jove she shall go to the Stygian waters.*"
(Ovid iii, 4, 20.)

This mersion extends to the Styx; but mergo does not
denote a plunging which extends from the bright scenes
of earth to the gloomy banks of that river.   This passage
is provided for by "penetrârit," and to mergo is reserved
the office of expressing the condition.

This interpretation is confirmed by the phraseology of
Seneca, where the word expressing the movement is
omitted—"Mergere aliquem ad Styga."

This omission does not confer on mergo the power to
express the idea of passing, penetrating, plunging; but
gives the mersion position and character, leaving the word
of movement to be supplied.

This is the explanation of all like cases.   And in this
there is nothing peculiar.   The usage is illustrated in all
words of the same class.   Take for example the word *bury.*

"Bury the dead body."   To fulfil this command, a pit
is dug, the body is lowered down, and it is filled up again.
Does "bury" mean to dig, to lower down, to fill up?   How
if the body be carried into a sepulchre hewn out of a rock,
and a stone be rolled against its mouth; does it, then, mean
to carry into, to roll against?

"An avalanche of ice and snow buried the entire hamlet." Does bury mean to fall down? "An avalanche of ice and snow *fell down* and buried the entire hamlet." Is not this only a more full statement of the other, placing the movement in its proper relation?

"The flock was buried by the falling snow." Does to bury mean to sprinkle with snow-flakes? "The entire crew was buried in the ocean." Does bury mean to sink? To merse may be accomplished by lowering down, falling down, carrying in, sinking, sprinkling over, and it expresses all these forms just as to bury does; no more, no less. And so, when bury is used without there being expressed, by an additional word, the act whereby the burial is accomplished, such word must be supplied, the nature of it varying greatly according to circumstances; but in no possible case can "bury" be converted into a word expressive of act or movement. All which is true of mergo. Bury is, also, used with *into*, without, however, in anywise changing its character. "He buried the knife *into* his body." "The cannon-ball was buried *into* the ground." Such phraseology does, as Dr. Conant says, express *the passing* from one point to another, but it is a mistake to say that such expression is due to "bury," or that it has anything, directly, to do with it. He buries the knife, *thrusting it* into his body. Does bury mean TO THRUST? The cannon-ball was buried into the ground by its *projective* impetus. Does bury mean "to project"?

In, compounded with bury, in-bury, in-tomb, has as little power to change the character of the word. It only emphasizes the inness of condition. The same is true of *in* joined with mergo; and when our Baptist friends take occasion, from the use, at times, of the Latin preposition to denote motion, to engraft this idea on im-mergo, immerse, they do what is incapable of justification. It is, however, on this ground (and failure to supply the executive verb) that the meaning, dip, plunge, has been erroneously attributed to this word, with some appearance of truth; while, its true nature and proper usage allowed it to be used in cases where dip and plunge were inadmissible. Therefore, dip and plunge have been used where they could be, and immerse has been used where it must be, with the assumption that it was a kindred word with them, and expressive of act and movement. This duplicity of use (I mean not to reproach, but only to show that Latin terms Anglicised may change their value) must be abated, even though it should cost our Baptist friends the very serious and painful loss of dipping as an act of divine command.

FAILURE.

Having now listened with patience, and not without much interest, to all which Baptist writers have to say as to the meaning of βαπτίζω, with the conviction, that if they could make good a moiety of their unqualified assertions farther investigation would be precluded, I must confess myself not a little suprised at the result.

Where is that one, clear, precise, and definite meaning? Certainly it is not in Baptist writings. Where is the evidence that βάπτω and βαπτίζω have, precisely, the same meaning, form, force, and effect? Not, assuredly, in Baptist writings. Where is the evidence that βαπτίζω expresses an act, a definite act, mode, and nothing but mode, to dip? Not a particle is to be found in Baptist writings. Where is the evidence that βαπτίζω expresses in secondary use the act (dipping), which is attributed to it in primary use? Baptist writers have not furnished it.

Where is that English word, the daguerreotype of the Greek word, which was to flash forth the one, clear, and definite meaning, so that " a wayfaring man though a fool need not err therein"? There is not a Baptist writer, during three hundred years, who has offered such a word with the attempt to carry it through Greek usage.

And where is that translation which was to rebuke the disloyalty of the Christian world, and indicate the unswerving fealty of the few? "It is found in *im-merse.*" And if the Holy Spirit employs a word (as we are told that he does) which "means im-merge, sub-merge, dip, plunge, im-bathe, whelm," by what authority are these six defining terms rejected and the seventh taken? Or if, as we are also told, and as Greek usage proves, forty other acts may execute the will of this Greek word, why are the thirty-nine rejected and the fortieth taken to represent, just and no more, the mind of the Spirit? If "im-merse" is used in the sense to dip, to plunge, it does most essentially fail to reflect the Greek word; if it is not used in that sense, then away with the definition—dip, plunge; or away with the "one meaning through all Greek literature."

An inspection of Baptist writings does not confirm the notion, that the work of defining this word has been done by them so thoroughly and so exhaustively of truth, that all farther inquiry is a work of supererogation.

ADMINISTRATION OF THE RITE.

Before instituting any inquiry of our own as to the meaning of this word, let us hear, still farther, what is to be said as to the practical administration of the rite, and the reduction of the theoretical meaning of the word to concrete practice.

We may, reasonably, expect to find, here, harmony with announced principles, if not absolute truth.

The Confession of Faith of the Baptist Churches (A.D. 1644), 40th Article: "The way and manner of dispensing this ordinance the Scriptures hold out to be dipping or plunging the whole body under water."

Booth (p. 146): "The ordinance should be administered by immersing the subject in water."

Ripley (p. 120): "The candidates being placed under water."

Wayland (p. 87): "We believe that the ordinance of baptism is to be administered by the immersion of the body in water."

Curtis (p. 68): "Baptism as a symbol necessarily embraces an immersion or burial of the body in water."

Jewett (p. 13): "The immersion of the subject in water is essential to the ordinance." (p. 46): "In baptism we are commanded to perform the act represented by the word baptize."

Stovel (p. 417): "What is to be baptized? The answer is, persons." (p. 495): "The act, therefore, is not sprinkling or pouring; but the motion takes place in the man, and ceases when the man is baptized in the water."

THE ACT—THE OBJECT—THE END.

In these statements respecting the administration of the rite three things are presented as of cardinal importance: 1. The act required to be performed. 2. The object to which that act is addressed. 3. The end toward which the act carries its object. Let us consider what is said of these severally.

1. *The act.*—Are we to understand that a definite act is taught or not? Surely this matter ought not to be left in the dark. Prof. Jewett seems to speak plainly: "We are commanded to perform the act represented by the word baptize." Very well; if we are "commanded" by God "to perform an act," it is very important that we should know what that act is. Will the Professor give us the information? Certainly; it is the act of "the immersion of the subject in water." Very good. And now may we ask what is the act in "the immersion of the subject in water"? Undoubtedly, it is "the act which we are commanded to perform by the word baptize." Indeed! After such a lucid *circular* exposition, who can complain that "the act commanded" is not perfectly "clear, precise, and definite"?

When we turn to Dr. Wayland, we are again confronted with an "immersion of the body in water." And so with Curtis, with the addition, "or burial." Booth reiterates,—"immersing the subject in water" is the way "the ordinance should be administered." But, here, we have at least a negative guide to the act; it cannot be *plunge*, for this writer says that word "makes our sentiment and practice ridiculous." What act, then, do Wayland, and Curtis, and Jewett propose when they say: "We are commanded to perform the act," but it is not "plunge"? Stovel, too, helps us, negatively, when he says: "The act is not sprinkling" (although there was a very extensive baptism by sprinkling when Noah sought refuge from it in the Ark); "nor pouring" (although his friend Fuller thinks that the act of pouring is quite competent to effect a baptism); but the act consists in "moving a man until he is baptized in water." Such, then, positively, is "the act commanded;"—to baptize a man is to "*move* a man until he is baptized"! An act of singular lucidity—"clear, precise, and definite."

Prof. Ripley eschews the use of immerse, with its doubleness, as, also, "the moving a man until he is baptized," and adopts phraseology which neither expresses a definite act nor movement of the object to be baptized.

The Confession of Faith, venerable with the years of a third century, unlike its more modern representatives, gives forth no uncertain sound: "The way or manner of dispensing this ordinance the Scriptures hold out to be dipping or plunging."

This doctrine, or its plain, outspoken English utterance, is becoming quite old-fashioned. New terms in theological issues seldom fail to foreshadow a departure from the old "way and manner." It will, most probably, be found, in the present case, that a Latin derivative has been resorted to for the purpose of covering over the abandonment of those ruder spoken terms, *dip* and *plunge*, as the exponents of "the act commanded."

If there is a consciousness of error in giving such meaning to the word, let the acknowledgment be made as frankly as by Morell: "We give up, thus far, the cause of immersion." If, while abandoning these acts, it still be insisted upon that some act is commanded; and that "the act commanded" must be performed; then, in turn, we insist on being told what "*the* act commanded" is. Do not give us half a dozen different words varying in their forms of action, and say we may take our choice; we wish no greater liberty than "the command" gives; we are willing, anxious, to be bound by it. Tell us, then, "*the* act." There is but one word used in the text. You cannot "dip" in half a dozen different ways. If baptize means "to dip," you cannot obey the command by baptizing in a half dozen different ways; no, not by *plunging*, for Booth says these are essentially different acts; nor by *pouring*, although Fuller says you can; nor by *overflowing*, although Cox says you can. If the command is "to dip," and "the command is to be obeyed," then, thus far must we go, and no farther. If baptize does not, definitely, mean any one of these acts, but still does definitely mean action, movement, embracing them all, then let us be furnished with an English word of equal breadth (as "the translation is the easiest possible"), and let us hear no more of "*the* act commanded." But if the word does not belong either to the class of words expressive of definite forms of action; nor of action indefinite; but to that class which is expressive of state, condition, result, employing "forty" or four hundred acts for the accomplishment; then, do not give us seven defining words, neither of which, confessedly, measures the original, making up the deficiency by saying that they agree in "a ground idea." Give us a word which expresses, like the original, that "ground idea," and we will dispense with "the seven" which do not.

If I am commanded "to bridge a river," I protest against the interpretation of this command into an injunction to build—1, a *pier* bridge; or, 2, an *arch* bridge; or, 3, a *tubular* bridge; or, 4, a *suspension* bridge; or, 5, a *draw* bridge; or, 6, a *stone* bridge; or, 7, a *pontoon* bridge. I protest against all of these "seven" being taken as the representative of the original command, on the plea of agreement in a common "ground idea." And I protest against the use of any of these seven to translate "faithfully" into a foreign tongue the original command. It is my liberty to use "pier," "arch," "tube," "wire," "draw," "stone," "pontoon," any one or any combination; and no one has a right to infringe that liberty by putting into the command any one which he may fancy to select, and command me to build *that*.

If it should be concluded to abandon the idea that act, definite or indefinite, is commanded; and it be acknowledged that result, state, condition, constitutes the matter of the command; then we ask for a word which will definitely express that idea, and not something else. This will be easy for those to do who say, "difficulty of translation is all a pretence."

When such word is secured, we farther demand that it shall reign with imperial autocracy through all its usage, and that we shall no longer have a rebellious dip or plunge introduced to control translation or interpretation.

" *The act* represented by the word baptize," which "we are commanded to perform," seems to be left very much in the dark by Prof. Jewett and friends.

2. *The object.*—The object on which this act expends itself, next claims attention. Stovel says, "the man;" Jewett and Booth say, "the subject;" Wayland and Curtis say, "the body;" Ripley says, "the candidate;" and the Confession of Faith says, "the whole body."

Here there is neither ambiguity of phraseology nor conflict of sentiment. If Baptist writers exhibited as much clearness and unity in speaking of the act of baptism as of the object of baptism, they would be above reproach.

"Man," "subject," "body," "candidate," "whole body," presents diversity of phraseology, but unity of material object. This object is, also, presented in the same aspect; the act expends itself not on any of its parts, but includes the "whole."

Dip, plunge, imbathe, whelm, sink, overflow, exhibit no such unity of act under diversity of terms.

The universal faith of the Baptist Church is, that baptize commands " *the whole body* to be dipped or plunged in water."

Does classic Greek require this? Timon baptized a man

in water. Did he "dip or plunge his whole body"? No, he put more or less of his head under water, and so drowned him. Now, what shall be said of the position—"baptize requires the whole body to be dipped or plunged"? Is it not most evidently erroneous? But why does Lucian call pushing the head under water baptism of the man? Because the rest of his body was, already, under water, and what remained out was pushed under? No. (1.) This could never be called a baptism, if baptize requires the whole body to be dipped or plunged. (2.) If the head and body of this man had been under water, except his foot or hand, or leg or arm, and Timon had pushed that into the water, the Greeks would have smiled at the suggestion that such an act should be called a baptism of the man. Did the Greeks adopt the principle, that *any* part of an object being baptized, the whole might be said to be baptized? They did not; but they did adopt the principle (as this and other cases show), that where the head, the nobler part, was baptized, the man was, justly, said to be baptized; especially when that part influenced the whole man.

In Prussia, certain Baptists dip the head, only, into a vessel of water. "Regular" Baptists will find it hard to justify the withholding fellowship from these imitators of the old Greek, on the ground that baptize necessarily dips the whole body. Baptist sentiment and Grecian practice are at contraries.

But how is it as to the accord between Baptist sentiment and Baptist practice? Are they at one?

Hear Prof. Ripley (p. 76): "Prof. Stuart blends together two things that are perfectly distinct, viz., the going down into the water and the immersion into it. That the going down into the water was the immersion, no one believes; the immersion after the descent into the water is expressed by another word, he baptized him."

Is it not marvellous that thoughtful men can write after this fashion, having laid down the principle—"baptize dips or plunges the whole body?" Is the baptism which

Prof. Ripley describes modelled after that which Baptist sentiment demands, or after that which Lucian describes? He says: "No one believes" that "the going down into the water" is the baptism; "these two things are perfectly distinct;" the baptism takes place "after the descent into the water;" "it is expressed by another word." Very well; but if baptism is dipping the head into water after "the candidate" has done "a very different thing," to wit, "walked into the water," which "no one believes" to be baptism, why announce, as a sentiment of faith demanded by "fealty to God," that "the way and manner of dispensing this ordinance the Scriptures hold out to be dipping or plunging the whole body under water"? And yet the Professor describes the universal practice, which is in flat contradiction to universal sentiment.

Timon's baptism was by pushing the head under water after the unhappy man had gone down into the water, or had fallen into the water, or had been swept away by a flood, or in some other "perfectly distinct" way had got into the water, and was covered up with the exception of his head. And after the same model is Prof. Ripley's baptism. Baptists must change their principle or their practice. If their principle is right, there is no obedience to "the act commanded," and no baptism in their practice; and if their practice is right, there is no truth in their interpretation of the command, or in their principle which they deduce from it.

If to this it be, apologetically, answered: "All the body gets under water somehow, although not by the act of baptism, nor in obedience, therefore, to the mode in the command; and what is the difference if we substitute the act of walking for the act of dipping; the act of the candidate for the act of the administrator; the head for the whole body"?

Well, I do not know that it makes much "difference" to others, if Baptists are satisfied. It is their business to have some harmony between sentiment and practice, or not to throw very big "rocks" at other people's glass houses.

"But it would be exceedingly difficult 'to dip the whole body into water.' " That may all be very true; but it sounds passing strange from Baptist lips. "Difficulty" stand in the way of a faithful administration of baptism! Why, I thought that that line of argument had been settled against the Christian world long, long ago, by two words—"divine command." Are Baptists ready to eat up their mass of argumentation (not always flattering to self-esteem) on this point? Will they now say (what their opponents never said, and, through grace, never will say), that difficulty in execution is an apology for disobedience to a clear divine command? Others have said that difficulties claim consideration in making interpretation of a divine command, and for this and other good reasons they have judged, that "there is no divine command to dip the whole body into water;" and, therefore, do not do so. Baptists have judged that God has given such command in the most explicit terms of which language is capable; and yet have never, in one instance, for three hundred years, obeyed the command. They may be disposed to make light of this discrepance between their sentiment and practice, but it is vain; it is ruinous to their system as it stands.

Whatever the difficulty in dipping the whole body, it involves no impossibility. When others have suggested that it would be difficult to dip or plunge couches; the difficulty has been smiled away. "The whole body" is not as large as a couch. When it has been said, it would be difficult for the twelve to baptize the three thousand; the answer has been prompt: "If more were necessary, we will find them; where were the seventy"? If more are necessary "to dip the whole body," can they not be found? When it has been objected that it would be difficult for John to live in the water during all his ministry, dipping or plunging such multitudes; the answer has been prompt: "Then we will put him on the bank, and he shall dip them thence." Could not "the whole body" be slid off from the bank by a little clever management?

Is it possible that the rich invention which has sur-mounted so many obstacles can, at last, be exhausted? Can no way be devised by which the divine command can be met, and "the whole body dipped or plunged"?

May not a stimulus to genius be found in the happy bearing which it would have on the baptism-burial of Curtis? Would it not be far more like a burial to carry the whole body into the water and lay it in "the watery tomb," than for a living man to walk into the water ("which no one believes to be baptism"), and then to dip his head and shoulders? Besides, was not the body of the Saviour, "the whole body," thus carried and laid in the tomb; and are we not "buried with him, and like him, in baptism"? There is nothing in burial-baptism which has better authority than this. Why not adopt it, and ventilate a new argument, with whole obedience to the divine com-mand in "dipping the whole body into water?"

The practicability of the thing has been demonstrated. Eunomius and his disciples, we are told, did "dip into water the whole body," by the help of ropes and pulleys. Whether this feat was performed under the impulse of a conception of duty similar to this modern notion, I cannot say; but the thing has been done, and, therefore, can be done.

None need hesitate through fear that "ropes and pulleys" could not secure an orthodox Greekly baptism. Classic Greek gives us examples of just such baptisms; and Dr. Carson would, by like means, baptize "the couches" of Scripture. Eunomius cannot be made a heretic on the ground of his "act of baptism." And why be troubled with "unseemliness"? Has not every suggestion of this nature been answered, to all Baptist minds, with as much triumph as indignation? Why, then, not harmonize prin-ciple and practice?

"Dip the whole body," by some legitimate process, and do not put the larger part of the body under water by the walking of the candidate (which Professor Ripley says, "nobody believes to be baptism"); or, while baptizing a part only of the body, extend some grace toward those who do so in like manner.

3. *The end.*—Stovel says, " the act moves the man, and ceases when the man is baptized in the water;" that is, I suppose, when he is put under the water.

The Confession of Faith " plunges the whole body under water," and thus and there, ends " the way and manner of dispensing this ordinance."

Dr. Conant says (p. 60) : " The idea of emersion is not included in the Greek word. It means simply to put into or under water, without determining whether the object immersed sinks to the bottom, or floats in the liquid, or is immediately taken out. A living being put under water without intending to drown him, is of course to be immediately withdrawn from it; and this is to be understood whenever the word is used with reference to such a case."

This is hardly a fair statement of the case. It is true, that there is nothing in the word to prevent its object from being "immediately taken out of the water;" but it is also true, that the word never contemplates the removal of its object from the condition in which it has placed it.

There is nothing in the word *bury* to prevent its object from being "immediately taken out." It would, however, be a very extraordinary thing to say that "bury" determines nothing as to whether its object is to be immediately taken out of a state of burial. So far as bury is concerned it contemplates nothing else, and if the burial is but for a moment this word has nothing to do with it; neither can it be used to express the idea of a momentary burial. Boys may, in sport, bury one another in the hay-mow or in a snow-bank; a vessel may, for a moment, be buried under a wave; but such brief burial never converts bury into dip; nor is the idea in a dipping and in a momentary burial the same, whatever resemblance there may be in the brevity of continuance. Bury remains the strong word, and is used because of its power; while dip remains a feeble word. The same is true of βαπτίζω. It is never used to express a momentary condition; although that condition

may be, and in some very few cases is, of short continuance. But in such cases there is always an element present
which renders the word, in its peculiarity, appropriate;
just as in the case of bury. It is never used to express
the idea of βάπτω, even in brief mersions, any more than is
bury under like circumstances.

The statement respecting a living man put under water
without intending to drown him, and the necessity for his
"immediate withdrawal," is not better grounded in the
merits of the case. I remember but one solitary case in
the classics to which the supposed case is, at all, applicable.
"Wherever the word is used with reference to such a
case, he must be immediately withdrawn," has, therefore,
a very sharp limitation.

But even this case does not square with the language
used. I know not of one case where a living man is
simply put into the water, and withdrawn from it, by the
party putting him in. To dip, requires that the one dipping should withdraw the object dipped. If I dip a man,
I both put him in and take him out; but if I plunge a man,
or souse a man, or immerse a man, though I do not intend
to drown him, yet it is not implied that I withdraw him
from the water; I may leave him to shift for himself. The
withdrawing is necessary to a dipping; but the withdrawing would not necessarily convert a baptism into a dipping,
although I know of no such feature in any classic baptism.

Dr. Conant seeks to sustain the ritual dipping of a man
into water, and his instant withdrawal, by the usage of the
Greek word. It cannot be done. It cannot be done; not
simply because of the brief continuance under the water,
but because it is, and is intended to be, nothing more nor
less than a dipping.

If I put into, and withdraw promptly from water a bag
of gold, I dip it; but if it slips from my hand and it sinks,
although I may recover it within as brief a space of time
as in the other case, it is not a case of dipping. Any object may sink, and remain in this condition for the briefest
duration; still, sink is not converted into dip. Although,

therefore, Dr. Conant may find a very few cases in which
the baptism was for a limited period, he can find no case
in which a baptism can be converted into a dipping; therefore, he can find no case of the use of this Greek word by
which the ritual practice of dipping a man into water, as a
baptism, can be justified.

But it is said that "if a man is not taken out of the water
he will be drowned, and that was never intended by Christian baptism."

But why was the man put into the water? "Why, to be
baptized." Well, baptize will put a man into water, but
it never did and never will take him out. This Dr. Conant
admits; but, he adds, as the man is not intended to be
drowned, he must be taken out of the hands of baptize,
which otherwise would drown him. In other words, the
Holy Spirit has employed a word which requires, absolutely, disciples to be put under water without making any
provision for their withdrawal; and *Dr. Conant has to find
some way to remedy the defect*, on the ground of an inference
that they are not to be drowned! And all this when βάπτω
would have done just what Dr. Conant thinks necessary to
volunteer to do, namely, to put in momentarily and withdraw; which word the Holy Spirit never once uses. Now,
such an oversight (may the word be used without irrever-
ence?) by the Holy Spirit is infinitely incredible. And the
Baptist system, which is responsible for originating such
an idea, is, thereby, hopelessly ruined.

All Greek writers refuse to interchange βαπτίζω and βάπτω;
the Holy Spirit persistently refuses to employ βάπτω, or to
interchange it, in a single instance, with βαπτίζω in speaking
of Christian baptism; is it becoming in those who are
"very jealous for the Holy Spirit" to substitute another
word for that which the Holy Ghost teacheth? Or, retaining the form of the word, to supplant it by using the
meaning of a rejected word? But this is done by those
who substitute βάπτω for βαπτίζω; or, who give to the latter
word the meaning of the former.

Thus, as we give our attention to what Baptist writers

say in relation to the administration of the rite, we find that they break down at every point.

1. There is a hopeless disagreement as to the command; whether it enjoins a specific act or not, and, if so, what is its precise nature.

2. As to the object on which the act bears; the whole body says theory, a part of the body rejoins practice.

3. The language of inspiration (we are told) puts disciples under water, but makes no provision for getting them out. In this dilemma an unwritten command is added to the Scripture, on the authority of an inference (the necessity for which is self-created), and so life is saved!

VALID BAPTISM.

The Baptist system rejects, as without validity, every baptism which does not bear certain marks which it lays down as essential.

Professor Jewett: "The immersion of the subject in water is essential to the ordinance."

"In baptism, we are commanded to perform the act represented by the word baptize."

These quotations so thoroughly represent the Baptist sentiment, on this point, that the multiplication of quotations is needless.

Four things are declared "essential to the ordinance."

1. Immersion. 2. Immersion of the subject. 3. Immersion of the subject in water. 4. Immersion of the subject in water by the act commanded in baptize.

1. *Immersion.*—Although Baptist writers do not use this word either with precision or with uniformity, yet they will acknowledge that it carries inness of position with it. Now, we wish to ask, does this word, representing βαπτίσμα, carry with it any limitation as to the time of continuance? If there is no limitation of time in this word, is there any limitation of time in any word adjunct with it? If there is not, then, we ask, on what authority any limitation of continuance can be introduced?

We affirm that there is no limitation in the word, and that it cannot be used for a *momentary* mersion without an adjunct word expressing that idea; and that a designed "*momentary* mersion" is not *mersion;* but is mersion qualified, so as to transform it and make necessary the employment of another term for its expression, to wit, *a dipping;* which term is rejected by the Holy Spirit, and thus *a dipping* baptism is rejected. This is as certain as that Scripture is Scripture.

2. *Immersion of the subject.*—This feature has been already considered. If this be essential to validity, it is not more certain that a part is not the whole, than that dipping the head and shoulders is not valid baptism. Samson perishes with the Philistines.

3. *Immersion of the subject in water.*—Some Baptists feel a necessity for protecting the immersed from being drowned. There is good reason for the interposition of their kind offices. The facts to which they appeal are, however, not only inadequate for their purpose but inappropriate. They may prove that a person immersed in water need not, of necessity, be drowned; but they do not prove that "immersion in water" would not, of its own force (uninterfered with), drown any living man. The dipping into water of a living man will not, of its own proper force, drown any one. There is no need for the interference of any outside agency to save life. It is as much a part of the contract in *dipping* a man to take him out of the water as to put him into it. In immersing a man there is no such requirement. It is the mersion only, the position of inness, which is called for, and there the object mersed would abide, to all eternity, unless some outside influence should recover it.

The thought which is in immersion has no tendency to pass into the thought which is in dipping. Whatever common elements they may have, they still have a great gulf separating the conception in the one from the conception in the other. The command to hang a man is not fulfilled by suspending him FOR A MOMENT. The command to immerse a man is not fulfilled by dipping him for an instant.

The reply to this: "It is madness to suppose that the Scriptures command men to be drowned," is met by the echo, "It is madness" to suppose that the Scriptures command men to be put into *a condition* by a word, which unlimited necessarily drowns, without attaching any limitation to that word; while, all the time, they only meant to express *an act* of the severest limitations, and which brings no peril with it, and which might have been, precisely, expressed by another word.

Baptists put Christian disciples under the water, and are, then, under the necessity of saving them from their "watery tomb" by changing βαπτίζω into βάπτω.

We do not object to men being taken out of the water after they have been improperly put into it; but we object to men being dipped into water, and then claiming to have received a Greekly baptism.

There is nothing more true than the proposition, which is contradictory of that of Roger Williams's friend: "Dipping is" NOT "Baptizing, and Baptizing is" NOT "Dipping."

4. *The act.*—Valid baptism requires that "the act commanded" should be performed. The act performed by Baptists is that of *dipping*. This, then, must be the act commanded, and the act which stamps validity. But Baptist writers, now, admit that the commanding word does not "always" mean *to dip* (soon they will admit that it *never* means so); how do they know that it means so in this command? Such confession puts them all "at sea" as to the act commanded, and "valid baptism" floats away, beyond their grasp, into regions all unknown.

RESULT—EX PARTE.

The sentiment and practice of Baptists (as presented by themselves), on all the vital features of this controversy—the meaning of the word; the manner of administration; and the requisites to validity;—have, now, passed under review.

The object has been to hear what the friends of these

views had to say, and to suggest any difficulties which might lie on the face of their own statements; not to gather them up from other quarters. They have claimed that they were possessed of absolute truth on all these points; and, that that truth was of such transparent clearness, that failure to recognize it must be due not to intellectual unenlightenment, but to moral obliquity.

Against the latter part of this position I make neither complaint nor offer defence. It is a part of "the sentiment" which concerns much more those who give it utterance than those against whom it is uttered. In regard to the former part, I would say:

1. *As to the word.*—Baptist writers, speaking for themselves, show either, that they do not understand the meaning of this Greek word, or, they can find no representative word for it in the English language. (1.) Some (Carson) say: It means a definite act—to dip, and nothing but dip; while in cases of actual usage, when this word cannot be used, they employ plunge, sink, overwhelm, &c., *ad libitum.*

(2.) Some (Gale) say: It means a definite act—to dip; yet, perhaps, does not so much express the act, as the resultant *condition.*

(3.) Some (Cox, Morell, Fuller) say: It means a definite act—to dip; and, also, means various other acts—to flow, to rise up, to pour—which issue in covering over their object.

(4.) Some (Conant) say: It means an act—to immerse, to immerge, to submerge, to dip, to plunge, to imbathe, to whelm—and yet it means none of these, but a ground idea which is expressed by them all—to put into—or, to put under.

This elaborate explanation is an earnest endeavor to find a *nexus* binding all divergencies into unity. It is unsuccessful. Duplicity remains. Act and condition are both sought to be preserved, and the truth perishes between them.

2. *As to the ritual administration.*—The statement of their sentiment and practice in this matter, as given by them-

selves, shows not a diversity, but a contradiction as irreconcilable as the declaration that one thing is another and different thing; or that the whole and its part are equal to each other.

3. *As to validity.*—The elements essential to validity are given with unquestionable honesty of intent (as, undoubtedly, are all other views), inasmuch as their own fondly cherished form perishes in common with all others.

With such results of Baptist research standing out upon the face of their writings, it would seem to be neither a moral delinquency, nor even a work of supererogation, to institute an independent investigation of this subject, inquiring—" *What is truth ?*"

PART II.

INQUIRY ENTERED UPON INDEPENDENTLY.

METHOD OF INVESTIGATION.

UNDER the conviction, that the developments made indicate some essential error, which vitiates the results of Baptist investigation, we will enter upon an examination of the subject for ourselves.

If this is to be done with any degree of thoroughness, it will require patience to traverse the whole ground, knowledge of well-settled principles of interpretation, candor and competency in their just application, and common sense to know that a universal conclusion cannot, safely, rest on a single particular, nor on many, but only upon what remains after a matured consideration of the action and reaction of all cases of usage upon each other.

While a satisfactory result might be reached by an exclusive examination of the word in question, it is undoubtedly true that we shall find assistance by conducting the investigation side by side, with some closely related, yet essentially differing, word. Such a word is βάπτω.

It is, also, manifest that any conclusions reached will be more firmly established, if they shall be sustained by the usage of correspondent words in other languages.

The terms which in Latin correspond with βαπτίζω and βάπτω are mergo and tingo; and in English immerse (stripped of its Baptist usage), and dip. If these words, in these languages, show similar usage, resemblance, and diversity, moving side by side without coalescence, each with deeply marked and distinguishing individuality, then, we may be assured that these words do not represent a sameness of conception, or a difference founded on accident, but which is grounded in the necessities of thought and language.

We shall avail ourselves of this source of help toward the firmer establishment of truth.

Beside the general reason, now assigned for the introduction of a detailed consideration of the usage of βάπτω, there is a special, and imperative, reason found in the fact, that these two words have been confounded together under the assumption that they were of identically the same value.

While this statement has an application beyond our Baptist brethren, it applies to them with special force. It is only quite recently that they have acknowledged, under the leadership of Dr. Carson, that βάπτω was possessed of a secondary meaning (to dye), and that this meaning was independent of the modal act of dipping; so much so, indeed, that βάπτω could express dyeing effected by *sprinkling* as well as by any other mode. This admission is of moment both in itself and as indicative that long and earnest asseveration, as to what is or is not the meaning of a word, cannot, safely, be accepted for proof.

Dr. Carson, who has led his friends in this change, still asseverates that there is no difference between the primary meaning of βάπτω and the meaning of βαπτίζω, the latter not having the meaning to dye. No attempt is made to prove this by showing a coincidence of usage. Such attempt never will be made by any thoughtful man. It is a matter, however, of the first importance to Baptist "sentiment and practice" to make βαπτίζω responsible for a dipping; consequently the meaning of βάπτω has been, most illegitimately, bound on to this word, and is called into use on every convenient occasion; and is made of divine authority as "the act commanded" by words of inspiration.

If such relationship between these words is radically erroneous, then all Baptist argumentation upon the subject is thoroughly vitiated.

This we believe to be true. It is our duty, by adequate evidence, to prove that it is so. This necessitates a presentation of the usage of both words.

CLASS OF WORDS TO WHICH IT BELONGS.

It has already been stated that *to merse* is the primary meaning which we assign to this word; and that it does not, of its own force, express any form of act, but the result of some act, or acts (involved as necessary to the accomplishment of the effect, but) unexpressed. It belongs, therefore, to that class of verbs which make immediate demand, not for a definite act to be done, but for an effect, a state or a condition, to be accomplished.

As this meaning, at once and forever, effects a divorce between it and its fellow, it is desirable that it should receive illustration and enforcement by an appeal to a few words of the same class, and of similar, general import.

BURY—DROWN—WHELM.

1. To BURY.—This word does not announce an act to be done, but a result to be secured.

Horne Tooke says: "Burial is the diminutive from Burgh; a defended or fortified place. To bury means to defend; as Gray in his Elegy expresses it,—

'These bones from insult to protect.'

Sepelire has the same meaning,—to hedge, to keep out of field or garden."

To bury, then, demands protection for its object by position within some inclosing material. How, by what acts this end demanded is to be secured, the word says nothing. Many cases, of the primary use illustrating this statement, are unnecessary.

"Abraham buried Sarah his wife in the cave of the field of Machpelah."

The place of burial being a natural excavation, the acts necessary would be controlled by that fact.

" And laid him in a sepulchre which was hewn out of a rock, and rolled a stone unto the door of the sepulchre."

The preparatory and essential act, in this case, was the hewing out of the rock a receptacle wherein the body might be safely deposited. The act of rolling the great stone unto the door completed the security and the burial.

" The soldiers slain were buried in trenches dug on the field of battle."

Here a new act, *digging*, is introduced in the performance of the requirement.

" In the deep bosom of the ocean buried."

Quite a different class of acts are called into exercise in an ocean burial, from that demanded by a burial in a cave, or a rock sepulchre, or an earth grave.

" The daughter of the Indian chief was buried on a platform, raised some feet, on poles."

Such diversity of act, however, trenches in nowise on the requirement of " bury;" it said nothing in relation to act; its demand was that its object should be placed in some. protecting inclosure. This was done when the body was deposited and made secure in the cave, the sepulchre, the trench, the ocean cavern, or the elevated platform. Bury asks nothing as to the *quo modo* of the acts by which the end was secured.

The secondary or metaphorical use of this word is equally devoid of all reference to act.

It is desirable to note this usage, as we shall have much to do with similar usage of the word under special consideration, and our conclusions may be not a little influenced thereby.

" He *buried* himself in a monastery."

No act is suggested by the use of the word in this passage. No act can assist in the elucidation of the meaning. The act done was crossing the threshold and the closing of the door. Does the interpretation turn on these acts? It would not be difficult to show a resemblance between these acts and the carrying a dead body into a cave and closing its mouth by a stone; but does any sane man imagine that we are called, in the interpretation of this passage, to inquire by what acts a burial is effected? Is such secondary use of bury to be regulated by carrying into a sepulchre, lowering down into a pit, sliding off from a plank, or lifting upon a platform? Do not these various and contradictory forms of act show the absurdity of an interpretation which should proceed upon such a basis? Are we not compelled to put wholly out of view the acts, of whatever kind, by which the burial is effected, and take the resultant condition as that which, alone, claims attention?

It is, also, important to bear in mind that a secondary use which is based on an act has, of necessity, a severity of limitation which does not belong to similar use based on condition. An act is, necessarily, limited in its nature; it must take some specific character; it follows, therefore, that a metaphorical use must be characterized by like limitation.

It is not so with condition. There is room, here, for a variety of thoughts, and in specific cases one or another may be chosen and brought into special relief.

In the word "bury," the condition suggested may give rise to many varied shades of thought. Among these may be enumerated concealment, removal, restraint, deep penetration, &c.

In the present case, it is obvious that the idea intended to be expressed is that of concealment. There is no suggestion of a funeral procession. There is no picture designed to be drawn by the writer; but as an object buried is, thereby, concealed, shut out of view, separated from other things, the use of the word is justified as expressive of the idea of seclusion when applied to one entering into a monastery.

If it be said, the phraseology—"buried *in* a monastery"—

implies figure; I answer, the phraseology is made to harmonize with *bury;* but does not, therefore, require any
picturing of the imagination. Should figure and picture
be still insisted upon, I, then, ask for the sketch. (1.) What
shall the monastery represent? A cave like that of Machpelah, or a pit dug in the earth? (2.) Is the occupant of the
tomb to be represented as dead or alive? (3.) Who effects
the burial? The text says, the buried man "buried himself." How shall this be pictured?

Is it not obvious that, in such phrases, neither can
"bury" nor "in" be pressed, hardly, upon for the proof
of figure; but that a meaning is to be attached to them,
derived from the primary use, such as the case demands.

"Thy hand, great Chaos, let the curtain fall;
And universal darkness *buries* all."

Will any one insist upon "the act" of burial here?
What will be made out of "letting fall the curtain"? Is
this the manner in which graves are dug?

If any one will say that Pope has given us a figure in
the first line, I will, most cordially, assent. No one need
be troubled to find the picture. It is all drawn for us—
"great chaos"—"thy hand"—"curtain falling"—the elements of a grand and awful picture are all there; but
when any one goes on to join with such a scene another
figure, in which a tomb, &c., loom up, they must think
that the writer is bereft of his senses.

Darkness and the grave are always associated, and, in
fact, are concomitants. Both hide their objects from view.
So much, therefore, of the word *bury* as expresses this
idea, may be taken when that term is used in connection
with *darkness*, and all else pertaining to it be dismissed as
inappropriate. This is so done here. Such modified use
of words is better designated as a secondary use than as
figure.

> " I have, as when the sun doth light a storm,
> *Bury'd* this sigh in a wrinkle of a smile."

Shall I, again, ask for " the act of burial"? Shall I, again, ask, whether we are to convert, under the demands of figure, " a wrinkle of a smile" into a grave? Is such a method of interpretation in harmony with the comparison? What is the point of resemblance between " the sun lighting up a storm" and "putting a sigh into a grave"? As sunbeams do not dig graves for storms, neither do smiles for sighs.

Is it not true, and is it not enough to say; an object which is buried is, thereby, made to disappear; and as a sigh is made to disappear by a smile, therefore a smile may be said to bury—cause to disappear—a sigh?

A word, in such secondary use, must not be interpreted as expressing all that can be put into it, in view of its primary use, but just so much as the peculiarity of the case may demand.

"Princeton has gone on in the accustomed way; Professors *buried* in the immensity of their subjects."

Does the sentiment turn on act or condition? An object which is buried is placed in a condition which removes it from the surface. Professors, engaged in study, advance beyond the surface of things, progressing into the depths of their great themes; and to express this shade of thought, profound and not superficial study, " bury" may be used. In such, all thought of a grave is out of question.

> " *Brutus.* Give me a bowl of wine :
> In this I *bury* all unkindness, Cassius.
> *Cassius.* My heart is thirsty for that noble pledge :
> I cannot drink too much of Brutus' love."

" The act" of burial, here, is the drinking of a bowl of wine. Does the sentiment turn on the act of drinking? The wine-cup, emptied in friendly pledge, put away, buried " all unkindness." This is the idea made emphatic

and impressive by the use of a word with modified meaning and out of its ordinary application.

" But in your bride you *bury* brotherhood."

Poetry would become marvellously prosaic under the
attempt to transfer such language, interpretatively, to the
canvass. The "bride" being converted into a plot of
ground into which a pit is sunk, while coffined "brotherhood" is being sadly deposited in its depths!

Better let the poetry remain, and call on secondary use
to show how, that as an object buried is destroyed, therefore, when marriage destroys "brotherhood" it is proper
to say: " In your bride you bury brotherhood,"—meaning
that the bride is the occasion of the destruction of fra-
ternal affection.

" He lay *buried* in the deep lethargic sleep which was
his only refuge from the misery of consciousness."

"The act" of burial, here, was drinking to excessive
intoxication. Does such "act" govern the interpretation?
Common sense, no less, revolts at such interpretation as
would convert sleep into a pit—a "deep" pit—in the earth
or a cavern in the sea, at the bottom of which should "lie"
the drunken sleeper, covered over, buried, with earth in
the one case, or with sea billows in the other.

When it is said of a man who lies at our feet, in full
view, that "he is buried in sleep," is it not patently absurd
to say that, in such case, "bury" means to cover over, "to
hide from view"? Is not the man uncovered? Is he not
in full view? Does the speaker mean to stultify himself,
or those whom he addresses? Such interpretation is out
of all question.

An object which is buried—or burghed—is protected
from anything which would assail it; but this very protection becomes the cause of restraint. What protects the
buried from the approach of enemies, at the same time
prevents the buried from going forth out of the protecting

inclosure. Protection and restraint, therefore, are ideas which equally belong to the idea of burial; and either of them, according to the indication of the case, may be taken out of a buried condition. Now, the only idea which is admissible in the case before us is that of restraint, or in intimate conjunction with protection. The sleeper is held bound, in every sense, physical and intellectual, by profound lethargy; and while he is thus under restraint from which he is powerless to escape, he has sought this very bondage "as a protection, a refuge from the misery of consciousness."

"Buried" does, most legitimately, mean, in such use, *to be under the power of;* and such burial becomes a protection, a refuge, *a burgh* from a stinging conscience.

I mention but one other case:

> "Before I freely speak my mind herein,
>   You shall not only take the sacrament
>   To *bury* mine intents, but to effect
>   Whatever I shall happen to devise."

This presents an absolute use of the word. Are we to be guided by "an act" (to dig, for example), to the right understanding of it? Where is the grave to be dug in which "mine intents" are to be interred?

Every object "buried" is placed in a covered condition. Every such covered object is concealed. To bury embraces the idea of concealment. This is what is demanded by the speaker; "take the sacrament *to conceal* mine intents." "Bury" expresses the thought emphatically—conceal profoundly, so that they shall be protected against the knowledge of all persons.

These, and like cases of usage, prove: (1.) Bury does not belong to the class of words which gives expression to an act to be done; but it makes demand for a condition to be effected, leaving the act unexpressed as to its form, and which it may take at will.

(2.) Such usage is not well designated as figure, but should be regarded as a secondary use in which a modified meaning (readily deducible from the original meaning) is presented, while the structure of the phrase is made conformable to the leading word.

(3.) Greatly varied shades of meaning, and sometimes even material diversities of thought, may be exhibited in the secondary use of this class of words.

2. To DROWN.—No definite act is expressed by this word, nor is its import in anywise dependent on any form of act. It expresses, primarily, the condition of an object covered by water; and then the effects, the influence exerted, upon such objects by such covered condition; and then, by an additional step, influence, of a correspondent character, where there was no, real or supposed, covering with water.

That modification of the original meaning, which embraces the influence exerted over the life of living animals, and covered by water, is now the most common; and is likely, unless guarded against, to give coloring to the use of the word where such coloring should find no place.

This modified use of a word, originally expressive of such condition, is most natural, not to say most necessary, and will find exemplification in other kindred words; especially in that word, to determine the usage of which is the object of this inquiry.

" A great waue of the sea cometh sometyme with so great a violence, that it *drowneth* the shyppe: and the same harme doth sometyme the small dropes of water that entreth through a lytell creueys, in to the tymbre and in to the botome of the shyppe, yf men be so negligente that they discharge hem not by tymes. And, therefore, although there be a difference betwixt these two causes of *drowning*, algates the shyppe is *drowned*."—*Tale of Chaucer*, fol. 74, p. 2.

This quotation shows an object "drowned" that is desti-

8

tute of life. No immediate or special influence is exerted over it by the condition into which it is introduced, although from the nature of the case it perishes.

It, also, furnishes us with evidence, that as long ago as Chaucer's time it was a settled matter that the act by which the drowning was brought about had nothing to do with giving character to the drowning. It might be the on-rushing of a mountain billow or tiny drops distilling through a " lytell creueys," "algates" (in all ways) "the shyppe was drowned."

> " At length his courser plunged,
> And threw him off; the waves whelmed over him,
> And helpless in his heavy arms, he *drowned*."

This is a perfectly clear case, in which—(1.) Drown does not express either plunge, throw, or whelm,—the acts engaged in the drowning. (2.) Nor does it express the covered condition by water, as in the case of the "shyppe." Such condition exists, unquestionably; but it has been already expressed by " the waves whelmed over him," and, therefore, cannot be repeated by this word. (3.) It does express, directly, the influence exerted by such condition on a living man,—it extinguishes life.

" These were events of such magnitude, it would seem to silence its tongue and *drown* its voice."

This absolute use as clearly expresses influence, without any covering by water or anything else, as does the preceding case express influence exerted by the covering material. This conclusion is based, not merely on the absence of any literal or figurative covering element in the statement, but because that which "drowns" is so represented as to preclude its being used for any such purpose. It is the "*magnitude* of events" that "silences and drowns." The magnitude of events is not a drowning material, although well calculated to exert such powerful influence (destructive in character) as "drown" fitly represents.

———————

"Till *drowned* was sense, and shame, and right, and wrong."

"What is this absorbs me quite?
Steals my senses, shuts my sight,
Drowns my spirit, draws my breath;
Tell me, my soul, can this be death?"

In both these passages Pope uses "drown" to express, directly, a destructive influence. To introduce an explanatory water-flood is to *drown out* every feeling of propriety and just criticism.

I will, only, farther call attention to the use of this word where the form of figure is used. It is of importance to have clear and just views as to the principles on which such language is employed, and the basis on which the interpretation must proceed.

———————

"All drown'd in sweat the panting mother flies,
And the big tears roll trickling from her eyes."

"Drown'd in sweat" is conceivable as a literal, physical fact. "Sweat" is a liquid capable of drowning a living animal covered by it; and we can conceive of it as being so multiplied as to be sufficient to drown, literally, the hind chased by a lion, of which Pope here speaks. Some insist on the most severely literal interpretation of such language, and demand that the imagination shall be taxed to picture this animal as lying under a pool of "sweat" until "drown'd;" for has not the poet said, "drown'd *in* sweat?"

Most persons will be too much disgusted by such "a picture" to care to look long upon it; so we turn away satisfied that "drowned in" does not, after all, mean covered over to suffocation "*in* sweat."

We are compelled to qualify such language by the exigency of the case. "Drown" can only be used to express, with deep emphasis, the profuseness of the sweating; and "*in*" is used as the necessary particle to harmonize with drown, and is no more to be pressed, on the ground of its meaning in cases of literal drowning, than in the word (drown) which originates its use. This particle, here, merely serves to point out that which "drown" declares to have been in excessive profusion, and all idea of inness is necessarily dropped. There is a superficial covering with the fluid.

"My man monster hath *drowned* his tongue in sack."

Again; "drowned in sack" is a physical possibility, and, more, has actually been done. Is it meant, by Shakspeare, that this language should be understood literally? He does not mean "drowned" in the sense—deprived of life; "the tongue" is not so drowned. He does not mean "drowned" as simply covered over; such was neither the fact nor to the writer's purpose. He uses it to denote the destruction of the power of speech by excessive wine-drinking. As wine is a liquid and drown is destructive, the loss of the power of speech by drunkenness is well described as "a drowning of the tongue in sack." "In," here, being used simply as the natural appendage to drown, cannot be pressed in its independent meaning; such meaning is unsuitable here. It points out the source of influence which so drowned the tongue by its intoxicating quality as to destroy the power of intelligent speech; not the mode of doing it.

"And *drown'd*, without the furious Ocean's aid,
In suffocating sorrows, shares his tomb."

"Drown'd in suffocating sorrows" is, literally, an impossibility. Understood as figure, how is the language to be interpreted? (1.) "In," does not necessitate the imagining "sorrows" to be a pool of water in which a drowning or a covering over must take place, any more than the

same particle requires that "the hind" or "the tongue"
should be thus introduced within "sweat" and "sack."

(2.) "Drown'd" does not require the destruction of life;
because "sorrow," with which it is associated, and the influence of which it develops, does not destroy life. necessarily. (3.) But life is, in this case, destroyed, and is indicated by "suffocating" and "tomb." "Suffocating" is not
employed with a view to its own proper force (for it has
no such force here), but in subordination to the use of
"drown." We take out of "suffocating" so much as is
indicative of death, and leave the special mode of death,
indicated by this word, go, as inappropriate. In this we
have confirmation of the explanation already given of
"in." We take from this word so much as indicates the
source of influence, and reject the form of inness as unsuitable to the case. A water picture of drowning is, expressly, rejected.

" In sorrow drown'd—but not in sorrow lost."

As "sorrow" does not kill by its own nature, "drown'd"
becomes restricted, when used in connection with it (as well
as in all other like cases), to a development of its influence
as excessive and eminently painful.

As in the previous case the appendages showed that the
drowning was fatal, so, in this, Young shows us that it was
not,—" drowned, but not lost."

" But though man, *drown'd* in sleep
Withholds his homage, not alone I wake."

If the mind receives the impression from "drown'd" of
a covering fluid, it, at once, corrects itself as it encounters
"in sleep," and says, "I was mistaken; there is no reference here to water, but to sleep; the drowning must be
qualified by the adjunct." Sleep cannot "drown;" but it
can powerfully influence, and hold in still repose every
faculty both of body and mind; and as an object "drowned"

is held under the influence of water in the highest degree, the phrase " drowned in sleep" must mean that the influence of sleep is exerted over its object in a controlling degree, but not by being put into a pool. Sleep is not measured by quantity but by quality. It does not drown by its bulk, but by its intensity. Therefore, sleep which drowns is commonly represented as induced by the *sprinkling* of soporific dew. Sprinkling can drown *in sleep*.

> " The grunting hogs alarm the neighbors round,
> And curs, girls, boys, and scolds, in the deep base are *drown'd*."

It would be a most notable figure which would require the transformation of " the grunting of a hog" into a pool of water in which were exhibited—" scolds, boys, girls, and curs," struggling, sinking, and drowning!

Pope has scarcely indulged himself in such a freak of imagination.

If it be said that "curs, girls, boys, and scolds" are not to be drowned, but only their noises, then I ask for special instruction as to the mode by which "noises" are drowned *in a pool of water!*

If any are better pleased to understand " drown" as representing a destructive influence proceeding from "the deep base" of the grunters and overpowering all lesser noises, we shall make no objection.

One or two instances, where there is no form of figure in the phraseology, and where none is intended, but a direct expression of influence, without any water imagery inducing death or covering, will now be adduced.

> " What is a drunken man like, fool?
> Like a drown'd man, a fool, and a madman:
> One draught, above heat, makes him a fool;
> The second mads him, and a third drowns him."

Here are four stages in the progress of wine-drinking, as described by Shakspeare: (1), it heats; (2), it fools;

(3), it mads; (4), it—"puts in a pool of water"! or (if preferred), inside of a full cask of wine!

Is this such interpretation as befits the dramatist? To
make this interpretation harmonize with the entire passage, "to heat" should put the wine-bibber into the element
up to the knees; "to fool" should place him in up to the
breast; "to mad" should raise it to his lips; while " to
drown" should give the *coup de grace* and put him under.
A final "draught" might render a man "*dead* drunk," but
could hardly (by figure) flood him.

Shakspeare uses "drown" in this passage without reference to suffocating or covering, but directly expressing the
power of wine to control and to stupefy every physical and
intellectual power. Wine *heats* literally; *fools*, literally;
mads, literally; *drowns*, literally; in the secondary sense,
here employed, namely, suspending the exercise of every
faculty, physical and intellectual.

"But, adieu! these foolish drops
Do somewhat drown my manly spirit; adieu!"

"Somewhat" is not a proper qualifying term to apply to
the extinction of life, or to the covering over with water.
It is a very suitable term to qualify the exercise of influence exerted to a limited degree. Tender emotion
softens the sternness of a manly spirit; such emotion is
shown by tears; tears suggest the use of "drown;" and
drown is employed to denote the destructive influence of
tender emotion, as manifested by "foolish drops" upon a
"manly spirit."

To magnify "foolish drops" into a pool of water, into
which "manly spirit" is introduced and covered over until
"somewhat" suffocated, may afford exercise to an erratic
imagination; but it is a work in which common sense will
decline to have any part. Such usage shows that drown
has passed from its original use expressive of covering

over with a fluid, and, specifically, extinguishing life by
the influence of such covering; as, also, that it has laid
aside the mode of figure as the vehicle for the expression
of its thought, and does directly express a destructive
influence tinged with such individuality of character as is
inseparable from its origin.

In this varied usage of drown there is no form of "act"
which appears to give it existence, or to determine its import at any point whatever.

In cases of figure, there is no justification for putting
the object into a pool of water, the form of the figure
being designed, merely, to give strong development to the
influence of the adjunct; nor is it necessary to conceive
the object as placed within this adjunct (sometimes impracticable, and sometimes unsuitable), for the purpose
of developing its influence, and this is thoroughly done by
the word "drown."

The usage of this word shows: (1.) A condition—object
covered by a fluid.

(2.) The influence exerted over the object so covered.

(3.) Influence exerted over an object without covering,
real or supposed.

3. To WHELM.—Expresses no form of act, but condition
effected by a variety of acts. This condition is, like the
preceding, a covered condition; but the covering substance
is more commonly brought over the object, and, as especially characteristic, with a power which cannot be successfully resisted. This peculiar feature adapts this word,
especially, to mark irresistible influence; and having no
such special limitations as belong to bury and drown, it is
adapted to a much wider range of application. As there
is a variety of words which express covered condition without adaptation to a broad application, "whelm" has a less
common use to express a physical covering, and a much
more extended application to metaphysical, or all unphysical influences which are irresistible in their power.
Whelm and overwhelm do not differ in value. The latter

simply expresses what is essentially implied in the former. Whelm *over*-comes by coming *over* irresistibly.

" By the mysgydynge of the sterysman he was set upon the pylys of the brydge, and the barge *whelmyd*, so that all were drowned."—*Fabian, Chronicle*, 1429.

" On those cursed engines' triple row,
 They saw them *whelmed*, and all their confidence
 Under the weight of mountains bury'd deep."

" Plung'd in the deep forever let me lie,
 Whelm'd under seas."

These three passages show "whelm" used in connection with "drown'd," "bury'd," "plung'd," and in marked distinction from each of them. In the last "plunged" is stated to be "the act" from which the whelming results; and in every other case there is an act by which this covered condition is induced which is not expressed by whelm.

" The water is ever fresh and newe
 That *whelmeth* up, with waues bright,
 The mountenance of two fingers hight."

" How must it groan in a new deluge whelm'd,
 But not of waters."

" To *whelm* some city under waves of fire."

 "Old Dulness heaves the head,
 And snatched a sheet of Thulè from her bed,
 Sudden she flies, and *whelms* it o'er the pyre;
 Down sink the flames, and with a hiss expire."

" Covereth it by *whelming* a bushel over it."

 " *Whelm* some things over them and keep them there."

The acts involved in these transactions are diverse in their forms, but all effect a covered condition which over-comes by its power. It is, also, to be noted that there is no such limitation of this word to fluids as to require the interpretation of figurative, or secondary use, on the assumption of such primary use.

———————

"Before her mother Love's bright Queen appears
  O'erwhelm'd with anguish and dissolved in tears."

"Those hangings with their worn out graces,
  Long beards, long noses, and pale faces,
  Are such an antiquated scene
  They *overwhelm* me with the spleen."

"Guilty and guiltless find an equal fate,
  And one vast ruin *whelm* the Olympian state."

"Some accidental gust of opposition
  O'erturns the fabric of presumptuous reason,
  And *whelms* the swelling architect beneath it."

"Of grievous mischefes, which a wicked fay
  Had wrought, and many *whelm'd* in deadly pain."

"Joy
  Invades, possesses, and *o'erwhelms* the soul
  Of him whom Hope has by a touch made whole."

"*O'erwhelmed* at once with wonder, grief, and joy,
  He pressed him much to quit his base employ."

"And moated round with fathomless destruction,
  Sure to receive and *whelm* them in their fall."

"Who perish at their request, and *whelm'd*
  Beneath her load of lavish grants expire."

"At the first glance, in such an *overwhelm*
  Of wonderful, on man's astonished sight
  Rushes Omnipotence."

"An *overwhelming* apparition. Like an apparition from the grave, you startled me from my self-possession and judgment."

"He came down from his throne; he struggled forward a few steps, like one who is weak from some *whelming* emotion, and laid his trembling hand" . . .

———————

> " To overthrow law and in one self-born hour,
> To plant and *o'erwhelm* custom."

It is unnecessary to dwell on the specialties presented by these cases. They show the broad use of the word applicable to any case of overcoming influence. Anguish and joy, wonder and fear, emotion of any controlling kind gives occasion for its use. A gust of opposition, mischiefs of a fay, old tapestry hangings, as well as the wonders of the infinite firmament, may, equally, whelm.

Such usage makes manifest the error of interpreting whelm by the form of an act or by a rush of waters.

A few examples of the usage of a word expressing a definite form of action will place in bolder relief the difference between such usage and that of a word expressing not the form of an act, but resultant condition.

Take the word *plunge*, which expresses an act characterized by rapidity and force of movement, entering, usually, into a fluid element without return.

> " He said, and climbed a stranded lighter's height,
> Shot to the black abyss, and *plung'd* downright.
> The Senior's judgment all the crowd admire,
> Who but to sink the deeper, rose the higher.
> Next Smedley div'd; slow circles dimpled o'er
> The quaking mud, that clos'd and op'd no more.
> All look, all sigh, and call on Smedley lost:
> Smedley in vain resounds through all the coast.
> Then * essay'd; scarce vanished out of sight.
> He buoys up instant, and returns to light."
> *Dunciad*, 285-296.

The annotator on Smedley's case remarks: " The allegory evidently demands a person dipped in scandal, and deeply immersed in dirty work."

His comment on the person denoted by " *" is, "A gentleman of genius and spirit who has secretly dipt in some papers of this kind."

This whole passage is one of honest figure. In true picture figure there is no change in the meaning of words employed, and, therefore, we can learn, here, the meaning of "plunge," and other words, as well as if an actual transaction was recounted. The passage is of special interest, as it presents, not only the characteristic use and meaning of "plunge," but, also, of *sink, dip,* and *immerse.*

"Plunge" here, as elsewhere, expresses an act characterized by rapid and forcible movement entering into a fluid element without return.

"Dive" expresses an act with similar characteristics with the peculiarity of entering the element head foremost.

"Sink" expresses an act characterized by a downward movement without return.

"Dip" is not found, verbally, in the text; but its nature, as an act, is very graphically described—"Scarce vanished out of sight, he buoys up instant and returns to light." Unlike plunge, dive, sink, *dip* makes provision for the return of its object out of the element into which it has been introduced. By this characteristic it is radically separated from these and all like words which carry their object into an element but do not bring it out. The secondary usage of these words is controlled by, and made wholly diverse in conception by reason of, this distinguishing feature.

The commentator on the text uses the word *dip,* but not in its primary meaning. "Who was secretly *dipt* in some papers of this kind." Here "dipt" cannot be used in figure, properly speaking; for in figure the primary meaning remains unchanged, while dipping into papers is an impossible conception and cannot be employed as a figure. We are necessitated to give to it a secondary meaning, namely, "*slightly* engaged" in. This is an obvious secondary meaning, resulting from the primary, literal, entering slightly into a fluid. "*In* papers," as already stated, does not require *inness* of position, but is used to be in harmony with dip, and with that word modified must not be pressed upon. But dip is, also, used by the annotator in a quite different sense; "dipped in scandal" is phraseology based on the idea of *dyeing,* and "scandal" is represented as a *dyeing* material. "Dip" may, therefore, be taken as expressing directly *to dye*, or, indirectly, as the result of dipping into a coloring element, represented in the text by "quaking mud," and in the note by "scandal." To dip *wets, dyes, stains, defiles*, according to circumstances. "Immersed in dirty work" harmonizes, as to strength (while differing in conception), with "dipped in scandal;" the unity arising from the power which is in "scandal" to effect a strong and abiding influence; it is the very opposite, as to strength, from "dipt in some papers." There is nothing in "papers" to give any adventitious power to the essential feebleness which belongs to "dip," while "immerse" literally denotes completeness of intusposition, and in secondary use complete, controlling influence, or *thorough* in contradistinction from *superficial* engagedness.

It is seldom that we have so many of these words brought together with their peculiarities and modifications so sharply defined. Plunge, dive, sink, dip, express sharply defined acts, with clear, distinguishing differences, separating each from each, but especially *dip* from all the others. Immerse expresses no such act, but condition of intusposition the result of any competent act.

> "Profounder in the fathomless abyss
> Of folly, *plunging* in pursuit of death."

> "So from the king the shining warrior flies,
> And *plung'd* amidst the thickest Trojans lies."

> "If glorious deeds afford thy soul delight,
> Behold me *plunging* in the thickest fight."

> "Or *plung'd* in lakes of bitter washes lie,
> Or wedged whole ages in a bodkin's eye."

> "O conscience! into what abyss of fears
> And horrors hast thou driv'n me? out of which
> I find no way; from deep to deeper *plung'd*."

It is obvious, without multiplying quotations, that the word maintains in metaphorical use its peculiarities as an act, expressing something which is done in a manner which demands a descriptive term denotive of earnestness and force. It expresses an act defined by certain characteristics in opposition to a condition.

It is to the class of words represented by *bury, drown,* and *whelm* that βαπτίζω belongs; while βάπτω belongs to that other class which is represented by plunge, dive, sink, dip, but specifically agrees with dip in bringing its object out of the element into which it has briefly and superficially introduced it.

MEANING MORE FULLY STATED.

Having exemplified the important point by which words demanding a condition to be secured, and a definite act to be performed, are distinguished from each other; and placed the word in question in the former class; I now proceed to unfold its meaning more fully.

1. The following points are essential to a proper understanding of the meaning of βαπτίζω. (1.) Its import is in nowise governed by, or dependent upon, any form of act. (2.) Its import is vitally dependent upon, and governed by, the idea of intusposition within a closely investing element. (3.) Its import is as vitally connected with a continuance within the element for an indefinitely protracted period of time. It can never be used to express a mere superficial entrance and a designedly momentary continuance. This would wholly change its character, removing it from its own proper sphere, and make it a usurper of that of βάπτω.

It is proper, here, in view of the distinction made and the importance attached to the difference between condition and act, to recall the language of Gale on this point: "The word, perhaps, does not so necessarily express the action of putting under water, as in general a thing's being in that condition, no matter how it comes so, whether it is put into the water or the water comes over it."

Dr. Carson, as we have seen, does, very earnestly, reject this statement as inconsistent with Baptist sentiments. Dr.

Conant, however, seems to agree, substantially, with Gale, when he says, that it is not in their peculiarity that immerse, or immerge, or submerge, or dip, or plunge, or bathe, or whelm, represents βαπτίζω; but by reason of some "common ground element," which can only be *condition*.

On the statement of Gale, Dr. Halley remarks: "Had he said 'coming into that condition' instead of '*being in* that condition,' he would have exactly expressed our meaning."

Prof. Wilson says: "Dr. Gale rowed hard to bring modal exclusiveness to land; but finding it a troublesome passenger, amid the storm of theological controversy, he adopted the more prudent course of throwing it overboard." He adds: "Our general statement is, that the verb βαπτίζω, unlike βάπτω in its primary sense, is not tied to any exclusive mode, but embraces a wider range, and admits of greater latitude of signification. Let the baptizing element encompass its object, and in the case of liquids, whether this relative state has been produced by immersion or by affusion, or by overwhelming, or in any other mode, Greek usage recognizes it as valid baptism."

Such testimonies give emphasis to the position assumed as fundamental to the interpretation of this word, and challenge for it a favorable consideration. All idea that a definite act is demanded by the primary, literal use, and all idea that the metaphorical or secondary use is in anywise based on such act, must be abandoned.

2. The idea of intusposition—inness—necessarily carries with it that of *completeness*. An object baptized is completely invested by the baptizing element, whatever it may be. In some cases (much the fewer, however, in number), the thought may rest here. When a stone, a pole, the sea shore, is said to be baptized, the nature of the object naturally arrests the conception, and bounds it with the simple investiture.

In most cases the baptism of an object carries with it more than the complete intusposition. Comparatively few objects can be wholly enveloped by a fluid, semi-fluid, or

other substance, without experiencing a very special and
very thorough influence as consequent upon such position.
Place a "ship" in such position, and it perishes; place a
"bag of salt" in such position, and it dissolves; place a
human being in such position, and he drowns.

It is obvious that influence, of the most thorough character, is inseparable from the idea of baptism, in most
cases which are physical in their nature.

Controlling influence being established as the ordinary
attendant upon such envelopment; and such influence, in
one form or another, being developed every day in the out-
working of life, where there is no physical envelopment,
it follows, rationally, if not necessarily, that the exigencies
of language would lay hold of the term with whose physical use such idea was associated, and apply it, indifferently, to all cases where controlling influence was operative, wholly regardless of the absence of a physically
investing element, the original form and means whereby
such influence was developed. It is purely gratuitous to
say that this must always be done by formal figure, or that
there must be an imaginary, shadowy something moulded
after the original style of encompassing waters to serve as
a substitute for it, when not actually present. It is abundantly sufficient to recognize the original source and
ground of the usage, and then freely and directly to employ the term as expressive of controlling influence, however, and by whatsoever, exerted.

But we may go, we must go to meet the facts of the case,
yet one step farther. When a word of a general character
has been employed very often, and through a long time,
to express a controlling influence of a particular kind, it
may come to have a specific meaning characterized by
such special influence. Drowning is the result of the influence of encompassing waters fully exerted upon a living
man; to express such envelopment βαπτίζω was employed;
the cases for such application would be frequently occurring, and would be perpetuated from generation to generation; it would, therefore, necessarily follow that this

word, sooner or later, would be understood as expressing not merely the fact of envelopment, but, directly, the condition resultant from it, namely, THE DROWNING.

By a similar process—*mutatis mutandis*—it might come to express, directly, the peculiarity of influence exerted by intoxicating liquors when drank to excess, viz., *to make drunk*.

3. These things being so, there is an absolute barrier to any connection ever being established between βαπτίζω and *dip*. Neither in primary, nor in secondary use, can these words ever come in contact. And, indeed, as a matter of fact, no two words in the Greek language are kept more distinctly and uniformly separate in their usage than are βαπτίζω and βάπτω.

REPRESENTATIVE WORD.

It is necessary not only that the meaning of a word should be described, but that such description should be embodied in some representative word.

It has been already seen that Baptist writers have entirely failed to furnish us with such a word. The failure, however, has not been because no attempt was made to meet the demand. Now, one word has been announced as having the precise form and force required; and, then, another word, essentially differing in form and force, has been declared to be just what was demanded; and yet, again, a third word has been brought forward, radically differing from both of these, as, unquestionably, the right one. Such failure, so manifest and so often repeated, constrains us to doubt, not the scholarship (Greek or English) of these writers, but the existence of any word in the English language which fully represents the broad and varied usage of the Greek word. This we shall consider, until better informed, to be incontrovertible truth.

Take up what word you will, in use with us, and employ it as the substitute for the Greek word, and you will very soon find it running out. Try a second, and it, speedily, meets the same fate. Try a third, and it has no better issue.

9

Under these circumstances it becomes a necessary question—whether we shall adopt several words to express the modifications of meaning, or whether we shall adopt some one word, as near as may be to the fundamental idea of the original, and carry it throughout the entire range of Greek usage without regard to the existence, or otherwise, of a corresponding English usage. Both these courses of procedure present advantages.

The use of one word, invariably, for the translation of the same word, commends itself, especially in controversy, as fit and obligatory, unless there be imperative reasons to the contrary. The English reader sees, by this course, much more satisfactorily what is Greek usage, and, also, in what measure, and at what points, it becomes divergent from English usage. He is, also, at liberty to substitute, at his own option, other words, according as he feels the necessity, without the bewildering, and oftentimes misleading, translations of the controversialist.

On the other hand, failing to find one word which moves on, *pari passu*, with βαπτίζω, throughout its entire range, if we can find a word which naturally, or by definition, accurately expresses one form of usage, while another word·may be found which accomplishes the same for another form of usage, there would be an advantage in so doing for many readers who might feel embarrassed in making a satisfactory selection for themselves.

If we could find a word which was not invested with embarrassing circumstances, arising out of its already established usage, we should be placed on vantage ground. To find such word is difficult, if not impracticable.

To drown, is in some respects quite a favorable representative word.

It is so, because: 1. It expresses the entire envelopment of an object by a fluid element. 2. It expresses the influence exerted over an object by such envelopment. This is its special use. 3. It expresses influence where there is no enveloping element. 4. It expresses, specifically, the influence of intoxicating liquors when drank to great excess. 5. It has no dependence on any form of act. 6. It expresses no limitation as to the continuance of the state induced.

In these particulars are embraced all the elements which enter into the usage of *βαπτίζω*; but in translating "to drown," we should, assuredly be embarrassed by the greatly predominant meaning—to destroy life by suffocation under water. Nevertheless it is of importance to state, distinctly, that this Greek word is fairly, though inadequately, represented by *drown*.

To whelm presents some special claim for consideration. 1. It envelops. 2. It influences by envelopment. 3. It influences without envelopment. 4. It is not limited by form of act. 5. It is without limit of time.

Its special claim lies in its usage under the third particular. Whelm (and overwhelm, the same word emphasized) has a secondary usage giving expression to fully developed and controlling influence, which, by its nature and breadth, represents the Greek word better, perhaps, in its like usage, than any other English word. Its deficiency consists in the predominant thought of the liquid sweeping over its object with force. Such specialty is not in the Greek word. This, however, largely, if not wholly, disappears in secondary use, leaving only the grand idea of controlling influence.

To merse has just and strong representative claims within certain limits.

"Im-merse" is peremptorily excluded: 1. Because compounded with a preposition, which the original word is not, and for which there is no conceivable necessity. 2. Because im-merse is the proper translation of *εμ-βαπτίζω*, and which should (if *im*-merse is the translation of the uncompounded word) be translated *im-im*merse. 3. Because the preposition has been abused and misinterpreted, as indicative of movement, while its force was merely local, as a proper examination, both of Latin and English usage, will fully establish.

In all cases where the simple envelopment of the object,

only, is concerned, no word, probably, is more unexceptionable than *merse*.

1. This word is of common use in cases where an object is placed in a fluid, semi-fluid, or any easily penetrable material.   2. It depends upon no form of act.   3. It is without limit of duration.

But where the design is to express influence, whether as a consequence of envelopment, or controlling influence without envelopment, this word, markedly, fails. Such usage is a leading feature in the Greek word, claiming special attention, and demanding expression.

The secondary use of merse (or immerse) does not correspond with that of βαπτίζω. "I am mersed in study," and "I am baptized by study," are phrases expressive of very different ideas. The former expresses *thorough intellectual engagedness;* the latter expresses *thorough intellectual prostration.*

Steep approaches toward the idea, yet falls essentially short of it. To be steeped in any influence is to be thoroughly interpenetrated by it, yet so that the influence remains under our control; to be baptized by any influence, is for us to be thoroughly under its control.

Whelm expresses this additional idea, and it is the only word, that I think of, which does do so in so satisfactory a manner.

In the first examination of this question, "merse" was carried through every case of the usage of the Greek word; but in doing so the necessity arises for the origination of usage unknown to our language. This is embarrassing. Unity of word and clearness of thought cannot be combined. It may be better (though we cannot but greatly regret the necessity) to sacrifice verbal unity to a clear statement of the thought.

Merse (immerse) fails to represent the Greek word in another particular, namely, its absolute use.

When it is said of a man, absolutely, that he was "baptized," meaning that he was *drowned,* we have no corresponding use of *mersed* (immersed). When it is said, in like absolute use, he was "baptized," meaning *stupefied* by an opiate; or "baptized," *bewildered* by questions; or "baptized," *intoxicated;* or "baptized," *purified;* we have no like usage of *merse* (immerse).

The fitness of merse (immerse) to represent βαπτίζω is good within certain limits; but those limits are decidedly restricted, unless the mind be educated to the interpretation of unfamiliar combinations.

To inn is a word of our language, although of infrequent and restricted use. Its radical idea of *inness* affords the essential idea requisite to develop a usage which would faithfully represent this Greek word. The usage would have to be formed out of this radical idea, for it has no present existence; but this is, measurably, true of every other word. The advantage would be, that we should not have to unlearn old and unsuitable ideas. In some cases, this word (because so much unused) would bring with it less *clog* to embarrass the thought than any other, more familiar, word.

The idea of *inness*, and of inness expressive of influence, is one of greatest familiarity to our language. If this thought were embodied in the verb *to inn*, and applied as the sole representative of the Greek word throughout the entire range of its usage, it would be as little liable to exception as any other one word, while it would have, in some cases, special advantage.

I make this suggestion not with any design to adopt it as a translation, but that it may serve, as a truth laid up, to get rid of some of the false notions which have gathered around this debated word, by reason of the use of a certain set of terms as representative words.

To steep.—Steep and dip, in their relation to each other, and in their distinctive usage, illustrate, very forcibly, the two Greek words. Like them, steep and dip come from the same root; and, like them, each has a deeply marked individuality. Dip represents βάπτω, steep represents βαπτίζω. Steep expresses no definite act; it does express envelopment by a fluid; envelopment, for the sake of influence; pervading influence without envelopment; and has no limitation of time. Dip and steep present strong claims to a front place as the English representatives of βάπτω and βαπτίζω. If, however, we had a verb *to deep*, then, to dip and to deep would exhibit the fundamentally distinguishing characteristic, and could well serve as duplicates of these foreign words.

To baptize.—After a thoughtful consideration of every, apparently, appropriate word, I am induced to believe that it would be well to employ *baptize* to represent the secondary use, defining it as expressing controlling influence; the particular nature of the influence being determined by the specialty of the case. We would be less embarrassed, in the use of this word, with previous and irrelevant conceptions, and the mind would be left more untrammelled in its effort to extract the thought presented.

After all, however, has been said as to the advantages and disadvantages in the use of particular words, there may be controversial considerations which will outweigh all others, and determine it to be best to use a single word, to represent the single Greek word, throughout the whole extent and under all the modifications of its meaning.

The best word, probably, all things considered, is Merse.

The statements already made will show that this word is not without its imperfections, while they may help to relieve them. Nor is it without advantage that the word, in this uncompounded form, has no common use. We shall find, on this account, greater facility in associating with it any modification of thought, desirable, above what would be the case with *im*-merse.

By such use of this word our Baptist friends will be deprived of all possible ground of complaint, while we shall show our unbounded confidence that the sentiment of passages adduced will be sufficiently clear and powerful to correct, and to control, any water tendencies which may pertain to the word, from more familiar usage, in that direction.

DEFINITION.

Defining—*to merse, to drown, to whelm, to steep, to inn,* in primary use, as causative of the condition of an object within a closely investing element, without any limitation as to the character of the act inducing such envelopment, and without any limitation as to the time of its continuance :

And defining—*to merse, to whelm, to steep, to baptize,* in secondary use, as causative of a condition induced by a controlling influence unlimited as to source, form, or duration :

I would define βαπτίζω to mean, primarily,

1. To INTUSPOSE: to merse, to drown, to whelm, to steep to inn; and, by appropriation, *to suffocate within a fluid* (to drown).

2. To INFLUENCE CONTROLLINGLY: to merse, to whelm, to steep, to inn, to baptize; and, by appropriation, *to intoxicate.*

In this secondary use, the word, or an organic phrase, or the word as embodying such phrase, may be translated with the utmost fidelity—*to stupefy, to bewilder, to pollute, to purify,* &c., &c.

Each of these words expresses a condition induced by some controlling influence. The nature of the influence is a matter of as absolute indifference as is the means and mode by which it is produced. One drop of prussic acid is as thoroughly competent to effect a baptism, secondary, (perhaps the more common form of baptism expressed by the Greeks), as is an ocean to effect a baptism, primary.

The meaning thus assigned to βαπτίζω must be sustained by an appeal to the facts of usage.

Every passage of what may be termed *Classical Greek* (liberally interpreted), which I have met with, either as the fruit of my own direct examination, or that of others, has been adduced. The period embraced within these quotations is about a thousand years. There will, therefore, be the fullest opportunity for the *usus loquendi* to give its authoritative utterance.

If any one, after seeing the usage of the two Greek words side by side, can hesitate to acknowledge that they are radically different in meaning, as radically different in reference to the act of dipping as in reference to effecting a dyed condition, I shall be greatly surprised.

If the conclusion reached should meet with general assent, then the bands by which dipping and baptizing have been so long bound together must be pronounced to be unlawful, and proclamation made that there are insurmountable impediments which forever forbid that these "twain should be made one."

What farther bearing this meaning, assigned to $\beta\alpha\pi\tau\iota\zeta\omega$, has upon Christian baptism, will be seen when that subject shall come before us for consideration. It will not, at present, be introduced into the discussion.

ΒΑΠΤΩ.

ITS MEANING AND USAGE.

It will facilitate our ultimate purpose to consider first, the usage of βάπτω, and other words whose meanings are designed to elucidate, by agreement or disagreement, the meaning of βαπτίζω.

It has been confidently affirmed that βάπτω has but the two meanings *to dip* and *to dye*. Usage will show that this latter position is as untenable as the earlier one which denied that it had more than one meaning—*to dip*. But it is unnecessary, here, to particularize; the quotations will speak for themselves.

We have a right, however, to note all such errors, as justly enfeebling our faith in other conclusions which we are called upon to accept. The commission of frequent, and manifest errors, should induce some hesitancy in affirming that "it is not so much evidence that is wanted as Christian honesty" to cause the acceptance of such positions as are, still, zealously pressed by our Baptist brethren.

To dip has been placed first in order among the meanings of βάπτω; but whether dip or dye be regarded as the primary meaning, the meaning is *dip* and not plunge, or sink, or any other word whose meaning characteristically differs from dip. By "dip" is meant a downward movement, without violence, passing out of one medium into another, to a limited extent, and returning without delay. *Plunge* differs essentially from this word in that it demands rapidity and force of movement; and, more especially, in that it makes no demand for a return. In critical, or controversial writing no word can, fairly, be substituted for dip, which has characteristics alien from and contradictory to its nature. I know of no instance, where βάπτω is used to put an object into a fluid to remain there permanently, or for an unlimited time. Nor do I know of any instance, where this word is used to draw up anything out of a liquid which it had not first put into it.

Dr. Carson gives more than fifty quotations from Hippocrates, in which, he says, "there can be no doubt but we shall find the characteristic meaning of Bapto." In all these cases there is the double movement of intrance and outrance. Whether this twofold movement be the result of the explicit demand of the word, or consequential on that which is immediately expressed, the result is the same; both find place in the "characteristic" use of the word.

To dye is now acknowledged to be a secondary meaning without any, necessary, dependence upon dipping. This doctrine was long and strenuously opposed by Baptist writers, who contended, then, that βάπτω had but one meaning, as, now, they contend that βαπτίζω has but one meaning; and that dyeing was a mere appendage to dipping, and an accident consequent upon a dipping into a coloring element. This position is, at length, thoroughly abandoned, and the admission made that dyeing by sprinkling is as orthodox as dyeing by dipping. In other words, it is now, however slowly, yet at last unreservedly admitted, that while βάπτω to dip expresses a sharply defined act; βάπτω to dye *expresses no such act; but drops all demand for any form of act, and makes requisition only for a condition or quality* of color, satisfied with any act which will meet this requirement. This being true; it is obvious that the difference between dip and dye, and dip and plunge, is not a difference of measure and form, but a difference of nature. Dip and plunge express forms of act to be done; dye expresses a condition or quality to be secured. Thus we secure a stepping-stone toward that truth which we would establish; to wit, that βαπτίζω, unlike βάπτω *to dip*, but like βάπτω *to dye*, does express *not a form of act, but a condition*— condition of intusposition, primarily, and condition of controlling influence, secondarily. Βάπτω, in one of its aspects, demands a movement which carries its object, momentarily, within a fluid element; and in another of its aspects, demands a condition which is met by flowing, pouring, or sprinkling: βαπτίζω, in one of its aspects, demands a condition which may be effected by flowing, pouring, or sprinkling; and in another of its aspects, demands a condition which may be effected by anything, in any way, which is competent to exercise a controlling influence over its object.

The two leading meanings, *to dip, to dye*, have, severally, modifications in usage which, as they shall be developed, will show that the refusal to accept of any farther modification, in the meaning of this Greek word, is not well grounded.

MEANING ESTABLISHED BY USAGE.

PRIMARY—TO DIP.

Στέφανον εἰς μύρον βάψας. *Ælian*, lib. xiv, cap. 30
Dipping the crown into ointment.

Ἐνέβαψεν εἰς τὸν κηρὸν αὐτῆς τὼ πόδε. *Aristophanes, Nubes*, i, 2.
Dipped its feet into the wax.

Τόδ᾽ ἐμβάψω λαβών. *Aristophanes, Peace*, 960.
I will dip—in, the torch, having taken it.

Εἰ εἰς κηρὸν βάψειέ τις. *Aristotle, On the Soul*, iii, 12.
If any one should dip into wax.

Βάψαι γὰρ δεῖ, καὶ τότ᾽ ἄνω ἑλκύσαι. *Aristotle, Mech. Quest.* c. 29.
It is necessary to dip and then to draw up.

Ἐς ὕδατα κρωσσὸν ἔβαψε. *Constantine, Epigr. of Hermolaus.*
He dipped a vessel into water.

Εἰς τὰς πλευρὰς βάψας τὴν αἰχμήν. *Dionys. Hallic. Ant. Rom.* lib. v.
Dipping the spear into the breast.

Καὶ ναῦς γάρ . . . . ἔβαψεν. *Euripides, Orestes*, 705.
If a vessel has . . . . dipped.

Βάψας, ἔνεγχε δεῦρο ποντίας ἁλός. Euripides, *Hecuba*, 608.
Dipping it, bring hither of the salt sea.

Βάπτειν ἐστὶ τὸ χαλᾶν τι εἰς ὕδωρ. Scholium, *Hecuba*, 608.
To dip is to let something down into water or some other fluid.

Οὐδὲ εἰς περιῤῥαντήριον ἐμβάπτειν. Iamblichus, *Vit. Pythag.* c. 18.
Nor to dip—into the periranterium.

Κρωσσοῖσιν ὀθνείοισι βάψαντες γάνος. Lycophron, *Cassandra*, 1365.
Dipping pleasure with foreign vessels.

Εἰς σπλάγχν᾿ ἐχίδνης αὐτόχειρ βάψει ξίφος. Lycophron, 1121.
Will dip the sword into the viper's bowels.

Τᾷ χάλπιδι κηρία βάψαι. Theocritus, *Idyl* v, 127.
Dip honey with a pitcher.

TO WET.

Βάψας κοίλην τὴν χεῖρα, προςραίνει τὴν δικαστήριαν. Suidas, *de Hierocle.*
Wetting the hollow of his hand he sprinkles the judgment seat.

TO MOISTEN.

Θλιβόμενος δὲ βάπτει καὶ ἀνθίζει τὴν χεῖρα. Aristotle, *Hist. Anim.* v, 15.
Being pressed it moistens and colors the hand.

Τὸ βάψαι, διῆναι κέκληκεν ὁ ποιητής. Plutarch, *Sympos.* Prob. 8, 6.
Βάψαι, the poet has called *to moisten.*

TO WASH.

Ποταμοῖο ἐβάψατο . . . ὤμους ἐκ κεφαλῆς. Aratus, 220.
Washed head and shoulders of the river.

Ἀνέφελος, βάπτοι ῥόου ἑσπερίοιο. Aratus, 858.
Cloudless, washes of the western flood.

Ἔβαψε ἑωυτὸν βὰς ἐπὶ τὸν ποταμόν. Herodotus, *Euterpe*, 47.
Washed himself, going upon the river.

Βάπτουσι θερμῷ. *Aristophanes, Eccles.* 216.
They wash with warm water.

SECONDARY—TO DYE.

Βάπτουσιν 'Αφροδίτης τὸν πέπλον. *Achil. Tat.* II, 87.
They dye the robe of Venus.

Τὸ φάρμακον ᾧ βάπτεται. *Achil. Tat.* II, 89.
The drug with which it is dyed.

'Εβάπτετο δ'αἵματι λίμνη. *Æsopi, Phry. Fab. Batr.* 218.
The lake was dyed with blood.

"Ινα μή σε βάψω βάμμα Σαρδιανικόν. *Aristophanes, Achar.* I, 112.
Lest I dye you a Sardinian dye.

"Ορνις βαπτός. *Aristophanes, Aves*, 526.
A dyed bird.

Καὶ τὰ ἀπ' αὐτῆς βαπτόμενα ἱμάτια. *Barker's Class. Rec.* p. 418.
And the garments which are dyed from it.

Τὰς τρίχας, ὦ Νίκυλλα, τινές βάπτειν σε λέγουσιν. *Bentleii, Ep. Coll.* 139.
Some say that you dye your hair.

Τὴν κεφαλὴν βάπτεις, γῆρας δὲ σὸν οὔποτε βάψεις. *Bentleii, Epigr. Coll.*
Thou may'st dye thy head, thy old age thou canst not dye.

Καὶ φαρμάσσειν τὸ βάπτειν ἐλέγετο. *Eustathius* ad Il. x, 32.
To drug was called to dye.

'Επειδὰν ἐπιστάξῃ ἱμάτια βάπτεται. *Hippocrates.*
When it drops upon the garments they are dyed.

Καθάπερ οἱ βαφεῖς προεκκαθαίροντες. *Iamblichus Vit. Pyth.* xvii.
As dyers cleanse beforehand.

'Ερεῖς δὲ βαφή χρῶσις, καταχρῶσις. *Julius Pollux*, vii, 30.
You will call βαφη color, paint.

Καὶ βάψομαι. *Menander, Frag.* 2, *Anger.*
And I will dye.

'Εὰν τέ τις ἄλλα χρώματα βάπτῃ ἐάν τε καὶ ταῦτα. *Plato, de Repub.*
iv, 429.
Whether one dye other colors, or whether these.

TO STAIN.

Ἔβαψας ἔγχος εὖ πρὸς Ἀργείων στρατῷ. *Sophocles, Ajax,* 95.
Is it well that thou hast stained thy sword with the army
of the Greeks?

TO SMEAR.

Λυδίζων, καὶ ψηνίζων, καὶ βαπτόμενος βατραχείοις. *Aristoph. Equites,*
523.
Playing the Λυδοι and the ψην, and smeared with frog-colored
washes.

TO GILD.

Καὶ πενίην βάψας, πλούσιος ἐξεφάνης. *Jacob's Anthol.* iii, 145.
Having gilded poverty thou hast appeared rich.

TO TEMPER.

Χαλκοῦ βαφάς. *Æschylus, Agam.* 612.
Temperers of brass?

Βαφὴν ἀφιέναι. *Aristotle, Pol.* 7, 14.
To lose temper.

Ἐν ὕδατι ψυχρῷ βάπτῃ .... φαρμάσσων. *Homer, Odys.* ix, 392.
Working .... tempers with cold water.

Βαφῇ σίδηρος ὥς. *Sophocles, Ajax,* 651.
As iron by tempering.

Θηλύνεται βεβαμμένος ὑπὸ ἐλαίου. *Scholium, Ajax.* 663.
Tempered by oil it is softened.

TO IMBUE.

Βάπτεται γὰρ ὑπὸ τῶν φαντασίων ἡ ψυχή, βάπτε οὖν αὐτὴν τῇ συνεχείῃ τῶν τοιούτων, φαντασίων. *Antoninus M.* v, 17.
The soul is imbued by the thoughts, imbue it, therefore, by the habitude of such thoughts.

Διχαιοσύνῃ βεβαμμένον εἰς βάθος. *Antoninus M.* iii, 6.
Imbued by integrity to the bottom.

Ὅρα μὴ ἀποχαισαρωθῇς μὴ βαφῇς. *Antoninus M.* vi, 25.
Beware of Cæsarism, lest you be imbued by it.

Μοῦσαν ἐχιδναία πρῶτος ἔβαψε χολῇ. *Bentleii, Epig. Coll.* p. 156.
He first imbued the Muse with viperish gall.

Χολῇ βεβαμένοις ὄφεων ὄϊστοῖς. *Strabo*, xvi, p. 1117.
Arrows imbued with the gall of serpents.

Ἀναλάβῃ τὸ πάθος τοῦ βεβαμμένου. *Epictetus, Arrian*, xi, 9.
Should adopt the character of one imbued.

Οἱ βάπται. *Eupolis.*
The Baptæ.

ΒΑΠΤΩ—PRIMARY.

TO DIP.

All the quotations showing the primary, literal use, confirm what Aristotle says, that the act expressed is one which carries its object, superficially, into a fluid and brings it out. The act is, emphatically, one of limitations, —limitation of force, limitation of extent of entrance into the element, limitation of time of continuance within the element, and, by consequence, limitation of influence. It is, also, noticeable that the objects are limited in magnitude, although there is no other necessity for this than the limitation of human strength, in its ordinary exercise, by which objects are usually dipped. Euripides speaks of

the dipping of a sailing vessel; but it is not the entire vessel that is dipped, but merely the rising and falling produced by the wind. The case, more fully stated, is this:
"Has a ship, with sheet hauled close, struck by the wind,
dipped? She will right again if the sheet be loosed."

The following quotation illustrates the passage: "As
the squadron rounded the buoy the wind was free and
the sheets were eased off; the vessels righted at once."
The dipping is not directly stated, but is involved in the
"righting." Some have translated this passage—"if a
vessel has *sunk*." There is no sanction here, or elsewhere,
for translating βάπτω *to sink.* It is never applied to vessels,
or anything else, sunk; βαπτίζω, exclusively, is used in connection with such facts. This case proves that a part,
only, of an object may be dipped, although there be no
express limitation in the statement.

Carson objects to this (p. 21): "Grave doctors make
themselves fools" by saying that the phrase, "they dipped
the man in the river, does not necessarily imply that they
dipped him all over." Euripides was not a "grave doctor," and so may escape the unenviable brand which the
Doctor of Tubbermore applies so sovereignly to his fellow
"doctors." The vessel is dipped (by a sudden blast) into
the sea without being "dipped all over," and Euripides
was, surely, no "fool" in his knowledge of Greek. Besides,
Dr. Carson, and other "grave doctors," speak, daily, of
"dipping men in the river," when they, in fact, dip but a
part of the body (head and shoulders), and I never heard
of any one calling them "fools" for such use of language,
however much they may be judged liable to the charge
of inconsistency in carrying theory into practice.

The preposition employed in all these passages (where
any is expressed) claims attention. 'Εις is always employed, with its appropriate case, and the verb in the
active voice directly expressive of the act performed. This
is the natural use of the word in its primary sense, and
whenever otherwise used there is reason to believe that
there is some modification in the meaning of the word.

The use of βαπτίζω will be found to be in marked contrast with this. It is used, infrequently, in the active voice with ἐις, in its primary sense, because such is not the natural grammatical construction of this class of words, although they may be so employed with a verb understood.

MEANINGS GROWING OUT OF DIPPING INTO WATER.

1. To WET.—This is an unavoidable consequence of dipping anything into water; and it would be in perfect harmony with the laws of language to use the word, whose act produces the effect, to express such effect when not produced by its form of act. It is difficult, if not impossible, to translate by *dip* in the passage from *Suidas*, and it seems to be a necessity to translate by *wet*.

2. To MOISTEN.—In the quotation from Aristotle *dip* is out of all question, and *dye* seems to be as much so, in consequence of the use of "ανθίζει." Two words are not needed to express dyeing; while the *moistening* by the juice of the berry pressed is essential to dye, stain, or color the hand.

We the more readily adopt this meaning, as Plutarch expressly says that the word is used in this sense.

3. To WASH.—Aratus speaks of a crow washing itself "of the river." The phraseology indicates that *dipping* is not intended. The scholiast omits the limitation ("head and shoulders") in the text, and says, "washes itself"—βάπτει δὲ ἑαυτην ἡ κορνίκη—including the whole, while a part only is washed.

In the second quotation from the same writer the form of the phraseology is similar, and is indicative of a similar use. The importance of the form of expression is obvious in the translation of Carson—"if the crow dips his head *into* the river." "Into" has no existence in the text, and whatever Carson may think, others will be likely to judge that "into the river" and "of the river" are phrases of very different value.

Herodotus.—The quotation from Herodotus is thus translated by Carson : " The Egyptians consider the swine so
polluted a beast, that if any one in passing touch a swine,
he will go away, and dip himself with his very garments,
going into the river."

Unless the text of Dr. Carson differed from that before
me, we have, here, another of those broad discrepancies
so often found in the translations of this writer as compared
with the original.   There is nothing said about " going
into the river;" the text is "going *upon*" (the bank of)
" the river."   If, however, it be assumed, as an unstated
fact, that after having come upon the river, he, also,
" went into the river" and then " dipped himself," we
learn from Dr. Carson that, after all, the dipping of the
head and shoulders may be accepted as the dipping of the
man, " himself," into the river.

The same writer tells us with some degree of exultation,
" Here is a religious baptism, and it is by immersion."   As
depicted by Carson, this Egyptian " baptism" into the
Nile is a perfect model for those more modern " religious
baptisms" with which he is familiar.   " Going into the
river," "with clothes on," dipping the head and shoulders;
these are the necessary elements.   If, now, Herodotus
were Matthew, and Egypt were Palestine, and the Nile
were Jordan, and last, but not least, if βάπτω were βαπτίζω,
and the facts were as the translator represents, then, to the
narrative might be appended an unanswerable Q. E. D.

But the equanimity with which this transaction is referred to as a solution of the mode of baptism must be
disturbed.   It is not called a " baptism" by Herodotus, but
by Dr. Carson, and with self-inconsistency, for elsewhere
(p. 48) he says, that this word should never be used with
bapto.   Herodotus understood Greek too well to use anything else than βάπτω, here, whether it means to dip or to
wash, and we cannot allow Dr. Carson to correct, or to
pervert, his language by transforming βάπτω into βαπτίζω.
The fact is that this transaction, as represented by Carson,
is fatal to the Baptist scheme.   According to it, a true

Greek calls their ritual service a *bapting;* this we cheerfully admit it to be; but this will not quite answer; so the
attempt is made to convert it into a *baptizing.* The Egyptian *bapting* may be pleaded as a precedent for modern
dipping, but it must be just as it is, with no surreptitious
conversion of the transaction into a *baptism.* The more
strongly this dipping is leaned upon for support, the more
utterly is Christian baptism abandoned. Βάπτω and βαπτίζω
are non-interchangeable terms. The Scriptures adopt the
latter, and know nothing of Egyptian bapting. Herodotus is right in the use of language; dipping is bapting,
and Carson must be satisfied with bapting or change his
practice.

The Doctor attempts, in vain, to bridge over the gulf between these two words by saying: "The person dips himself; therefore it is bapto to dip, and not baptizo to cause
to dip." The attempted distinction has no real existence.
When I dip my pen into the ink I cause it to dip just as
much as when I dip the upper part of a man's body into
the river. Besides, this reasoning is nullified by the writer
himself when he speaks of Naaman, finding no embarrassment from the presence of βαπτίζω; but makes him, by this
word, "dip himself," entirely oblivious of the necessity,
arising from this word, that somebody else should be there
"to cause him to dip."

It remains, then, classically true, that "Bapting is dipping, and Dipping is bapting;" but this truth throws the
rite of our friends entirely out of the range of Scripture
phraseology.

What this swine-polluted Egyptian did, whether he went
into the river and *dipped* his head, or remained on the bank
and *washed,* has some bearing on the meaning of βάπτω; it
has none on βαπτίζω. It expounds the dipping of Baptists;
it has no bearing on the baptism of the Scriptures.

Aristophanes.—"They wash the wool with warm water."
Carson admits that this translation "gives the sense, but
not the exact version of the words; what is asserted is, that
they dip, or immerse, or plunge the wool into warm water."

I am sorry that I cannot say that his translation either "gives the sense or is an exact version of the words." Of what use is it for a controversialist to translate βάπτουσι θερμῷ, "they dip *into* warm water"? And of what use are grammatical forms, if such as that before us is to be converted, by some *prestidigitation*, into another essentially different? The form and the nature of the case unite in sustaining the conclusion, that the dative is instrumental, and that there must be a corresponding modification in the use of the verb.

Some things may be washed by dipping, but a greasy fleece of wool is not among the number; a dipping, therefore, is not the thing that is here called for, but a washing. It is admitted that "Suidas and Phavorinus interpret baptousi by plunousi;" but "it argues shallow philosophy to suppose that on this account the words are perfectly synonymous." The "shallowness" may be found to be in Dr. Carson's examination of the case; but whether or no, I leave it to lovers of truth to determine, assured that, however determined, the result bears more strongly on general truth than on the specific issue before us.

ΒΑΠΤΩ—SECONDARY.

TO DYE.

Dr. Gale, representing Baptist writers up to that time, says: "The Greeks apply the word to the dyer's art, but *always* so as to imply and refer *only* to its true, natural signification TO DIP."

This position was tenaciously held for more than a hundred years, notwithstanding all the mass of evidence accumulated against it. At length Dr. Carson arose, and sharply rebuked his friends for attempting to advocate so untenable a position. He boldly affirmed that βάπτω, "from signifying mere mode, came to denote dyeing in any manner. This serves to solve difficulties that have been very clumsily got over by some of the ablest writers on this side of the question. Hippocrates employs βάπτω to denote dyeing by dropping—'When it drops upon the garments they are dyed'—this surely is not dyeing by dipping."

This reasoning is presented by Dr. Carson as unanswerable, and it has been accepted, from him, by Baptists, as truth, although rejected a thousand times when stated by their opponents. And, yet, when identically the same argumentation is adduced to prove that βάπτω may mean *to wet*—Nebuchadnezzar being bapted by drops of dew—it is rejected as a mere nullity, and βάπτω can mean nothing else but *dip!*

Gale's position in reference to βάπτω, which Carson repudiates (with the Baptist world crying, "Well done!"), he most cordially adopts as true, in relation to βαπτίζω; "the Greeks apply this word to cases where there is no immersion in fact, but always so as to imply and refer only to its true, natural signification, *to dip*." And, again, the Baptist world exclaims, "Well done!"

It may be of but little avail for us to bring evidence, "clear as holy writ," in disproof of this position; but I suppose we must continue to do it until another Carson, wilful, but honest and trusted by his friends, shall arise and teach them that "from signifying intusposition, and complete influence from intusposition, it came to denote baptizing," *i. e.* influencing completely without intusposition and in any manner. "This seems to solve difficulties that have been very clumsily got over by some of the ablest writers on this side of the question." And him they will hear.

"*Bapting* by sprinkling" was once regarded as a very fair subject for the exercise of the powers of ridicule; but that time has passed, and, in order to cover the confessed error, the task is assumed of making doubly ridiculous "*baptizing* by sprinkling." Truth can wait; but she will not have to wait long before the confession will, once more, be made—"there are difficulties very clumsily got over by some of the ablest writers" who have ventured to indorse this Baptist position—"baptizing by sprinkling is an absurdity."

Βάπτω to dye has a far more practical and instructive relation to βαπτίζω, than has βάπτω to dip; because the former meaning is not, like the latter, a demand for an act, but for an effect, and there is a consequent harmony in grammatical forms, and, measurably, of thought branching out of it. This will be seen to be true by the facts of usage. As a dyed condition may be effected in almost endless variety of ways, even including the paradox, "dipping by sprinkling," so, a baptized condition may be effected in ways no less numberless, even including "the absurdity" baptizing by sprinkling.

We might decline to use dye to express the modified meaning of βάπτω, and retain dip, throughout, as the Greeks retain βάπτω.

There would be a propriety in doing so; because, 1. It would perfectly reflect the Greek practice. 2. Because dip, in English, also, has the meaning to dye. 3. Because thrown on to the sentiment and the syntax, to learn the modification of the primary meaning, there would be some equalization of the case with that of βαπτίζω, when it is compelled to vindicate its claim to modified meaning under the uniform use of a single word through all its usage.

But we will not insist on putting a similar burden on βάπτω; but cheerfully assume the unequal task, believing that the word is able to vindicate its rights even under such unfavorable circumstances.

———————

"The lake was dyed with blood."

It would be quite unnecessary to dwell upon any of these quotations, if the only purpose was to establish the meaning to dye; this has been thoroughly done, and is universally accepted; but there are other reasons, connected with the grammatical structure, modified translation, varied agencies, the introduction of distinct words to express the form of action, as they bear upon and illustrate kindred peculiarities in the usage of βαπτίζω, which make a rapid survey of particular passages desirable.

The above passage from Æsop, attributed to Homer, is instructive by reason of the manner in which it has been treated in the earlier period of this controversy, as well as for the reasons prompting to the abandonment of the ground then taken.

Dr. Gale says: " The literal sense is, the lake was dipped in blood. And the lake is represented, by hyperbole, as dipped in blood."

Dr. Carson replies to this: "Never was there such a figure. The lake is not said to be dipped, or poured, or sprinkled, but dyed with blood. The expression is literal, and has not the smallest difficulty."

It is desirable to note several particulars ruling in Dr. Carson's interpretation:

1. The repudiation of Gale's view on the ground of extravagance in the figure.

2. The rejection of all figure by the introduction of a secondary meaning.

3. The denial that the act by which the dyeing takes place is expressed by βάπτω. "The blood was POURED into the lake," but "βάπτω does not, therefore, signify TO POUR."

4. The rejection of the local dative and the substitution of the instrumental.

5. The necessity for this as grounded in the meaning of the verb as modified.

So long as Gale insisted on the act dip, he was compelled (whatever might be the amount of violence done to the construction, or whatever might be "the perversion of taste") to make the dative represent that in which the act took place, for "blood" could not be instrumental in a *dipping;* in like manner, when Carson rejected the act (dip) and took the condition (dye), he was shut up to the necessity of interpreting the dative as instrumental; for "blood" can *dye* while it cannot dip.

6. The dative is made instrumental, notwithstanding

that it represents a fluid element in which (its nature only considered) a dipping could readily take place.

All these elements which enter into the rejection of Gale's interpretation (who in this matter does not stand as a simple individual, but as the representative of the entire Baptist body) will come into frequent play in the exposition of other passages where Carson will be found attempting to sustain a similar position in relation to βαπτίζω, with that of Gale to βάπτω, which he has so remorselessly overturned.

One more point in connection with this passage and we may leave it.

"βάπτω, from signifying mere mode, came to be applied to a certain operation usually performed in that mode. From signifying dip it came to signify to dye by dipping." And, according to this interpretation, and elsewhere, it came, by yet another step, to signify to dye *without dipping;* to dye in any manner. That is to say, the original peculiarity of the word, *the name remaining the same*, is entirely lost sight of: 1, to dip; 2, TO DYE *by* dipping; 3, *to dye without* dipping. Apply, now, this developing process to βαπτίζω, and we have, 1. To intuspose within a fluid. 2. To influence controllingly *by* intusposition within a fluid. 3. To influence controllingly *without* intusposition.

In the first process βάπτω remains, in all its literal integrity; but dip is wholly eliminated from its signification. In the second process, βαπτίζω exhibits every letter in wonted position, while it has, bodily, come forth from intusposition in water or in anything else.

However much it may be denied that this latter word has such development, in fact, it is beyond denial that such development *may be* (unless we are to go back to the antiquated interpretation of "the lake dipped, hyperbolically, in a frog's blood"), and if it may be, then, the cry of "absurdity" is absurd.

What are the facts as to this development, we can better determine when they shall have passed before us.

"The garments which are dyed from it are called byssina."

The use of the genitive (ἀπ' ἀυτῆς) excludes all idea of dipping which might be forced upon the dative. Even Gale could not say, here, "the garments are dipped *in* it." Although the garments should have been dyed by dipping, still, the βάπτω, in this construction, could have neither part nor lot in any such dipping. If this act should be desired to appear, and appear under the auspices of βάπτω, this word as signifying *to dip* must be called into requisition; as meaning *to dye*, in this passage, its power is exhausted, and the dipping must be supplied from some other quarter.

No word can have, at the same time, two meanings. No word can mean, in the same passage, both dip and dye.

"And I will dye."

No regimen is expressed. "I, also, was once young; but I was not washed, then, five times a day; but now I am; nor had I, then, a fine mantle; but now I have; nor had I ointment; but now I have; *and I will dye.*"

To dye *himself* did not require that he should dye his whole person, but the hair and beard—"*crines et barbam pingebant,*" a commentator observes. On the process of dyeing a writer from India says: "On reaching the village I observed an aged man, the lower part of whose face was covered with bandages, beneath which stuck out the edges of green leaves besmeared with a black stuff. I inquired into the cause. The reply was that he had colored his beard, and that the bandage was worn until the color had well dried upon the hair. The coloring of the beard is a very usual custom."

We, here, learn how absolutely dipping has disappeared from dyeing. The Christian missionary (J. H. Orbison) repeats what Nearchus said two thousand years ago— "the Indians dye their beards."

The mode, as well as the custom, probably remains the same.

"When it drops upon the garments they are dyed."

This statement goes beyond the others in the exclusion of dipping, in that while they expressed this by construction and by sentiment, here, we are expressly furnished with a word (επισταξη) expressing an act of an entirely different character, by which the coloring material is brought in contact with the material to be dyed. Professor Wilson remarks: "The great critical value of this example consists in its stripping βάπτω completely of all claim to modal signification, by employing another term to denote the manner in which the dye was applied to the garments."

We have, here, a favorable opportunity to indicate and make the attempt to correct, an error constantly outcropping in this controversy.

No Baptist would say that βάπτω, in the phrase " to dye by dropping," expressed the act *to drop;* no such person should say that βάπτο in the phrase, "to dye by dipping," expressed the act *to dip;* and, yet, there is a constant identification of βαπτίζω with the act (whatever it may be) by which its demand is effected.

It is possible that it may yet be confessed that it is quite as *facile,* and fully as legitimate, to baptize by sprinkling as to βαπτειν by dropping; while in so doing, although the sprinkling effects a *baptism* as truly as that the dropping effects a *bapting,* yet βαπτίζω has just as little responsibility for the expression of the *act* of sprinkling, as βάπτω has for giving expression to the *act* of dropping.

"Whether one dye other colors, or whether these."

"No matter what dye they are dipped in," is the translation of Gale and Carson, and is, surely, loose enough when used as an element for a critical judgment. It shows no regard to the syntax. The comment of Halley is just: " Whether the χρῶμα was the dye into which the wool was dipped, or the color imparted to it, is not the question. Be it which it may, it is the object of βάπτῃ; it has gained in the syntax the place of the material subjected to the process; and, therefore, pleads a law of language, that βάπτω in the passage does not, and cannot mean to dip, as the color cannot be dipped whatever may be done with the wool."

" *Colors* dipped in Heaven" (Milton) is a parallel passage; where "dipped" necessarily means *dyed*.

" Lest I dye you a Sardian dye."

" Lest I dip you into a Sardinian dye." (*Carson.*) Such translation makes a recast of the syntax. And by so doing opens the way for the introduction of the primary meaning, in contradiction to the principle laid down by Buttman and Kühner—" when the verb is followed by the corresponding or kindred abstract substantive,"—which would necessitate the translation, " *dye* a Sardian *dye*," or " *dip* a Sardian *dip*."

The apology offered by Carson for his translation is: " As the reference is to the art of dyeing, so the expression must be suited to the usual mode of dyeing." Against such reasoning we protest. There is nothing whatever suggestive of " the usual mode of dyeing." Gale might as well say, " the lake was *dipped* in blood," because, " as the reference is to dyeing, so, the expression must be suited to the usual mode of dyeing." If Aristotle had a right to speak of dyeing by *pressing* a berry, and if Hippocrates had a right to speak of dyeing by drops *falling*, why is Aristophanes to be interdicted from speaking of dyeing by *bruising?*

The tendency to fall back on dipping as here, and elsewhere, manifested needs to be corrected.

MODIFIED MEANINGS OUTGROWTHS OF DYE.

TO STAIN.

"Is it well that thou hast stained thy sword with the army of the Greeks?"

"Ajax is represented by Sophocles as *dipping* his sword *into* the army of the Greeks;" so says Carson. Had any one else translated πρὸς by *into*, none would have frowned upon the extravagance more indignantly than Dr. Carson. And such unwarranted translations to force in *dip*, by an opponent, would have brought down coals of fire on his head.

As swords are not properly dyed with blood, but only *stained*, temporarily, this and other passages may be regarded as exemplifying that modified idea.

TO SMEAR.

"Playing the Λυδοι and playing the Ψην, and smeared with frog-colored washes."

"Magnes, an old comic poet of Athens, used the Lydian music, shaved his face, and smeared it over with tawny washes." (*Gale* and *Carson.*) The Lydian music and shaving the face are introduced through some misconception. The passage alludes to two plays, as above designated. What, however, especially claims attention is the translation of βαπτόμενος by *smear*, with the remark: "Surely, here, it has no reference to its primary meaning. The face of the person was *rubbed* with the wash. By this example it could not be known that βάπτω ever signifies to dip."

Why Dr. Carson should so unreservedly exclude dip, here, and insist upon its introduction in other passages, I do not know. "The allusion is to the art of dyeing," and why we are not compelled "to suit the expression to the most usual mode of dyeing" does not appear. We have, however, the translation—"βάπτω, *to smear, to rub!*"

TO GILD.

"Having gilded poverty thou hast appeared rich."

The intimate relation between dyeing and gilding is obvious. In this passage, and in others, the thought expressed seems to have passed into this modification. It is the case of a person who had become wealthy from a state of poverty.

TO TEMPER.

"Working . . . . tempers with cold water."

It might, at first, be thought that "to temper," as a meaning of βάπτω, should be traced *to dip* rather than *to dye;* but the tempering of metals is regulated not by the act of dipping, in contradistinction from other modes of using water and oil, but by the color and dye of the metal; I, therefore, trace this meaning to dyeing rather than to dipping.

"The razor blade is tempered by heating it till a brightened part appears a *straw* color. The temper of penknives ought not to be higher than a *straw* color. Scissors are heated until they become of a *purple* color, which indicates their proper temper."—*Ency. Amer., Art. Cutlery.*

A friend, connected with one of the most highly esteemed edge-tool manufactories in the country, having come into my study, confirms the above statements.

As the tempering of metals is not the performance of any modal act, but the inducing a peculiar condition of the metal, in the accomplishment of which water and oil are used as agencies; it follows that these fluids should be spoken of, in this connection, as instrumental means by which an end is to be secured, and not as elements into which an object is to be dipped.

Carson says: "No one who has seen a horse shod will be at a loss to know the mode of the application of water in this instance. The immersion of the newly formed shoe in water, in order to harden the metal, is expressed by the word *baptein*."

If βάπτω means to "harden the metal," to temper, nothing is more certain than that it neither does, nor can, express the immersion of the metal; supposing that an immersion took place.

The admission is made that the immersion is *in order to* harden; how facile the transition to express directly the effect—*to temper*. Such transition is most common; why not exemplified in this word?

As for the necessity of dipping, I have seen, in a blacksmith's shop, in routine work, sprinkling, pouring, and dipping, all used within about ten minutes.

" Tempered by oil it is softened."

"*Dip* by oil" is an impossible translation; "*dye* by oil" is equally so; *temper by oil* is an every day-transaction. We seem to be shut up to this translation.

Whatever plausibility there may be in a plea for dipping, when the dative, especially with a preposition, is used, there is none with the genitive. And if, in this case, the oil must be an instrumental means to an appropriate effect; then we are justified, in similar circumstances, in arguing that the dative is used instrumentally.

It is clear that if in this passage βάπτω signifies *to temper*, and the tempering should be by dipping into oil, yet, this βάπτω cannot express such *dipping*. Plain as this is, the contrary is so often assumed that the statement needs repetition. In any case the oil is spoken of as instrumental means.

The tempering of metals by water, or by oil, results in characteristic differences. The result is not determined by the mode of application of these fluids, but by their peculiar qualities; hence the tempering is *by* water and *by* oil, whether it be *in* water, or *in* oil, or otherwise.

TO IMBUE.

"The soul is imbued by the thoughts; imbue it, therefore, by the habitude of such thoughts."

"Imbue" is, perhaps, somewhat too strong to meet the requirements of the passage; and yet seems to be the word most suitable, on the whole, to this and kindred cases.

To dip involves a very extravagant figuring by which "the thoughts" receive personality, and seizing the soul dip it into the dye-tub! Is this any less "perversion of taste" than "the lake" dipping?

Gale gives an active form to the phraseology, "the thoughts dip or *tincture* the mind;" but he has excluded himself from the use of "tincture;" and, besides, this mode of translating and defining by "dip *or* tincture," "dip *or* immerse," is very unsatisfactory in a critical controversialist.

Carson, as not unfrequently, exercises a sovereign license in the treatment of the passage. His substitution is, "the thoughts are tinctured by the mind." A statement not calculated, by its profundity, to enhance in any very eminent degree the reputation of the imperial philosopher.

Carson has not cut himself off from the use of *dye*, as has Gale; but has he any better right to employ "tincture," here, than has his friend?

Is "tincture" used as entirely synonymous with *dye?* If so, why not use dye? Those who insist on single, barren ideas, as running through the whole compass of a language, for long ages, should magnify their work by illustrating it in their practice. "Tincture" is as far from being used as the mere equivalent of *dye* as is *smear, stain, color*, and it is just because of its difference that Dr. Carson uses it, here, to the rejection of dye; we cannot allow such rigidity of definition and such looseness of translation.

"Tincture" does not necessarily involve *color*, much less *dye*. A pharmaceutist informs me that some "tinctures" are colorless. A passage before me speaks of "water being tinctured by a little *lemon-juice*." Is this dyeing, or coloring, or the imparting of a colorless quality,—*acidulation?* So, in the passage under consideration, it is not the communication of color which is spoken of, but of *quality, character.*

A habitude of thinking imparts a quality or character to the soul kindred to its own.

"Imbued to the bottom with integrity."

This is the summing up of the character of a man uncorrupted by pleasure; unbroken by misfortune; undisturbed by envyings and jealousies; triumphant in self-control—"*imbued to the bottom with integrity.*"

Dip is out of the question. Dye is as little in place. Integrity, justice, has no dyeing qualities any more than has pure water. Its glory is to be void of color; to exhibit a transparent pureness.

Gale is, again, hampered and confused by his erroneous conception of the word; "dip'd, as it were, in and swallowed up with Justice; that is perfectly just: as we say, persons given up to their pleasures and vices, are immersed in or swallowed up with pleasures or wickedness."

All this mixing up of things that differ, shows, 1. The error of limiting βάπτω to *dip.* 2. The error of supposing that βάπτω can mean, at the same time, to dip, and, also, to swallow up and to immerse. And, 3. The error of confounding the usage of βάπτω and βαπτίζω, now transferring dipping from the former to the latter, and now claiming, in return, *mersing* to be handed over from the latter to the former.

No passage can be adduced in Greek where βάπτω, or, in English, where *dip*, signifies to be "immersed or swallowed up in pleasures, or wickedness," or in anything else.

This explanation is not satisfactory to Carson while he offers nothing better. "I would not explain this, with Dr. Gale, 'dip'd, as it were, in or swallowed up with justice.'

Justice is here represented as a coloring liquid, which imbues the person who is dipped in it. It communicates its qualities as in the operation of dyeing. The figure can receive no illustration from the circumstance that 'persons given up to their pleasures and vices are said to be immersed or swallowed up with pleasures or wickedness.' The last figure has a reference to the primary meaning of βάπτω, and points to the drowning effects of liquids; the former refers to the secondary meaning of the word, and has its resemblance in the coloring effects of a liquid dye. The virtuous man is to be dipped to be dyed more deeply with justice; the vicious man is drowned or ruined by his immersion."

Dr. Carson speaks as though this honest man were to be dipped "to the bottom" of *the dye-tub*, instead of imbued to the bottom of his own soul.

Such extravagant interpretations, manifestly groundless and framed to meet a case, will prepare us to appreciate others of like characteristics in connection with βαπτίζω.

"Beware of Cæsarism, lest you be imbued by it."

" Don't make the former emperors the pattern of your actions, lest you are infected or stained, or as it were dipped and dyed, namely, in mistakes and vices."—*Gale.*

This road to dipping, through "infection," and " staining," is rather roundabout, and hardly worth the trouble of passing over, inasmuch as, after thus reaching " dipping," the Doctor makes no tarrying, but passes on to " *dyeing.*"

This is another illustration of the inconsistency of Baptist writers in affirming that a word has but one meaning through Greek literature, and, then, availing themselves of the use of half a dozen different meanings whenever the exigency of the case requires it.

Carson is never embarrassed by any difficulty; the knot which his principles cannot untie, is always resolved by

11

the edge of his knife. When neither dipping nor dyeing will answer his purpose, he, very sovereignly, asking permission of none, adds to or takes from these agencies at will. " He uses the same word, also, when the dye injures what it colors. He cautions against bad example, *lest you be infected.*" The notion of a dye injuring the fabric is that of Carson, not of Antoninus. To make injury to the fabric the basis of the interpretation, is to go entirely beyond the record. A dye capable of giving a good or bad color is one thing; a dyeing material which benefits or injures, apart from the color, the object dyed, is quite another matter.

" To infect" is a translation to which Dr. Carson has no right so long as he says that βάπτω has but two meanings, *to dip, to dye;* " to infect" is neither the one nor the other. As conjoined with *Cæsarism,* and regarded as receiving the contagion embodied in that word, it may be so translated. We not only have no objection to the principle, that a leading word may embody the sentiment of a phrase, and be treated as its representative; but we do most cordially accept of it, and shall insist upon it in cases where Dr. Carson may give but reluctant consent. Infection is a consequence of being imbued with Cæsarism. There is no dyeing, but a transference of moral qualities. The idea of color is lost.

The qualities of honor or dishonor, of truth or falsehood, of justice or injustice, of integrity or treachery, are as distinguishable as the colors of the rainbow; but they are not colors; and when βάπτω is used to express the communication of such qualities, language will no more consent to be chained to the dye-tub than will Samson yield his strength under the fettering influence of the "seven green wythes." *Imbue* expresses this modification of thought, and is equally applicable to any quality, good or bad.

" Adopt the character of one imbued."

The interpretation of this passage has caused no little

embarrassment, and given rise to various translations and expositions.

Professor Stuart quotes and comments thus: "Why dost thou call thyself a Stoic? Why dost thou deceive the multitude? Why dost thou, being a Jew, play the hypocrite with the Greek? Dost thou not see how any one is called a Jew, how a Syrian, how an Egyptian? And when we see any one acting with both parties, we are wont to say: He is no Jew, but plays the hypocrite. But when he takes on him the state and feelings of one who is washed or baptized, and has attached himself to the sect, then he is in truth and is called a Jew. But we are παραβαπτίσται, transgressors as to our baptism, or falsely baptized, if we are like a Jew in pretence and something else in reality."

"A great variety of opinions have been given on this passage. Some think that Arrian, here, refers to Christians; but I see no good ground for such a supposition. De Wette says: 'The passage is too obscure to gather anything certain from it.'

"I can scarcely doubt that the writer refers to the Jewish ablutions. Paulus has endeavored to explain away the force of the whole passage. Bauer suggests that βεβαμμενου may refer to a Christian whom Arrian confounds with a Jew. On the whole I conclude this to be a difficult and obscure passage, in some respects."

Dr. Halley (p. 346) thinks that reference is made to Christian baptism, and that Arrian, a heathen, has failed to discriminate between βάπτω and βαπτίζω, as does the New Testament.

Gale presents this view: "After baptism, and the public profession, they were accounted, and really were, true Jews or rather Christians."

There is no evidence that Arrian confounded either the distinction between βάπτω and βαπτίζω, or that between Jews and Christians. The supposition is violent and without any real necessity, so far as this passage is concerned.

Attention has been directed, so far as I am aware, exclusively to the primary meaning of βάπτω, or to a meaning (connecting it with baptism) of which it is not possessed. The clue to the interpretation lies, I think, in the secondary meaning and its modification.

I would translate: "When one takes up the character (state or condition) of one *imbued* and convinced, then, he is in reality and in name a Jew."

When the passage is considered alongside of those already examined, can there be a reasonable doubt that this is the true interpretation? Usage sanctions the translation, and the passage is made luminous by its application.

The notion of Jewish ablutions or of Christian baptism is quite inadmissible—1, because of lack of evidence; and, 2, because they render no service when introduced. Ritual ablutions have no power to discriminate between real and assumed character; they have no power to unmask a hypocrite or to stamp honesty on profession; and this is the point made by Arrian. The "character of an imbued man" is a positive and known quantity; the character of a Jewishly washed, or Christianly baptized man, is a variable and unknown quantity.

The interpretation is farther established by a reference to the language of Plato, Iamblichus, Theo. Smyrnæus, and others, who speak of the effect of a thorough training and instruction as a $\beta\acute{a}\varphi\eta$, a dye. Not hereby expressing a dipping (Gale), nor a coloring (Carson), but a distinguishing and abiding quality of the mind.

The legitimacy of the use of $\beta\acute{a}\pi\tau\omega$ and $\beta\acute{a}\varphi\eta$ to denote the communication of some quality devoid of color needs no vindication as an abstract proposition; the evidence for the usage as a matter of fact, is before us.

"That they may receive the laws in the best manner, as a dye."

Plato, having described the great pains taken by dyers in order to secure a dye which would be unchangeable and ineradicable, applies this to the pains taken in training soldiers, which he says is in order to their receiving the laws or ordinances like a dye—which cannot be washed out by pleasure, grief, fear, &c.

By this comparison, made between a military training and dyeing, Plato does not represent the soldier as either dipped or colored; but indicates the thorough preparation which is practised in both cases, and the similarity of results, so far as inducing a permanent quality was concerned, namely, permanent color in the one case, and permanent, soldierly character in the other.

To the same effect is the language of Iamblichus and Theo. Smyrnæus, when speaking of the effects of a well-conducted course of instruction. "As dyers cleansing beforehand." "Afterwards they receive instruction as a dye." Pupils in the school and soldiers in the gymnasium receive their training like a dye, being imbued with abiding qualities.

How much wisdom would there be, on the basis of this allusion to a dye, to convert the school of Pythagoras and the gymnasium into places filled with dye-vats, where philosophers and drill sergeants should be busily engaged in dipping pupils and soldiers into their appropriate dye?

Extravagance like to this we shall often find in the interpretations of Baptist writers, rather than abandon the notion of a cast-iron inflexibility which they have attributed to a Greek word.

ΒΑΠΤΑΙ.

This is the title of a play written by Eupolis, much the greater part of which has been lost.

The word also occurs in *Juvenal* ii, 92.

> Talia secretâ coluerunt Orgia tædâ
> Cecropiam soliti *Baptœ* lassare Cotytto.
> Ille supercilium madida fuligine tinctum.

The annotator on this passage says:

Baptœ. 'Απο το' βάπτειν, *lavare* dicti: quia aquâ calidâ

tingebantur illis Sacris Cotyttus initiati. *Polit. Miscell.*
cap. 10. Porro, Baptæ, titulus Comœdiæ Eupolidis Poetæ,
in qua viros Athenis ad imitationem fœminarum saltantes
inducit, et psaltriam lassantes. *Vet. Schol.* Cùm autem
Baptarum lasciviam Eupolis proscripssisset, ab illis in mare
præcipitatus et submersus fuisse dicitur.

Feeling a special interest in this word as appropriated
to designate a particular class of persons, and finding the
materials out of which to form a conclusive judgment as
to its precise usage quite limited; I ventured to ask information from others who might be supposed to know all
that was knowable in the case, and whose scholarship gave
them a right to speak so as to challenge the respectful attention of all. The information sought was grounded
solely on the interest of those addressed in the solution
of a purely classical question, and neither of the respond-
ents had the remotest idea of the special inquiry in which
I was engaged. While I do not feel that I have any right,
at all, to mention the names of the writers, yet I am sure
that they would not object to the use of their statements
as showing the position of a, confessedly, obscure question,
namely: What is the precise import which should be attached to the δι βάπται of Eupolis?

The following is one of the replies kindly returned to
inquiries bearing on this question:

" There is no doubt that the note on Juvenal ii, 92, refers
to the same persons whom Eupolis calls Baptæ. An old
scholiast on that passage of Juvenal gives us valuable
information concerning the play. 'Baptæ ergo molles,
quo titulo Eupolis comœdiam scripsit ob quam ab Alci-
biade, quem imprimis perstrinxerat necatus est.'

" The latter part of this scholium appears in another
shape, as edited by George Valla, in the 15th century,
thus: 'Ob quam Alcibiades—necuit ipsum in mare præ-
cipitando, dicans, "ut tu me in theatris madefecisti, nunc
ego te in mare madefaciam." '

" A scholiast on the rhetorician or sophist Aristides (ed.

Dindorf 3. 444), gives the following lines from some one, which must refer to the same event:

Βάπτες μ' ἐν θυμέλησιν, ἐγὼ δέ σε κύμασι πόντου
Βαπτίζων ὀλέσω νάμασι πικροτέροις.

"Where βάπτω, βαπτίζω, answer to the madefacio of the scholiast on Juvenal. And this makes it altogether likely that βάπται meant *dippers* or *washers* rather than *dyers*. But the thing is uncertain, opinions differ, and I cannot give you absolute light as to the original sense of Baptæ.

"1. Probably Eupolis had it for his object to satirize the secret orgies of Alcibiades and his vicious companions, by directly introducing on the stage the orgies of the Baptæ, priests of Cotytto, who was then worshipped at Corinth, with which state Athens was then at war, and was not yet worshipped at Athens.

"2. Βάπτης can mean *tinctor*, *dyer*, as well as *dipper* or *washer*. Some learned men have supposed, that, as washings or lustrations were common to all rites, it is not likely that a distinctive name would be derived from this custom in this case. But they fail of explaining the other signification from dyeing, and have nothing but hypothesis to build on.

"3. I have called the Baptæ priests of Cotytto; probably it would be safer to call them worshippers, 'sacricolæ.' "

Another, and wholly independent response, is as follows:

"1. I remark that the *Baptæ* of Eupolis is not extant; that a few lines, only, have been preserved, and that the fragments of Eupolis are to be found in Meineke's Fragments of the Greek Comedians.

"2. The βάπται were effeminates who in many respects imitated women. They were accustomed to paint, or stain their faces and eyelids. It is sufficiently well known that the play of Eupolis, called Ὁι Βάπται, was written to expose and censure the licentiousness of such characters.

"3. The verb βάπτω is used freely in the sense of to dye, to stain, or to paint—so the Latin *tingo*. The application of the derivative noun in the play of Eupolis is to the effeminate practice above mentioned.

"4. Considering the character of Cotytto, there can be little doubt that such is also the meaning of the word as applied to her priests—her priests were βάπται.

"5. The annotator on Juvenal is correct when he gives βάπτω as equivalent in this respect to *tingo*. And *tingo* is quite correctly used in respect to both bathing and staining with color, and, like βάπτω, sometimes to paint."

"In the note the Latin is modern, but the use of the word is classical. But the first part of the note concerns a different thing from the latter part, and they are not to be confounded. For the former of the two statements the authority quoted is Politian, an eminent scholar of the fifteenth century. In this note the two things mentioned are brought together, most likely, from the fact that Juvenal satirically presents the Baptæ as worshippers of Cotytto, with poetic if not with historical truth."

Professor Ewing (*Essay on Baptism*, Glasgow) makes the following remark:

"The fellows called βάπται in Juvenal ii, 92, were not so called because they had been immersed in a dyer's vat (although they would have been well served had they been so treated), but because they were *painted*, from βάπτω to paint, that is to lay on colors."

Robinson, *Greek Arch.*, p. 317. "Κοτυτης, Cotytto, her priests were called βάπται, from βάπτειν, to paint."

It will be perceived that these eminent scholars, on the question, "To which branch of βάπτω, *to dip* or *to dye*, should βάπται be traced?" are inclined to take different views; the one leaning to dip, the other to dye; yet neither of them disposed to insist upon the modal act of dipping, or the technical process of dyeing.

It is certain that the word might be traced to that side of βάπτω which exhibits the use of an uncolored fluid, and in its use exhibit only a lustral washing, which might be administered as properly by *sprinkling* "warm water" as by *dipping* into cold water; or it might be traced to that side where we find a colored fluid, while the facts showed, 1, a bapting, a dyeing without any dipping, the modal act having passed into pressing, bruising, sprinkling, and thus entirely disappearing; or, 2, a bapting, a dyeing, *without any color*, but simply the communication of a quality or trait of character.

If the statement of "dyeing without coloring" seems, on its face, to be paradoxical, yet, it is no more so than the earlier change—"dipping by sprinkling." And, on consideration, it will be adjudged to be as philosophical as it is paradoxical.

To dye is to communicate a quality, the specific quality of *color;* but there are qualities, devoid of color, which are communicable, and which from their nature are associated with color, spots, stains, the communication of which qualities, by the most facile extension of the word, might be represented by *dye*. Dr. Gale says, "Stains on linen, or anything white, take from its beauty and clearness; so ill reports, &c., lessen and impair the purity of a man's reputation, and are to it what stains are to clean linen." Again, there are qualities without color, such as Justice, Integrity, Honesty, which by their pureness are not conceived of by any color, but by the absence of all color, absolute whiteness, which yet may, under the demands of language necessitating the extension of the meaning of words, be spoken of by the term *dye;* quality is communicated, but not of *color*. And the facts of usage, which have been already considered, show that βάπτω was applied to the imaginary staining of Cæsarism and to the unspotted pureness of an absolute integrity. Under this usage the Baptæ of Cotytto would be her priests who imbue with Cotyttoism, or her disciples imbued by Cotyttoism.

The result of a general consideration of the elements entering into a determination of the meaning of the word βάπται, would present several words as worthy of thoughtful consideration, among which appear—the dipped, the washed, the dyed, the imbued.

THE DIPPED.—Dr. Conant adopts this translation, yet not without intimating that he was not entirely satisfied with it.

I am not aware of any special reason which can be offered in its support. If these persons dipped their bodies into water, or were dipped by one another, were they the only persons who did so? Is there any reasonable foundation for grounding a distinguishing title, separating them from all others, on such practice? But, again, if the practice of *dipping* the person, more or less, into water gave origin among the Greeks to the title βάπται, who shall, against the Greeks, set up the title βαπτισται as designating a similar class of people? Unquestionably, the proper word to use in such case is that of *Bapters*, and not Baptists; and thus, again, we are brought, face to face, with the error of our Baptist friends in attempting to convert a *bapting* into a baptizing, a *dipping* into an immersion.

If Dr. Conant is right in translating βάπται *dippers*, then Baptists are wrong in their name as denoting their mode of performing the Christian rite, and in attempting to substitute a *bapting* (Egyptian or Cecropian in form) for our most holy *baptism*.

THE WASHED.—The opinion that a *washing*, in some form, is designated by this word seems to have met with considerable favor.

The annotator on Juvenal says that it is from βάπτειν, *to wash*, and that those who were initiated into these mysteries were washed (*tingebantur*) with warm water. Valla expresses the idea using *madefacio, to make wet*.

The Scholiast, who quotes Alcibiades, may be adduced as favoring a dipping, or wetting, or washing, according to our views derived from other quarters. It is obvious, however, that the opposition between βάπτες and βαπτίζων makes the latter the stronger word. The difference is such as between dipping and mersing, *drowning*.

It does not follow, however, that the verb in the epigram is used in the same sense as the derivative noun in the comedy; it may be a congruity purely verbal and not of sense which is designed.

The meaning, "washings, lustrations," has been objected to on the ground that these were common things, and could not be supposed to give rise to a distinctive name for any class of persons.

The force of this objection is tacitly admitted by the author of the first communication; but his reply is—no adequate, positive vindication of any meaning based on dyeing has been presented. If this should be done, the force of the objection will have full operation.

THE DYED.—This meaning, while having no less claim than those preceding, on general grounds, can present a stronger special plea than either. The evidence that these persons did *dye* is more complete than that they did either *dip* or *wash*. Dyeing was a well-known characteristic of this class of persons, and Juvenal expressly states this as one of their practices. There is no difficulty, therefore, either from the word used, or from the facts of the case, in this particular, in employing "the dyed" as the translation of δι βάπται. But there are two difficulties, notwithstanding, which confront us. 1. All "dyed" persons did not belong to the class spoken of, and therefore this meaning lies under the same disability as these preceding. Dyeing was a very common practice, as well as "dipping," and "washing," and, therefore, could not be employed to denote a limited class among those to whom the characteristic was common. 2. While dyeing is spoken of as one feature marking these people, it is only spoken of as one among many others, and those others immensely more important as elements of character.

It is impossible, therefore, that "the dyed ones" could exhaust the import of δι βάπται; and whatever fitness it might have in its bearing upon a single particular, and that of the least possible importance, it cannot meet the case except as regarded as a finger-board pointing on toward that which it is unable of itself, directly, to express. But in that case it cannot retain its original limitation of meaning, but must attract to itself, by its association, a newness and a fulness of meaning not before possessed. In other words, the suggestion of color is lost, merged in other, more momentous, elements of character.

THE IMBUED.—The vital element to be regarded in the interpretation of this word is found in the fact that it designates a limited class of profoundly marked character. Neither "the dipped," nor "the washed," nor "the dyed," in their own proper meaning meets such a case. Undoubtedly either of these expressions might be modified and extended by appropriation; but in the case before us the one most likely to be selected for such service is the last.

It is quite possible that these Baptæ introduced some peculiarity in the process or extent of the dyeing. Juvenal may refer to this where, after describing the dyed *eyebrow*, he adds, "*pingitque trementes attolleus oculos.*" The painting of the eyelids, or the eyelashes, may have been introduced by these persons, and thus made their class emphatically "the dyed or painted ones." But if such were the origin, and primary force of this term, it certainly did not continue to have such narrowness of import. Juvenal, certainly, did not so use the term. Eupolis, almost as certainly, did not. Now, embody the idea in what one term we may, the fact is certain that "the Baptæ" were those, priests or disciples, or both, who were *imbued with the spirit* of Cotytto, "the Goddess of Immodesty."

Whatever Baptæ may have originally expressed, or whatever may have been the immediate exciting cause to give this word such direction, it was appropriated to designate a class of persons singularly debased and debauched; effeminate, voluptuous, and licentious—priests and people of a dancing courtesan, deified.

In view of a fact like this, it becomes a matter of very secondary interest to know from which stem of βάπτω this derivative proceeds, for in either case, as *dipped* or *dyed*, it must accept the meaning which results from appropriation. Whatever may have been the original meaning of the term "Methodist," or whatever may have been the original ground of its application, such original meaning and ground of application very speedily disappeared from the appropriated title, "the Methodists." The same is true of the term *Quaker* as applied to "the Quakers." Can there be any doubt that "δι βάπται" is to be explained in the same way, and that the Baptæ designated neither "the dipped" into water, nor "the dyed" with blackened brows, but those who were dipped deeply into, dyed in, imbued with, *Cotytto-ism?*

In a word, this derivative expresses not quality of color, but has passed on to express *quality of character.*

This investigation as to the meaning of βάπτω appears to justify the following conclusions:

1. The severe limitation of this word to the two meanings *to dip, to dye,* is no better grounded than the limitation to a single meaning, to dip.

2. The natural and prevailing syntax used with βάπτω *to dip* is to place the element, into which the dipping takes place, in the accusative with ἐις; while βάπτω *to dye,* as naturally and prevailingly, requires the element, by which the coloring influence is to be exerted, to be put in the dative, usually, without a preposition.

3. *Βάπτω,* after having exercised its powers in communicating the quality of color through dyeing, staining, painting, passes on a step farther, and expresses the communication of qualities which are devoid of color.

And in this extreme development βάπτω makes its nearest approach to assimilation with βαπτίζω.

TINGO.

ITS MEANING AND USAGE.

The meaning of *tingo* is so well understood and so universally accepted, that the passages about to be adduced are not cited, so much, to show what is the meaning of that word as to reflect light upon the more controverted Greek word.

If in any language we meet with a word whose usage in a particular sense is questioned; and we find the corresponding word in another language clearly used in such sense; the usage, before doubtful, becomes greatly confirmed, if not established. The usage of βάπτω and *tingo* is as nearly identical, under every phase, as the usage of two words, in different languages, could well be. They mutually illuminate each other. A few passages will abundantly illustrate this statement.

PRIMARY.

TO DIP.

Spongia in aceto tincta.   .   .   .   .   .   . *Celsus.*
    Sponges dipped in vinegar.

Tingunt faces in amne.   .   .   .   .   .   . *Ovid.*
    They dip the torches in the river.

Primumque pedis vestigia tinxi.   .   .   . *Ovid.*
    And first I dip the soles of my feet.

Protinus eductam navalibus æquore tingi, .   .   . *Ovid.*
Aptarique suis pinum jubet armamentis.
    And orders the vessel to be dipped in the sea.

Arctos metuentes æquore tingi.   .   .   .   .   . *Virgil.*
    The Bears fearing to be dipped in the sea.

Nec tingueret celeres plantas æquore.   .   .   . *Vi˙gil.*
    Nor would she dip her swift feet in the sea.

These passages are too clearly self-interpretative to need any comment.

"The Pine," or vessel, of which Ovid speaks as being "dipped in the sea" when launched, and which, then, rises again to its natural position on the water, shows that an object may be dipped, without being covered, when no part is specified. It illustrates, also, the limitation of the use of *tingo*, as applied to ships, compared with *mergo*. *Tingo* applies to the momentary descent of a vessel into the water, beyond what is usual, in the launching, but is never used to express a permanent, indefinite, or sunken condition of a vessel. The same distinction obtaining as to the usage of these words, in this respect, as in the case of βάπτω and βαπτίζω.

The act expressed by *tingo* is one which, evidently, carries its object only temporarily and superficially within a fluid. The dipping, by launching, spoken of by Ovid, is illustrated by the following quotation: "On Saturday morning the Dunderberg was launched. The launch was in all respects successful. The vessel went into the water beautifully. She *dipped some water, but immediately rose to her place* and sailed handsomely to the middle of the channel." Could you say she *immersed* some water?

TO WET.

Tingere pascua rore. . . . . . . *Calpurnius.*
  To wet the pastures with dew.

Et mero tinguet pavimentum. . . . . *Horace.*
  And wet the pavement with wine.

Neque enim celestia tingi ora decet lachrymis. . *Ovid.*
  Nor is it becoming that celestial faces be wet with tears.

Necdum fluctus latera ardua tinxit. . . . *Virgil.*
  Nor yet has the wave wet his lofty sides.

In these, and like passages, *to dip* and *to dye* are impossible meanings. We are shut up to the translation *to wet*.

The instrumental case, without a preposition, is used as is the dative with βάπτω in its secondary meaning.

TO WASH.

Nuda superfusis tingamus corpora lymphis. .   . *Ovid.*
> *Let us wash our naked bodies with water poured over them.*

Lydia Pactoli tinguit arata liquor.   .   .   . *Propertius.*
> *The river Pactolus washes the Lydian fields.*

Quia aquâ calidâ tingebantur.   .   .   . *Juvenal* (note).
> *Because they were washed with warm water.*

TO MOISTEN, TO ANOINT.

Tingere membra Pallade pingui. .   .   .   . *Ovid.*
> *To moisten the limbs with rich oil.*

Sæpe oculos memini tingebam parvus olivo. .   . *Perseus.*
> *I often moistened my eyes with oil.*

In such passages, the nature of the case and grammatical construction unite to declare that the element is used as an agency; and to exclude the meanings, both, of dip and dye. Yet, in the first passage, if we had not, by express statement, the word by which the water was applied to the body, we should be doomed to hear the exhaustless argument—"*tingo*, βάπτω, βαπτίζω, mean to dip; naked bodies are suitable objects for dipping; water is the very element for the purpose; and there is a plenty of it—THEREFORE, *this was a case of dipping.*" The passage from Ovid is utterly destructive to such reasoning. The dipping was by pouring! Where the word expressive of the act is not stated it cannot be found in *tingo*, or, in such cases, in any other corresponding word.

Whether Gale would say of this passage—"dipped *as it were* by pouring over;" or Carson—"it means in this passage to dip just as much as any other, one mode of action being put, by *catachresis*, for another mode of action;" or Fuller—it means dip, being an "extravagant and impassioned" utterance for "*drench*,"—I do not know; but I do know, that in like cases a sound discretion is, as absolutely, abandoned.

SECONDARY.

TO DYE.

Vestes Gætulo murice tinctas. . . . . . *Horace.*
> *Garments dyed with Gœtulian purple.*

Supercilium madida fuligine tinctum. . . . *Juvenal.*
> *The eyebrow dyed with moist soot.*

Phocaico bibulas tingebat murice lanas. . . . *Ovid.*
> *Dyed the absorbing wool with Phocean purple.*

Tanta est decoris affectatio ut tingantur oculi quoque. *Pliny.*
> *Such is the longing for beauty, that the eyes, also, are dyed.*

Tinguntur sole populi. . . . . . . *Pliny.*
> *The people are dyed by the sun.*

The remark of Pliny, that the dyeing "the eyes" was something unusual, and regarded as a mark of extravagance, in connection with the statement of Juvenal that the Baptæ not merely dyed their brows but "painted their eyes," shows that there is some foundation for supposing that their name originated, not in their practice of dyeing and painting as commonly practised; but in some peculiarity or extravagance; and, then, embraced a class distinguished for all extravagance and immoral excesses.

The allusion to the "dyeing" of the body by the rays of the sun, is parallel with that by Achilles Tatius in speaking of the East Indians: "*Καὶ τηρεῖ τὸ σῶμα τοῦ πυρὸς τὴν βαφήν—the body takes the color of fire.*"

The phraseology attaches no limit to the mode of dyeing. In no case is the object dyed represented as put into the dyeing material. To dip the people *in the sun* would be an embarrassing undertaking. The sun's rays dye by falling on the body. *Tingo* does not mean *to fall.* Such word must be understood. So in every case where a condition or result is expressed, such expression exhausts the word making it; and it cannot, also, express the act by which the condition or result is effected. This is true of tingo, *to dye,* βάπτω, *to dye,* and of βαπτίζω through all its usage.

TO PAINT.

Tingit cutem Marinus, et tamen pallet. .   .   . *Martial.*
    Marinus paints his skin, and yet is pale.

TO STAIN.

Victima, pontificum securim, cervice tinguit. .   . *Horace.*
    The victim stains the axe of the priests with its neck.
Et virides aspergine tinxerat herbas.   .   .   . *Ovid.*
    And stained the green grass by the sprinkling of the blood.
Musto tingue novo mecum dereptis crura.   .   . *Virgil.*
    Stain with me the bared legs by the new wine.

None of these cases can, properly, be considered as
cases of dyeing. They are, also, far removed from the
form of dipping. The blow of an axe, the dropping of
blood from a wound, the trampling of grapes, which,
severally, meets the demands of *tingo*, show that this
word, like βάπτω, has ceased to make demand for modal
action. Even "sprinkling" can meet the requirements
of this modified dipping.

Conant translates "ἐπεθύμει τὴν δεξιάν τῷ λαιμῷ βαπτίσαι τῷ
πατρικῷ—he desired to *plunge* his right hand *in* his father's
neck." *Horace* suggests, "baptize, merse, cover with blood
by his father's neck," since he says, "the victim stains the
axe *with* its neck," not *in* it.

TO TEMPER.

Et Stygiâ candentem tinxerat undâ. .   .   .   . *Virgil.*
    And tempered it glowing hot with Stygian water.

The act by which the sword was subjected to the peculiar influence of "the Stygian water" may have been that
of dipping, and yet "tinxerat" not used for the purpose
of expressing such act. When *tingo* is used to denote
dyeing, although that result should be accomplished by
the process of dipping, the word which expresses the

result cannot at the same time express the process. Tingo cannot express both *to dye* and *to dip*. When tingo expresses the tempering of metal, it cannot, also, express the dipping (if that be the process), any more than it can express sprinkling, if that be the process.

TO IMBUE OR TO TINCTURE.

It has been already remarked, in speaking of this class of meanings in connection with βάπτω, that *imbue* was felt to be too strong a word to use in this case; but that, no better presenting, it was adopted. Perhaps *tincture* would be preferable. These words are used interchangeably; yet the latter has less breadth of application, and less power in its import, while it may express the communication of quality irrespective of color, with which it stands, verbally, related.

In making use of tincture, in this relation, it is regarded as thoroughly divorced from all coloring element.

Non ego te meis immunem meditor tinguere poculis. *Horace.*
　　I do not purpose to tincture you with my bowls.

Orator sit tinctus literis. . . . . *Cicero.*
　　An orator should be tinctured with letters.

Romano sale tinge libellos. . . . . . *Martial.*
　　Tincture the writings with Roman salt.

Vis aurea tinxit flumen. . . . . . . *Ovid.*
　　The golden potency tinctured the river.

Et incerto fontem medicamine tinxit. . . . *Ovid.*
　　And tinctured the fountain with the ambiguous virtue.

Cum dira libido . . . . ferventi tincta veneno. . *Perseus.*
　　Fierce passion tinctured with fiery poison.

Ignibus et sparsâ tingere corpus aquâ. . . *Ovid, Fasti.*
　　To tincture the body with fires and sprinkled water.

Hæc, quibus, tingendus est animus. . . . *Seneca.*
　　Those things with which the mind must be tinctured.

Hoc fimo tinctum in scrobem demisit. . . . *Seneca.*
　　This tinctured with manure he put down into the trench.

This usage exhibits tingo (in common with βάπτω, having already laid aside modality of act, *dyeing* by sprinkling, &c.) as laying aside, now, *dyeing*, and imparting any quality whatever. 1. The intoxicating quality of wine, *to a limited extent.* 2. The quality of transmuting into gold, imparted to a river. 3. The quality of transforming the human person, communicated to a fountain. 4. The quality of pureness given to the human body by " fire and sprinkled water."

I am aware that *tangere* has been proposed as a substitute for " tingere;" but would retain tingere—1. As, apparently, the more difficult reading. If we attempt to translate this passage from the Fasti (iv, 790) by a mere reference to *dip* and *dye*, we are at once involved in inextricable embarrassment, and look around for succor. This is found, as supposed, in *tangere;* but before a reading, which involves some difficulty, is rejected, would it not be well to inquire, whether we may not have overlooked some usage of the word which will fully vindicate its retention in the passage?

2. As the much superior reading when fairly interpreted.

There is nothing of elegance or fitness in " tangere" to meet the demands of the passage. The most that can be said in its favor is, that it relieves, measurably and awkwardly, of a difficulty from which no better way of escape was seen. But the difficulty is of our own creation. "Fire and sprinkled water" do, unquestionably, according to ancient rites, purify the body. Let Ovid say this; let tingo express this; and what use have we for " tangere?"

3. Such use of tingo is in proof. And this very passage gives evidence, not least in force and beauty, in its support. The purifying quality which belongs to sacrificial fires, and to water ritually sprinkled, is exerted over the body which is brought within their influences; and they tincture it with their characteristic quality, expelling impurity and imparting pureness.

4. Those purified by "*sprinkled* water" would be, properly, designated as—*Tincti.*

Two other passages may be sufficient to exemplify the meaning under consideration.

Non illa, quibus perfundi satis est, sed hæc tingendus est animus. *Seneca.*

Not those studies with which it is sufficient to be sprinkled, but those with which the mind should be tinctured.

This passage is parallel with those from Antoninus; and, like them, exhibits quality without color communicated to the mind. We have, also, in this passage, incidental proof of this interpretation, in the contrast between *perfundo* and tingo. The former, certainly, has nothing to do with color, and the word with which it is contrasted cannot. No one would contrast sprinkled water and a dyed color; nor can the contrast be between sprinkling and dipping, for they both represent, in themselves, but a very feeble effect; while Seneca means to contrast superficialness with thoroughness. The fitness of tingo to express what is penetrative and abiding, comes from its use in the sense of *dyeing;* and after it has dropped the idea of color. Hence *perfundo* denotes what is superficial; and tingo an incorporated quality.

"Tinctum," in the second passage from Seneca, expresses the reception of the virtue of the manure by the olive tree. This is a case neither of dipping nor dyeing.

Quam qui dona tulit Lernæo tincta veneno
Euboïcasque suo sanguine tinxit aquas. *Ovid, Ibis.*

*He who bore the gifts tinctured with the Lernæan poison,
And tinged the Eubœan waters with his blood.*

This passage reminds us, forcibly, of the epigram on Eupolis:

βαπτες μ' εν θυμελησιν . .
βαπτιζων, ολεσω ναμασι . .

There is in both, the suffering of individuals—Hercules and Alcibiades; and in both, the death by drowning, of the authors of that suffering—Lichas and Eupolis; and in both, a play upon words expressive of the suffering and the punishment—Ovid employing the same word with different meanings, and Alcibiades employing similar words of different meanings.

"Dona tincta" were gifts neither dipped nor dyed in Lernæan poison, but tinctured with it; the poisonous quality belonging to the Hydra had been imparted to the garment; and it is this quality only which is brought into view. "Tinxit aquas" just as clearly means to dye, to impart color, although, as a matter of fact, there was no such thing; the opportunity to introduce the same word to express death, in a rhetorical manner, is seized upon.

So, Alcibiades employs βάπτω and βαπτίζω, allied in origin and sound, to express widely different meanings, and designing by their likeness in letter, to give emphasis to their unlikeness in meaning. Eupolis would *dye* him in plays; he would make Eupolis *die* in the sea.

It would be difficult to find two words, in different languages, which, starting out with sameness of meaning, continue *pari passu*, through all their development to exhibit such thorough sameness, in all their changing phases, as do βάπτω and tingo.

As they reciprocally illustrate each other, there is nothing wanting to the most satisfactory determination of the meaning of both.

TO DIP.

ITS MEANING AND USAGE.

To dip, in English, has a usage in marked correspondence with that of βάπτω, in Greek, and of tingo, in Latin. There is not, indeed, a perfect accord in every shade of meaning; there are some features of the Greek or Latin word which are not found in the English; and so, also, there are features in the English word which do not appear in the Greek or Latin; still, with these peculiarities of development, the radical elements are the same. A few quotations will place this statement beyond all question.

PRIMARY.

TO DIP.

' The landscape gives the summit of a ridge of land that suddenly *dips from sight*, in the mid distance, and *rises again* in the form of a dim line of high ground drawn along the horizon."

Rosa Bonheur.

" The minister dipping the scoop into the water."

Chalmers.

" The Lady Mayoress dipped the corner of the towel into it."

Id.

" Children should never be dipped more than once."

Sir A. Clarke

" The dip of oars in unison awake,
Without alarming silence."

Glover.

" So was he dight
That no man might
Hym for a frere deny,
He *dopped* and dooked,
He spake and looked
So religiously."

Sir T. More.

"And dipt them in the sable well,
The fount of Fame or Infamy.
What well? what weapon? (Flavia cries.)
A standish, steel, and golden pen!"

Pope.

"Dipping her fingers in a little silver vase of rose-water."

Sir W. Scott.

"The cloth thou dip'dst in blood of my sweet boy,
And I, with tears, do wash the blood away."

Shakspeare.

"The fleet dipped their colors to the Queen's yacht."

Fête at Cherbourg.

"Now wheeling and dipping toward it, as a butterfly."

Japan Legerdemain.

1. In the first of these examples showing the primary, literal use of dip, we have the modal elements which enter into this word distinctly stated: "Suddenly dips from sight and rises again." The "rising again" is essential to a dipping in its primary use; in this it is radically distinguished from plunge, dive, immerse, whelm, &c.

2. The objects which are dipped claim attention. These are "a scoop," "the corner of a towel," "children," "oars," "head and shoulders," "pen," "fingers," "cloth," "flag," "bits of paper." None of these are selected cases. The smallness of the objects is not matter of accident. It is a necessity resulting from the nature of the act. Every object which is dipped must be brought out again from the element into which it has been introduced. This requires that the introducing power should have full mastery over its object; but, in all ordinary cases, it is human agency by which the act is performed, and the power employed that of the hand or arm; consequently, the objects capable of being thus dipped are limited, and must be of trivial size and weight, as indicated by the examples adduced. Thus the nature of the objects gives testimony to the nature of the act.

3. Some modifications of usage require notice. Ordinarily a fluid element is present in a dipping; and, also, usually, the whole of an object is dipped when there is no limitation expressed; but Sir Thomas More says that the friar "dopped and dooked"—(dipped and ducked—"*dopped* being from *dippan*, the characteristic *i* being changed to *o*"); he did not dip into any fluid element, but merely performed the modal acts of depressing and elevating, not his whole body, but his head and shoulders; still the act is legitimately attributed to the whole man, and although our Baptist friends put, ritually, but the head and shoulders under water, it may lawfully, and of right can, be called only a dipping.

The case from Pope, also, shows that the "steel and gold pen" may be said to be dipped in the standish, although an unexpressed part, only, is so dipped. The last two cases, also, exemplify a dipping in which the modal act of lowering and raising a flag, or bits of paper by fanning, is performed without carrying the object into a fluid element.

TO WET.

"She fables not; I feel that I do fear
    Her words set off by some superior power;
    And though not mortal, yet a cold shudd'ring dew
    Dips me all o'er, as when the wrath of Jove
    Speaks thunder."   *Comus.*

"She alway smyled, and in her hand did hold
    An holy-water sprinckle, dipt in dowe."   *Faere Queene.*

Comus could not be dipped in dew under any circumstances, much less in drops, formed by fright, on his own body; we are, therefore, under necessity to understand "dip," here, as expressing not modal action but the effect, *wetting*, which is the usual consequence of dipping. This is, also, a fair and legitimate explanation of the second case, although the necessity is not, in all respects, so absolute. To lean heavily on "in" to oppose this interpretation, would be to lean on a reed, which might break and pierce the hand confiding in it. We speak of an object being "left out *in* the dew," although impossible that it should be, literally, *in* the dew. Gideon's fleece was thus "in the dew," and so was Nebuchadnezzar; and the condition of wetness consequent on such exposure, may be designated by *dip* or tingo, or, as in the case of Babylon's king, by βάπτω.

TO BATHE.

"He walked to the river to take his customary dip."
Judge Brackenridge.

"The dip was over, and dripping with brine, they hastened back."
Cape May Letter.

"In whose waters Cardinal Wiseman was dipped."
Letter from Wales.

Since, in bathing, the act of dipping the body more or less, is of common and frequent occurrence; that word has come to be familiarly employed to designate the whole transaction; and is equally applicable to the bathing, whether any, technical, act of dipping take place or not.

TO EXAMINE SLIGHTLY.

"Only to dip into a Hebrew or Greek Lexicon."
Booth, i, 115.

"I have just dipped into the works of such an author."
Id., i, 123.

"We have occasionally dipped into the novels."
Editorial.

"He resolved to dip into it, but took no serious notice of what he read."
Col. Gardiner.

"We first dipped into the pages of Whiston's Josephus."
Rev. Dr. Leyburn.

"Dip into the work where you like."
Review.

"I have dipped into Aristotle and several other masters of the science."
Rev. Dr. Thornwell.

Such usage is clearly based on the superficial entrance, and transitory continuance, of an object within a fluid element. The effect upon an object, under such limitations, must be trivial. To dip into a book is to make a superficial and transient examination of its contents. Therefore, Dr. Thornwell commits no offence against modesty when he claims to have "dipped into Aristotle;" but modesty would never have allowed him to say of himself, "I have been *immersed* in Aristotle and other masters of logic." So vastly diverse is the import of the one word and the other.

There are some who seem disposed to insist that these "Lexicons" and "Novels," as, also, "Aristotle and his Logical Compeers," should represent *pools of water*, because associated with "*dip into.*" Can such a demand escape the supremest ridicule? Grant that "dip into" is phraseology fashioned at the water-pool. What then? Does it follow, that when such phraseology is taken away from the pool and articulated with books and philosophers, that it has a charm whereby they are incontinently metamorphosed into water-ponds? But, even let the experiment be tried. Let lexicon, and novel, and Josephus, and Aristotle, be turned into any fluid that may please best. And what next? Why, then, we are to "dip into" them. Very good. And let that be done. What next? Why, then, I suppose we are to come out *a little wet*, which *dampness* is (by the force of a lively imagination) to be converted into a trifling amount of Lexicography, or Fiction, or Jewish History, or Stagiritic Logic, as the case may be!

This may be highly imaginative, yet be seriously deficient in homely common sense; which would teach us to modify the meaning of the foreign phraseology to suit its new relations; taking out of its original use what is demanded by its novel position, and allowing the remainder to tarry, still, by the water. Thus "dip into" is transformed into *examine slightly.*

TO ENGAGE IN, MORE OR LESS DEEPLY.

> " For warrants are already issued out :
> I met Brutidius in a mortal fright :
> He's dipt for certain, and plays least in sight."
> *Dryden.*

" When men are once dipt, they go on until they are stifled."   *L'Estrange.*

> "Full in the midst of Euclid dip at once,
> And petrify a genius to a dunce."   *Pope.*

" Dipping deeply into politics."   *Pursuits of Literature.*

" He was a little dipt in the rebellion of the Commons."
> *Dryden.*

" Who was secretly dipt in some papers of this kind."
> *Dunciad* (note).

" O'wer mony great folks dipped in the same doings."
> *Sir W. Scott.*

Qualifying adjuncts—"full in the midst," "deeply," "little,"—may increase, or diminish, that feebleness which, by nature, belongs to *dip*. The meaning exhibited in these passages is, obviously and essentially, different from the preceding.

TO MORTGAGE.

> " Put out the principal in trusty hands,
> Live on the use ; and never dip thy lands."
> *Dryden.*

"Lord T—— had dipped so deeply into his property."
> *Mrs. Sherwood.*

Money taken out of real estate, by mortgage, is called *dipping the land.*

By dipping with an empty vessel into a fluid we take out a portion of it; so, by a mortgage we take out a portion from our property and fill an empty pocket.

This idea is the ground of usage in the following passages.

TO TAKE OUT.

" She dipped up water in her hands and gave her child."
Wyoming Massacre.

" As they dipped their hand in Uncle Sam's pocket."
Current Literature.

" The ministers allowed the Prince to dip deep into the
national purse." Id.

As the empty hand, hollowed, dipped into the stream,
brought up *water;* so the empty hand dipped into the
nation's purse brings out *gold!*

This meaning the Greeks could readily understand; for
it is involved in τᾷ χαλπιδι χηρία βάψαι—*dip honey with a pitcher,*
Theocritus, Idyl 5, 127; but its specific application—"never
dip thy lands"—would, at first sight, prove embarrassing.

SECONDARY.

TO DYE.

" Fancy, that, from the bow that spans the sky,
  Brings colors, *dipp'd* in heaven, that never die."
Cowper.

" And made the symbols of atoning grace,
  An office key, a picklock to a place,
  That infidels may prove their title good
  By an oath *dipp'd* in sacramental blood." Cowper.

       " The middle pair
  Skirted his loins and thighs with downy gold
  And colors *dipt* in heaven; the third his feet
  Shadowed from either heel with feathered mail
  Sky tinctured grain." Milton.

       " Over his lucid arms
  A military vest of purple flow'd,
  Livelier than Melibæan, or the grain
  Of Sarra, worn by kings and heroes old
  In time of truce; Iris had *dipt* the woof." Milton.

" *Dip't* in the richest tinctures of the skies."
" Or *dip* their pinions in the painted bow." Pope.

> "*Dipt* by cruel fate
> In Stygian dye, how black, how brittle here!"
>
> *Young.*

> "Thy wondrous love,
> That arms with awe more awful thy commands,
> And foul transgression *dips* in seven-fold guilt."
>
> *Young.*

The usage of dip, in the sense *to dye*, is not, by any means, so thoroughly incorporated in the English language, as is that of βάπτω and *tingo*, in the same sense, in their respective languages. The above quotations, however, will show that such usage is distinctly recognized

TO STAIN.

"*Dipt* his hands in the blood of a noble Norman."
>
> *Sir W. Scott.*

"The troops would not dip their hands in the blood of their countrymen."
>
> *Tuscan Revolution.*

> "He writes
> My name in heaven with that inverted spear
> (A spear deep *dipt* in blood!) which pierced his side."
>
> *Young.*

These cases are essentially different from "the oath dipt in *sacramental* blood."

TO IMBUE——TO TINCTURE.

> "I'll make him *dip* my sword and pike for me in holy water."
> "And I have arrows mystically *dipped*."
>
> *Coleridge.*

"Custom *dips* men in as durable a dye as Nature."
>
> *Cur. Lit.*

> "Old Bavius sits, *to dip* poetic souls,
> And blunt the sense, and fit it for a skull
> Of solid proof, impenetrably dull;
> Instant when *dipt*, away they wing their flight."
>
> *Dunciad.*

> "*Dipt* me in ink."   *Pope.*

" For not to have been *dipt* in Lethe lake
Could save the son of Thetis from to die;
But that blind bard did him immortal make
With verses *dipt* in dewe of Castalie." *Spenser.*

" A person *dipped* in scandal." *Warburton.*

"Holy water" has no color to impart to "sword and pike;" but these are "dipt" for the purpose of securing, thereby, some quality or virtue; they must, therefore, be imbued or tinctured with some uncolored quality. The same is true of arrows "mystically dipped." They receive no quality which appeals to the eye, yet which is mysteriously powerful. Sword, and pike, and arrows, when taken out of the "holy water," *still remain dipped, i. e.* imbued, tinctured with the quality imparted; as, having been dipped into a dye, they would remain *baptèd* after removal out of the dye. Colored, or uncolored, the quality communicated equally remains. The dye which "custom dips," is devoid of color; yet her tincture is as abiding as that of Nature herself; for "Custom is second nature."

Poetic souls, dipped by Bavius into Lethe, may be tinctured very deeply with stupidity; but, when most deeply dipt, they fail to show any color of the rainbow.

Spenser alludes to the same transaction which gives basis to Pope's poet-dipping; and compliments the genius of Homer as accomplishing that, by his

"Verses dipt in dewe of Castalie,"

which the power of Lethe's waters had failed to effect. Verses, dipped in Castalian dew, are imbued with the spirit which reigns in that home of the Muses.

"Holy water," "Lethe lake," "dewe of Castalie," are supposed to possess characteristic qualities, which they impart to objects dipped into them in fact, or by imagination, or only of verbal suggestion; just as dye-water parts with its coloring quality under like circumstances.

This is a modified use of dip, and most justifiable extension of its meaning, in which is repeated the usage of βάπτω and *tingo.*

APPROPRIATION.

" Relenting forms would lose their power or cease,
  And e'en *the dipp'd* and sprinkled live in peace."

Cowper.

" The dipped," and not *the immersed*, is the title to be appropriated to those who receive the Christian rite by dipping the upper part of the body into water.

The βάπται and the βαπτίσται are separated by an immense interval.

"THE DIPPERS," *alias* SNUFF RUBBERS.

There is another appropriated use, not so generally understood, and which is thus explained: "It may be that some of your readers are not familiar with the practice of 'dipping.' I will say, therefore, that *a dipper* is one who, having separated the fibres of a hickory stick by chewing it, uses it, when wet with saliva, as the means of conveying snuff from the family box or pouch to the mouth."

Hon. W. D. Kelley.

Whatever the βάπται of Eupolis may have been, they certainly differed from these "dippers;" the nearest point of resemblance, probably, being that the latter dyed their mouths with *snuff*, and the former dyed their eyes with *soot*. In both cases, the origin of the name ceases to control its meaning, and becomes expressive of habit and character.

RESULTS.

Making no claim to having exhausted the great variety of usage which characterizes these words, enough has been exhibited to show:

1. *Βάπτω* signifies—*Primarily.* (1.) To dip, (2.) to moisten, (3.) to wash.

Secondarily. (1.) To dye, (2.) to stain, (3.) to paint, (4.) to gild, (5.) to temper, (6.) to tincture, without coloring.

2. *Tingo* signifies—*Primarily*. (1.) To dip, (2.) to wet, (3.) to moisten, (4.) to wash.

Secondarily. (1.) To dye, (2.) to stain, (3.) to paint, (4.) to temper, (5.) to tincture, without coloring.

3. *Dip* signifies—*Primarily*. (1.) To dip, (2.) to wet, (3.) to bathe, (4.) to examine slightly, (5.) to engage in, (6.) to mortgage.

Secondarily. (1.) To dye, (2.) to stain, (3.) to tincture, without coloring.

A glance at this statement shows that the Greek and Latin word has found fuller development in the direction of dyeing than of dipping; while the English word has received larger development under the leadership of the act without the element of color.

2. Each of these words expresses, primarily, an act characterized by the severest limitations in all directions. It is limited in force; it is limited in the extent of its fluid penetration; it is limited in the duration of continuance within the fluid; it is limited as to its objects, and it is limited, by the necessities of the case, in the influence which is exerted.

An invigorating element is introduced by the incorporation of color in the secondary meaning; the force of which still remains when color is merged in simple quality. And it is in this direction, only, that it makes any real approach toward sympathy with the usage and essential power of βαπτίζω.

3. One word reigns, unchanged, through all these Greek and Latin passages. This should be kept in distinct remembrance while we are told that βαπτίζω has but one invariable meaning, and is most easy of translation. If both these statements be correct, then that "readily found" Anglic representative can be carried without change "through all Greek literature." This has never been attempted. A like doctrine was long promulged respect-

ing βάπτω, and maintained in utter disregard of sentiment and construction.

It is obvious, that if the Greeks used the same word to express essentially different ideas, that they must have depended upon the sentiment expressed, and upon a modified grammatical structure, to throw light upon the meaning. "The berry pressed *dips* the hand." "Drops falling on garments *dip* them." "*Dip* other colors." These were phrases employed by the Greeks, but wholly unintelligible in the primary sense of dip; and yet by a metaphoric translation, and by a cloud raised under the name of "figurative language," they were compelled, by controversialists, to bear the badge of the original dip.

Severe pressure has constrained the admission of a secondary meaning; and with this admission has come a modified translation, and grammatical structure is allowed its rights; so that the lake is no longer "*dipped in* the blood of the frog," but "*dyed by* it." And while the Greeks still say that "garments are dipped (bapted) by *sprinkled drops;*" their translators no longer insist on their being dipped in them, but are content that they should be *dyed by* them. We, now, ask them to go a step farther, and admit that there may be a *bapting* without either a dipping or a dyeing, and, as well by sprinkling, as by any other mode. And, there, we will rest.

A similar pressure, from sentiment and syntax, has compelled some of the leading Baptist writers to revolutionize their position, as to an invariable act of dipping in βαπτίζω; thus, endeavoring to spike the grammatical guns whose fire could no longer be endured; while they held on to a dipping, "sometimes, and pretty commonly." To this we cannot assent; but ask a full surrender, or the endurance as well as may be, of continued syntactical bombardment.

Ten or a dozen words are required to represent βάπτω. Will one answer for βαπτίζω?

The Latins, like the Greeks, used but one word in all those passages, where we employ in translating, ten times as many.

They said: "*Dip* the pastures with dew;" "*Dip* the pavement with wine;" "*Dip* the face with tears;" "*Dip* the body by water poured over it;" "*Dip* the limbs and eyes with oil;" "The sacrificial victim *dips* the axe with its neck;" "*Dipped* the grass by sprinkling;" "*Dip* you with my bowls;" "*Dipped* the river by a quality communicated to it;" "*Dipped* the fountain" by similar means; "*Dipped* the sea by his blood;" "*Dipped* the body by sprinkled water."

These are remarkable phrases, and will repay close study. We shall have need of some of them hereafter.

Dip, in English, shows how sentiment and syntax must be our guide when a word is used out of its ordinary sense.

"Dew dips me all over;" "Dip into Aristotle;" "Dipped in those doings;" "Dip thy lands." These are phrases which, at once, say, "Look out for some other than the ordinary meaning."

If we meet with precisely similar phrases in connection with βαπτίζω, who can chide us for rejecting the iron clamp —" one meaning through all Greek literature?"

PART III.

IMMERSE.

ITS MEANING AND USAGE.

WE now proceed to examine the meaning of "immerse," as determined by general usage. This word is used, at will, by Baptist writers, as the equivalent of *dip*. They do not, indeed, employ these words, indifferently, in all cases; this they could not do; but where they *must*, they do discriminate, without any acknowledgment of the necessity; and where they *may*, without too open incongruity, there they confound and interchange.

Whether "immerse" be coincident in meaning with βάπτω, *tingo*, and *dip*, or whether it be separated from them by a line, clear, deep, and radical, the sovereign law of usage must determine. To that we appeal, and by its decree will we loyally abide.

MEANING.

To IMMERSE—*primarily.*—To cause to be in a state of intusposition (enveloped on all sides by, ordinarily, a fluid element), without any limitation as to the depth of position, time of continuance, force in execution, or mode of accomplishment.

All of these points are the contradictories of those which have been shown to belong to *dip*.

They are no less alien from the meanings shown to belong to the Latin *tingo*, and to the Greek βάπτω.

The usage of these words is too clear, too bold, too abounding, to allow of any doubt.

(196)

" The globe was in a state of immersion a much longer time than forty days."

" The next objection, that there is not enough of water on the earth to submerge it to the depth necessary to cover the tops of the highest mountains."

" The waters on the earth and under the earth could be so expanded by the rarefaction of the atmosphere, as to submerge the earth."

These three passages all relate to the universal deluge. They speak: 1. Of the condition of the object immersed; it was "*a state* of immersion." 2. Of the time of continuance; "a much longer time than *forty days.*" 3. Of " the depth" of the immersed object below the surface; the highest point being " fifteen cubits" beneath the rolling billows. 4. Of the mode in which it " could" be accomplished; " the waters could be *expanded* so as to submerge the earth." 5. Of the object immersed; " the globe."

Now, I would ask: 1. Was it ever said of an object *dipped* that it was in " a state" of *dipping?* 2. Was the continuance of a *dipping* ever known to last "much longer than forty days?" 3. Was a *dipping* ever known to put its object from fifteen cubits to half as many miles below the surface? 4. Was a *dipping* ever known to be effected by " the expansion" of the fluid until it surmounted its object? 5. Does *dip* number in the catalogue of objects which it takes up and places momentarily beneath the surface, such objects as this great " globe" which we inhabit?

The English language will be searched in vain for any such phraseology. The nature of the case does not admit of it. Dip does not put its object into " a state;" but merely carries it into, and out of, a fluid element without allowing it to gain any *status* in it. How vital this distinguishing difference is, in itself, is obvious; that the consequences, flowing from such diverse starting-points, must forever continue diverse, is no less obvious.

Booth thinks that "Baptist sentiment and practice is made ridiculous" by the use of "plunge;" would the finger of ridicule be pointed any the less sharply, if Booth and his friends would test their principles by employing *dip* to express such cases of "immersion" as that before us?

"A solid when immersed in a liquid becomes lighter by the weight of the fluid displaced."

"Representing a globe half immersed in water."

These statements necessitate a continuance of the state of intusposition. It is only as an object continues in a *state* of mersion that it becomes lighter. It is impossible to substitute *dip* for "immerse." The sentiment is, thereby, made untrue or impracticable. It is untrue that a dipped object is any the lighter for having been dipped; and it is impracticable to weigh an object which is, *in transitu*, going through the process of a dipping.

"Not rest until he found the persons who caused his immersion in the dungeon."

"We descended to the house, whence we emerged, on foot, upon the beautiful grounds."

"The party emerged from the vehicle that I had driven up."

Can you speak of a man shut up in a dungeon as being *dipped* into it? Can you speak of a company shut up in a house as being in a state of *dipping?* or, when coming forth from it, as *dipping* out of it?

Can you say of a party inclosed in a carriage that they are in *a state* of dipping? or, when they alight, that they dip out of it?

I do not ask, whether such phraseology is unusual; but

I ask, whether it is not absurdly impossible in the nature of the terms?

But it is most intelligible, most legitimate, and most nakedly true, that a man who is inclosed within the walls of a deep, dark "dungeon" is in *a state of mersion.* And it is no less true, that a company shut up in a house, or carriage, are also in *a state of mersion;* from which they "e-merge" in passing into the open air.

Where is the ground for equivalence between dip and immerse?

"Columbus is submerged, and the inhabitants are moving about in boats."

"The Great Eastern is submerged in steam blowing off from no less than twelve escape pipes."

Was the town of Columbus, or the Great Eastern, *dipped?* Would it be possible to say that they were, and to talk English?

"After sixty years' immersion the gold looks as fresh as if it had been taken out of the bank."

"Report in regard to the submerging of the Atlantic cable."

"Some authors of great name have maintained that this part of the globe had but lately emerged from the sea."

Is it customary to speak of a ship and her freight of gold being dipped in the ocean for the space of "sixty years?"

Is *dip* in English, any more than *tingo* in Latin, or βάπτω in Greek, ever applied to the loss of a vessel at sea?

Of the thousand times ten thousand speaking the English language, and who have spoken of the laying of the Atlantic cable, has there been one man, woman, or child, educated or uneducated, in Great Britain or America, who has ever spoken about "*dipping*" the Atlantic cable to the bottom of the Atlantic Ocean?

If a "part of the Earth" has remained since the morning of creation, until "lately," covered by the sea, can it

be said to have been "dipped" all that time? "Immersed"
it may have been for five thousand years, or five times five
thousand, in the depths of the sea; but no one will say
that it could, thus, have been *dipped*, except he should wish
to make "the sentiment" (or himself) "ridiculous."

"The lamp extinguished, he was immersed in total
darkness."

"Entreaties for aid, being drowned partly in the con-
cave of the steel cap in which his head was immersed, and
partly by the martial tune."

Does the extinguishing of the flame of a lamp, and consequent envelopment in darkness, expound the modal act
of dipping? It does expound *mersion.*

Is the placing "a steel cap" on the head an exemplification of the *modus* requisite *to dip* the head? Thus the
head is "immersed."

When a candle blown out can *dip* a body (without moving it a hair's-breadth) in darkness; and when moving a
"cap" to invest the head, can be said *to dip* the unmoved
head in the cap; then, we may be ready to hear what can
be said about the equivalence of *dip* and "immerse."

"Rolling over the edge of the moat was immersed in
the mud and marsh."

"A box on the ear overthrew the falconer into the cistern; his wrath was noways appeased by the cold immersion."

"Disgorging the sea-water which he had swallowed
during his immersion."

A man leaping over the wall of a town, and rolling into
the mud and marsh of the moat, does not present a good
picture of a dipping; either as to the mode or the *quantum*
of force.

A knock-down blow, tumbling a man into a cistern of

water, is as little orthodox in these particulars. To effect an immersion they will answer quite well; but another fashion and a gentler mode would be required by most who sought *a dipping.*

I call attention to the fact that these cases of mersion lasted but a short time. There is nothing in the nature of a mersion which requires that it should be protracted; but when it is most brief in its continuance, it is still, essentially, distinguished from a dipping. It is so in manner and intention. In both these respects the above cases differ from a dipping. A man who falls into the mud cannot be said to dip himself into it; nor can a man who receives a blow on the ear and falls into the water be said to be dipped into it by the striker.

It is especially to be noted, that in neither of the above cases does the immerser take out the object immersed. There was no limitation of the mersion on the part of the merser. Any of these parties might have continued to be mersed to the present hour, except they had, otherwise, recovered themselves from their mersed condition.

It is not so in a dipping. The dipper always intends to put the object dipped only momentarily into the element; and does recover it, himself, out of it. Unless this is done it is not a case of dipping.

The mere brevity of the mersion is no rational ground for confounding the *act* of dipping and the *state* of mersion.

A man who falls overboard or is knocked overboard, as in one of the above cases, and is speedily recovered from the sea, may be said to have been immersed; he cannot be said to have been dipped. A bucket which is let down from the same vessel, into the sea, for the purpose of procuring water, is properly said to be dipped into the sea. The time of continuance in the sea by the man and the bucket may be the same; and yet, by reason of the differences indicated, the only legitimate designation of the one is by immersion, and of the other by dipping.

It is, however, by the occurrence of these occasional

cases of brief immersion, that the semblance, and only the semblance, of justification, for the confounding of two terms whose broad usage is so diverse, can exist.

And why wish to establish such confusion? Why not be content to call "a spade a spade," and a dipping a dipping? The natural and unavoidable answer is: There is a necessity for confounding dip and immerse, because of the error which confounds βάπτω and βαπτίζω. Dipping has been introduced into the Christian ordinance under the plea (honestly meant no doubt), that "the word of inspiration demanded it;" but, on examination, *the Greek word for dipping is not to be found anywhere in the inspired record!* Then the position is assumed, that "the word that is there means the same thing." It is shown, however, not to mean the same thing; but to have a usage perfectly antipodal. Then there is an attempt to mix, "*through-other,*" this dip and immerse; and by discarding dip from the designation of the mode of administration, and by the use of immerse, to make some claim to the usage of βαπτίζω, from which usage dip is wholly excluded.

We cannot allow this mixing up of iron and clay. The magic stone of truth smites it, and it crumbles into its discordant elements. If the performance of a dipping be insisted upon, we insist on its being called just what it is —a dipping—and not an immersion, just what it is not.

INTUSPOSITION WITH INFLUENCE.

The cases of mersion, now stated, are not such as are accompanied with any marked influence on the object mersed. They were designed to show the radical idea of intusposition without limitation of depth, mode, force, or time. It is obvious, that any object so situated must be exposed to the fullest influence of the encompassing medium. The result of such influence will depend on the nature of the object exposed to it. A rock, and a bag of salt, a human being and a fish, will be very differently affected by encompassing waters.

One or two passages will suffice to present this aspect of the case.

> "His horse . . . .
> Rushed to the cliff, and, having reached it, stood.
> At once the shock unseated him: he flew
> Sheer o'er the craggy barrier: and immersed
> Deep in the flood, found, when he sought it not,
> The death he had deserved, and died alone."

> "At length, when all had long supposed him dead,
> By cold submersion, razor, rope, or lead."

"But among other nations 'submersion' (which is the French for 'drowning'), leads off as the most fatal of accidents."

What would be thought of the man who would introduce *dipping* into these passages as an equivalent? Neither dip, *tingo*, nor βάπτω drowns any one. Mersion does, and does by necessity of its nature, unless deliverance comes from some *ab extra* influence.

> "The clouds . . . .
> More ardent as the disk emerges more."

The influence upon the sun of an immersion within the clouds is to quench the effulgence of his rays.

> "The river flows redundant;
> Then rolling back, in his capacious lap
> Ingulfs their whole militia, quick immersed."

The mersion is destructive. The mode is by the water coming over its object. A movement by which a *dipping* cannot be effected. "Ingulf" is the equivalent of "immerse." Is it ever the equivalent of *dip?*

INTUSPOSITION FOR THE SAKE OF INFLUENCE.

This is a development quite in advance of the other, while it furnishes a stepping-stone for still farther progress.

> "Then on the warm and genial earth, that hides
> The smoking manure, and o'erspreads it all,
> He places lightly, and, as time subdues
> The rage of fermentation, plunges deep
> In the soft medium, till they stand *immersed*."

So Cowper describes the formation of a hotbed, and the mersion of seeds within it, for the purpose of bringing them within its full influence. In this instance the influence is not destructive, but vitalizing.

The passage, also, affords opportunity to see the discriminating difference between dip and "plunge." Plunge does not bring its object out of the element into which it carries it. Dip does. These words are never truly equivalent. Immerse agrees with "plunge," in not bringing out the object which it has caused to be introduced; but it differs from it, in that the latter term is limited as to the form of its action, and the nature of its force, and belongs to those words which are immediately expressive of action; and not of state or condition.

This is clearly exhibited in the above passage, where plunge expresses the act by which the condition denoted by "immersed" is secured. And as here, so everywhere there is some satellitic word of action attendant on immerse (expressed or understood), to perform its behests.

> "Whelm'd under our dark gulfs those arms shall lie,
> That blaze so dreadful in each Trojan eye;
> And deep beneath a sandy mountain hurl'd,
> *Immersed* remain this terror of the world.
>
> These his cold rites, and this his watery tomb."

By such mersion it was sought to destroy Achilles. The element, again, moves to invest its object, in contradiction of Dr. Carson's inconsiderately maintained position, that immerse must always dip. The act causative of the state of mersion is, here, "hurl'd," as before it was "plunge," and, yet previously was, "roll back," showing how absolutely free is immerse from all form of act. Whatever can effect a condition of mersion, immerse does not express but accepts as servitor.

" IMMERSED IN FURS."

The influence sought to be secured by this mersion was such warmth as might be, thus, attained in the Polar regions. So says Dr. Kane. He, probably, had good reason for his preference of a mersion in furs, over a *dip*.

The cases of mersion, thus far considered, have been all primary and physical. They have all been marked by influence in some aspect.

1. Capability for influence, rather than its actual exercise. 2. Controlling influence exercised, but without design in securing it. 3. Mersion sought for the sake of its controlling influence. This influence we have seen to be most varied in character, but always controlling in power. We have, also, seen that the state of physical mersion is induced in ways and by forces most various. And, farther, that the element may come to the object, as well as the object be brought to the element.

We have, also, seen that the mersing substance may be "furs," "clouds," "soft earth," "steel cap," "house," "carriage," "dungeon walls," &c., &c., as well as water.

Now, all these diversities uniting together in the unity of controlling influence, will prepare us, in passing from the consideration of physical mersions, to those which are not physical, to see a great variety of development as to forces and forms of agencies, while there will, everywhere, be present a resultant controlling influence. This is the grand resultant product of physical mersions. To secure this result as the end (and not the mersion), mersion has been sought.

Where no mersion can be secured, in the nature of the case, but where it is desired to express the controlling influence of any person or thing; it will be natural to employ such form of phraseology as is expressive of a mersion, although no mersion is designed, even in imagination, or, it may be, is conceivable, though we should tax our imagination to the uttermost.

We will see that this, in fact, has been done.

INTUSPOSITION, VERBAL, EXPRESSING INFLUENCE.

Forms of expression which are designed to express controlling influence; and which take their form from physical mersion as the source of such influence; may be regarded, sometimes, as properly figurative; but, most commonly, as a direct expression of the thought without any design to present it indirectly through a picture of a physical transaction.

The following passages may be regarded as designed picturings:

"The world was fast sinking into a sea of drunkenness; and the only wonder is that it was not entirely submerged under the flood."

"The tide of Southern bank suspension, in its sweep northward, submerged Philadelphia, but was stopped at New York."

But the following everyday phrases are not to be interpreted as formal figure; but as organic forms springing from a physical parentage whose lineaments they clearly reveal in their structure. The grosser elements of their original, however, they do not retain; but only an unsubstantial form, embodying, still, the vital spirit of controlling influence. These phrases, therefore, are to be regarded as organic unities, having a common life, and not as disjunct words.

"We are at last immersed in the horrors of civil war."

"Kings in the plenitude of power, if immersed in ignorance and prejudice, are less free than sages in a dungeon and bound with material chains."

"No longer immersed in the ignorance of heathenish idolatry."

"The Irish were a lettered people, while the Saxons were still immersed in ignorance."

"Some of the places were so completely immersed in Popish darkness as not to present the best points for missionary effort."

"Finding no foundation for a rational liberty on the emersion of the country from the corruption and tyranny of centuries, strove to save it by terrorism."

"Some time before commenced the pecuniary embarrassments of Sir Walter Scott, and his convulsive struggles to emerge from them."

"Instead of becoming immersed in secularity."

> "Of Calvary—that bids us leave a world
> Immersed in darkness and in death, and seek
> A better country."

In all these passages, "immersed" is combined with "ignorance, prejudice, tyranny, corruption, secularity, Popish darkness," &c., for the simple and single purpose of developing, in the completest manner, that influence which is appropriate to its adjunct. "In" is merely the formal *vinculum* necessary to the case; and is not to be pressed upon as though it made demand for a picture to be wrought out by the imagination. "*Immersed in*—ignorance," directly and prosaically declares that those spoken of are *under the controlling influence of ignorance*. Or, we must say, that "under," in this expression, demands figure, and pictures some poor wretch as crushed beneath some huge weight. Where, then, shall we find any direct channel for the utterance of our thoughts?

It is not the case, however, that "immerse," used with an unphysical adjunct, does necessarily express influence exerted over its object. We have seen that immersed objects are variously affected according to their nature; and that some (as a rock), when immersed, are affected only as occupying a position within the encompassing element. This affords the basis for the use, under appropriate circumstances, of immerse as simply indicating the fact of encompassing sources of influence, without their power being felt.

This usage is exemplified in the following passage:

"The missionary lives immersed in the sins of heathenism that he may raise them from death to a life of righteousness."

The missionary may, like Lot in Sodom, be "vexed with the filthy conversation" of the depraved around him; but, as the rock repels the encompassing billows, so he, while "immersed in the sins of heathenism," does, by divine grace, remain uncontaminated by their corrupting power.

"Immersed in sins" would, ordinarily, imply being under their full, morally corrupting influence; but applied to the preacher of the gospel encompassed by the immoralities of heathenism, it has no such meaning. The fact of intusposition, only, is indicated.

INFLUENCE WITHOUT INTUSPOSITION.

"Immerse" does not always bring into view intusposition, either in the limited measure, or as expressive of the ideas now considered.

The physical form ceases to be even a transparent shadow through which influence is made visible. Both the form of the shadow, and the nature of the influence, disappear together.

It is quite common to use "immerse" in phraseological combinations in which it expresses the most thorough engagedness; the most strenuous mental effort. If an explanation of the ground of this usage were asked, there might not be common consent shown in the reply; but this would only indicate how far, and how completely, the usage has been removed from the physical fact. The image has been worn off from the coin by long and varied handling.

Perhaps the passage, already quoted, respecting Sir Walter Scott's pecuniary embarrassment, may guide to the true solution. He being "immersed in pecuniary embarrassment," made "convulsive struggles" to extricate himself from it, and succeeded. Any man physically immersed must use all effort to save himself or perish. "Immerse" may thus come to be intimately associated with the effort necessary to escape from such position; and, then, with mental effort without such appendages. The use of "immersion," without any immersion, by Sir Walter Scott himself, may be here, appropriately, introduced:

"The boat received the shower of brine which the animal spouted aloft, and the adventurous Triptolemus had a full share of the immersion."

Here is an "immersion by sprinkling" from the showery brine. So we have seen a *bapting* by sprinkling among the Greeks, a *tinction* by sprinkling among the Latins, and a *dipping* by sprinkling in Milton's Comus. Do the framers of this phraseology (intending by it to construct a crown of supremest ridicule for their opponents), feel alarmed? "Stones thrown up into the air may come down on our own pate."

It is beyond all controversy, that one of the best writers of the English language does use the word "immersion" where no immersion, in fact, took place; but only a thorough wetting by means of a profuse sprinkling. This is the incontrovertible fact. Did "the Wizard of the North" write good English? Were the laws of language unknown to "the Great Unknown?"

Unless these framers of sentences will crown, with their handiwork, Sir Walter as "Lord of the Ridiculous," they must even accept of "Immersion by Sprinkling."

If, now, the author of Waverley is justified in writing, not under the poetic afflatus, nor as "one of the most impassioned of men" (the explanation given of a similar Greekly baptism by Dr. Fuller), but in homely prose, of *a thorough wetting* as an "immersion;" then, we are justified in speaking of *a thorough influence* as an "immersion" where no immersion takes place; or *thoroughly engaged*, mentally occupied, as an "immersion," when no immersion, real or imaginary, takes place.

It is this latter which it is proposed, now, to exemplify:

"While Dr. Chalmers, immersed in Parliamentary reports as to the operation of the Poor Laws, was engaged" . .

"November saw Dr. C. once more immersed in his professorial labors."

14

" The Secretary of War is immersed in business."

" I find myself immersed in the matters of which I know least."

" Men of business immersed in the cares of an extended traffic."

" We in England are generally immersed in our own concerns."

" Deeply immersed in calculations from the simple unit to millions, billions, and trillions."

" As he rode on immersed in these unpleasant contemplations."

" They rode as men deeply immersed in their own thoughts."

" Walking up and down the room immersed in thought."

" The busy, bustling merchant immersed in all the calculation of this world's traffic."

" He was a little too much immersed in worldly schemes. He attached himself so eagerly to business that he thought every hour lost."

" He was so much immersed in politics that he did not care to be annoyed with it."

" And immersed himself among a parcel of worm-eaten folios."

" Had taken up the Prayer-Book; she seemed immersed in devotional duty."

" Ha! yes, I was so immersed in my book."

" Continued immersed in the fascinating perusal."

" The noonday prayer-meeting comes, happily, at that hour when we would be most likely to be immersed in the business or pleasures of the world."

" The padre was on his way to church, and immersed in the study of his sermon."

" I've just dipped into the works of such an author. Now, this far from signifying that I feel my mind, as it were, immersed in the author's writings."

Whatever may be supposed to be the precise physical literality on which such usage of "immerse" rests; there can be no doubt, but that, without suggestion of intus-position, it does, directly, express *thorough mental engaged-ness.*

MEANING ESTABLISHED BY USAGE.

The examination of this word has been pursued suffi-ciently far for our purpose. The conclusions reached are:

1. Immerse expresses no form of act; but demands and secures for its object intusposition, without limitation of size in the object, force in the agency, depth in the ele-ment, or time in duration.

2. When the continuance of the intusposition is brief, it is not because of any limitation, or action on the part of immerse; but from causes foreign to it, and for which it has no responsibility. No alliance, therefore, can be established with *dip* on this ground, any more than be-tween dip and *sink*, or *ingulf*, or *swallow up*, &c.; all of whose objects may, by foreign influences, be recovered within a brief space from the condition to which they have been introduced.

3. The preposition in composition—"*in*"—merse,—has a purely local force, and does not indicate movement of the object *into*—put *into*, dip *into*—as some writers have as-sumed. It is as legitimate to "immerse" by bringing the water to the object, as by bringing the object to the water, notwithstanding that Dr. Carson (whose like we are told the world will not see again for "a millenary of years") declares, that put *into* is so ingrained in the word that when it does *not* "put into" it still means *put into.*

4. It may express *a thorough wetting* (without intusposi-tion), by sprinkling or otherwise.

5. It may express death by *drowning.*

6. It expresses *thorough influence* of any kind; the nature determined by the adjunct.

7. It expresses *thorough mental engagedness.*

8. Immerse is antipodal to dip. Baptist writings which make these terms equivalents can be of no controversial value. Baptist Bible translation which commands "immerse," and Baptist ritual practice which substitutes *dip*, have neither part nor lot in each other.

9. While dip, *tingo*, and βάπτω are joined in the closest bonds, immerse is, by nature, widely disjoined from them all.

MERGO.

ITS MEANING AND USAGE.

1. MERGO expresses no definite form of action; but makes the demand, in primary use, of intusposition for its object as its essential requisite.

This it secures by forms of action, and by forces of agency, in endless variety. The magnitude of its objects, and the depth of penetration to which it introduces them, are also most varied in character.

The duration of the mersion effected is without limit; although, as in any other case where an object has been sunk, ingulfed, or swallowed up, the object mersed may be recovered, from its state of mersion, by other influences.

2. Capability of influence, necessarily, attaches to such state of intusposition.

This influence will vary in development according to the nature of the object mersed, and the nature of the mersing element; which appears in Latin usage to take a somewhat wider range than in Greek or English.

3. The secondary use of this word has its development, necessarily, in the direction of a controlling influence. Physical investiture is thrown aside. As, in physical mersion, whatever force can secure intusposition is an equally legitimate representative of the will of *mergo;* so, in the secondary use, whatever agency (no matter in what form it may develop its power) is capable of exerting a controlling influence over its object, may claim *mergo* to express, not the form of action, but the measure of the influence.

4. To all these characteristics, primary or secondary, *dip* is, by usage, and must ever remain by necessity of nature, a perfect stranger.

PRIMARY.

ILLUSTRATION BY USAGE.

Primumque pedis vestigia tinxi:
Poplite deinde tenus. Neque eo contenta recingor
Nudaque mergor aquis. . . . . . . *Ovid.*
    And I am mersed naked in the waters.

In medias quoties visum captantia collum
Brachia mersit aquas, nec se deprehendit in illis! . *Ovid.*
    He mersed his arms into the midst of the waters.

        Juvat esse sub undis;
Et modò tota cavâ submergere membra pallude
Nunc proferre caput. . . . . *Ovid.*
    And to submerse all their limbs in the deep pool.

        Furit Æsacus, inque profundum
Pronus abit, lethiquè viam sinè fine retentat.
Æquor amat: nomenque manet, quia mergitur, illi. . *Ovid.*
    The name (mergus) remains to him, because he is mersed.

Et mergi projecta non possunt, licet gravia sint. . *Seneca.*
    Things cast into it cannot be mersed, although heavy.

Nihil mergitur in Siciliæ fonte Phintiâ. . . . *Pliny.*
    Nothing is mersed in Phintia, a fountain of Sicily.

The first of these passages shows the distinctive use of *tingo* and *mergo*. The foot playing in and out of the water is *dipped;* the body under the water "gliding hither and thither," is in a state of mersion. How the body became mersed, there is not a ray of light to indicate either from *mergo* or any other quarter. It may have been by walking gradually into deeper water; it may have been by leaping from the bank, at once, into deep water; or it may have been partially by walking, and, then, by slowly sinking down. We know that it was *not* by dipping, for dipping puts nothing into *a state* of mersion, but takes out, promptly, what it puts in, and is, *therefore*, what it is—*a dipping*.

It should be noted that *the head* remains unmersed,

while there is no limitation in the language—"I am mersed in the waters."

In the third quotation, the frogs are wholly under water, and we know that this is by *leaping;* but will any one say that "*mergo*" means *to leap?* Yet it does mean "to leap" just as much as it means any other act by which mersion is effected.

The last passage expounds the origin of the name "Mergus," a class of waterfowl. It arose from an attempt of Æsacus to drown himself in the sea; when he was changed by Tethys, in commiseration, into a *Mergus.*

MERSING MATERIAL VARIOUS.

Pandere res altâ in terrâ et caligine mersas. . *Virgil.*
　　To reveal things mersed in the deep earth and in darkness.

Ferrum mersum in robora. . . . . *Lucretius.*
　　Iron mersed in hard wood.

Mersis in Sinum manibus. . . . *Quintillian.*
　　Hands mersed in the bosom.

Flumen specu mergitur. . . . . *Pliny.*
　　The river is mersed in the cave.

Mergit se limo. . . . . . . *Pliny.*
　　Merses in the mud.

Mergere manum in ora ursæ. . . . *Martial.*
　　Merse the hand into the mouth of the bear.

Mersisque in corpore rostris. . . . *Ovid.*
　　Dogs' mouths mersed in the body (of Actæon).

Cæcis ego mersa cavernis. . . . . *Ovid.*
　　Immersed in dark caverns.

Membra simul pecudis. . . Mergit in ære cavo. *Ovid.*
　　Merses the limbs of the ram in the hollow brass.

Mersitque suos in cortice vultus. . . . *Ovid.*
　　And mersed her features in the bark.

This last passage, in which Myrrha is transformed into a tree, is in perfect harmony with a state of mersion; it can scarcely be made to accord with *a dipping.*

The following passages, showing the covering material brought over the object, are, in like manner, inconsistent with any other meaning than that of condition. The first refers to the general deluge; the second to the eyelid being drawn over the eye.

Aut mersæ culmina villæ navigat. . . . . *Ovid.*
> *Sails over the top of the mersed house.*

Lumina somno mergimus. . . . . *Valerius Flaccus.*
> *We merse the eyes in sleep.*

INTUSPOSITION WITH INFLUENCE.

Corporeasque dapes avidam demersit in alvum. . . *Ovid.*
> *Whoever first de-mersed flesh food into his greedy belly.*

Sive virgam, sive frondem demersis, lapidem post paucos dies extrahis. . . . . *Seneca.*
> *A twig or leaf having been let down, you may draw it out, after a few days, a stone.*

DROWN.

Tyberinus, qui in trajectu Albulæ amnis submersus. *Livy.*
> *Tyberinus, who in the passage of the river Albula was submersed.*

Albula, quem Tiberini, mersus Tiberinus in undis. *Fastorum.*
> *Albula, called Tiber, because Tiberinus was mersed in its waters.*

Hoc exilium est mihi instar procellæ quo agitor, non submergor. Summersus fuissem, si me interemisset.
> *Tristium,* xi, 13 (note).
> *This exile is to me like a storm by which I am tost, not submersed. I had been submersed, if I had perished.*

Vertere Mæonios, pelagoque immergere, nautas. . *Ovid.*
> *Could transform the Mæonian sailors, and immerse them in the sea.*

Ecce super medios fluctus niger arcus aquarum
Frangitur: et ruptâ mersum caput obruit undâ. . *Ovid.*
> *The bursting billow rolls over his mersed head.*

Coëunt, et saxa trabesque
Conjiciunt; mergunt que viros mergunt que carinas.   *Ovid.*
  They hurl rocks and beams, and merse men and ships.

Spargite me influctus, vastoque immergite ponto.   .   *Æneid.*
  Cast me into the waves, and immerse me in the deep sea.

Spumosâ undâ immerserat virum.   .   .   .   .   *Æneid.*
  The envious Triton mersed in the foaming wave the man.

Medioque sub æquore mersit.   .   .   .   .   *Æneid.*
  What God mersed you in mid ocean?

Nec me Deus æquore mersit.   .   .   .   .   - *Æneid.*
  Nor has any God mersed me in the sea.

Doctus eris, vivam musto mersare Falerno.   .   *Hor. Satir.*
  Merse it, living, in Falernian wine.

This common use of "mergo" to denote death by drowning, is, of itself, conclusive evidence that it cannot mean *to dip*.   There is no evidence that dip, in English, *tingo*, in Latin, or βάπτω, in Greek, has any such usage.

DESTRUCTIVE.

Mersâ rate, naufragus assem dum rogat.   .   *Juvenal.*
  One shipwrecked, his vessel mersed, begs a penny.

Unda . . .
Nec leviùs, quam siquis Athon Pindumve revulsos
Sede suâ totos in apertum everterit æquor
Præcipitata ruit: pariterque et pondere et ictu,
Mergit in ima ratem.   .   .   .   .   .   *Ovid.*
  *The wave, not lighter than Athos or Pindus, falls headlong;
  And equally by the weight and by the blow, merses the ship to
  the bottom.*

Mox eadem Teucras fuerat mersura carinas   .   .   *Ovid.*
  Scylla would have mersed the Trojan ships.

Pars maxima classis mergitur.   .   .   .   .   *Lucan.*
  The greatest part of the fleet is mersed.

Quassa, tamen nostra est, nec mersa, nec obruta navis.
  Tristium.
  Our ship is shattered, but not mersed or whelmed.

Quid navigia sarcinâ depressa—quo minus mergantur.

Seneca, Nat. Quæs.
What hinders but that vessels, depressed by their lading,
   may be mersed.

Again we must profoundly feel, that between such usage and *a dipping* there can be no common sympathy.

ASSIMILATION.

Fluvius in Euphratem mergitur. .   .   .   .   .   *Pliny.*
The river is mersed into the Euphrates.

The influence of water intusposed in water is the most complete incorporation and assimilation; the larger body controlling and absorbing the lesser.

This affords the basis for a secondary use of an important character. I do not know that I can point to any exemplification among Latin writers; but it is quite common, in English usage, in connection, not with *immerse*, but with *merge*. This word is employed daily in the sense expressive of incorporation and assimilation, but, almost, never in relation with physical elements.

A few passages will illustrate this statement.

"It provides for *merging* our Presbyteries into the Synods of the General Assembly. If we are to have union, let it be union; but if absorption, let it be so stated."

"The States are united, not *merged.*"

"The amendment *merging* the Minnesota with the Kansas bill was withdrawn."

"I am not prepared to be *merged* with the Old School."

"The banks of the Cavalla River gradually rise until they *merge* into the Gero and Pawh mountains."

"The carriage road *merges* into the bridle path."

"This is more than all the Popes, who ever lived, *merged* in one, would dare propose."

"*Merging* its members in the newly created Christian community."

"Her evening sun set, *merged*, at length, with joy in the endless life of heaven."

"The meeting will continue until 12 o'clock, and will, then, be *merged* into the prayer meeting."

"I may transgress the limits of propriety, and *merge* the pulpit in the rostrum."

"An ordinance to *merge* the department of the market-houses into that of the city property."

"Christians cannot *merge* themselves in the world, and yet live above the world."

"In the year 1457, the distinctive existence of the Taborites was *merged* in the Society of the Bohemian Brotherhood."

This usage is grounded in the controlling influence represented in *mergo*. The special form which that influence takes, in the present case, is that of absorption and assimilation. There is not mere mersion, but unification. *Merge*, in its ordinary English use, cannot translate βαπτίζω.

PURIFICATION.

Hæc sanctè utposcas, Tiberino in gurgite mergis
Mane caput bis terque, et noctem flumine purgas.   *Perseus.*
That thou mayest ask these things purely, merse thy head
In the river Tiber, twice and thrice, in the morning, and thus
purge the night by the stream.

Whether it be thought justifiable, or not, to say that "mergo," here, does, directly, signify to purify, it is certain that the end sought is purification. When Tiberinus was "mersed" in the Tiber he was *drowned;* and "mergo," as used by both Livy and Ovid to describe the fact, has this direct force—*to drown.* It would be unavoidable, but that the word, commonly used to describe similar occurrences, would secure to itself the power to express directly what originally was expressed, only, indirectly. In like manner, "mergo," used, daily, to express the development of a purifying influence by mersion, would, unavoidably, come to represent that influence, and not merely the intusposition procurative of it.

Thus, in the natural development of language, "mersus homo" might represent "a purified man;" because—1. He had been actually mersed in his whole body, and thus had received a fully developed purifying influence. 2. Because his "head" had been actually mersed, and thus the purifying influence had been received by the entire body. And, 3. Because complete purification had been received in some other way than by mersion, in whole or in part, whether by sacrifice, by fire, or by sprinkled water.

To say that a man thoroughly purified by sprinkled water may not be called "*mersus* homo," on the ground that "mersus" means *immersed*, is to "kick against the pricks," sharp and innumerable, projecting through all the history of language. The purifying power was in the water of the Tiber, and that power was not limited, in its development, to a state of mersion, but was equally secured by sprinkling.

Bis caput intonsum fontana spargitur unda

. . . .

Ter caput irrorat, ter tollit ad æthera palmas.   *Fast.* 4.

 Twice his unshorn head is *sprinkled* with spring water.

 . . . .

 Thrice he *sprinkles* his head, thrice he lifts his hands to heaven.

No one will question that this sprinkling induced condition of purification; no one (I will venture to presume, until advertised of the contrary) will question that "mersus" *may* denote a condition of purification (or any other condition), where no actual mersion has taken place; therefore, it is beyond all denial that "mersus homo" may represent, *not the act of sprinkling*, but a man who has been purified by sprinkling.

I do not say that, in the passage before us, mergo means to purify, although Perseus employs *purgo* to express its import alone, or that of the phrase of which it is a member, and the "interpretation" substitutes *lavo* for it. It is sufficient for my present purpose to establish an unquestionable possible use. Mergo used to develop a thoroughly purifying influence for its object by intusposition in river water, may, most legitimately, be used to express such purification in whatsoever way effected.

In reference to a resemblance between this mersion of the head, and a dipping, I would remark: 1. The distinction established between these words precludes their confusion here. 2. Any object mersed, and resting, most briefly, in that condition, for the sake of the influence of such condition, deprives it of the character of a mere dipping. 3. With the facts before us, it is madness to make mergo *mean* to dip. 4. Such usage of mergo brings it into fellowship, not with the primary meaning to dip, but with the secondary meaning *to dye*, and its extension to the communication of quality without color. This mersion was for the purpose of securing the quality of purification. As dipping sometimes took place for the sake of dyeing, and then ceased to mean to dip; and dyeing was effected by sprinkling, or in any way; so, mersion for purification ceases to mean to intuspose, and becomes to purify in any way. 5. The extent and mode of applying an element capable of producing a purification is purely arbitrary, and, in fact, endlessly varied. Whether the whole body be mersed, or the head or hands only; whether the whole body be poured upon or sprinkled; or whether the extremity of the lips only be touched; the purified one becomes equally a "*mersus* homo." *Mersus* in such case, of course, referring not to the manner in which the purifying element has been used, whether by mersion or sprinkling, but to the condition of purity induced. The following quotation is illustrative: "Let him first sip water thrice; then twice wipe his mouth; and lastly touch with water the six cavities before mentioned, his breast and his head. He who knows the law and seeks purity, will ever perform his ablution with the pure part of his

hand, and with water neither hot nor frothy, standing in a
lonely place, and turning to the east or north.

"A Brahmin is purified by water that reaches his bosom;
a Cschatriga by water descending to his throat; a Vaisya
by water barely taken into his mouth; a Sudra by water
touched with the extremity of his lips."—*Institutes of
Manu, Gr. Ch. Haughton*, London, p. 29.

Purifying water "touching the lips" constitutes an ablution, and makes a "mersus homo."

FIGURE.

Nescit quid perdat, et alto
Demersus, summa rursum non bullit in unda.   .   *Perseus.*
Demersed in the deep, he never again emerges.

Nimia facultate in voluptates mergi.   .   .   .   *Curtius.*
Mersed into pleasures by too great wealth.

Mersor fortunæ fluctibus.   .   .   .   .   .   *Catullus.*
Mersed by the billows of fortune.

Mersor civilibus undis. .   .   .   .   .   .   *Hor. Epist.*
Mersed by political waves.

These passages exhibit figurative use, in contradistinction from that simply tropical, turned or secondary use,
by which words of original physical application are so far
modified in meaning as to adapt them to express ideas
growing out of relations not physical. Perseus, clearly,
has a picture in his mind which he presents for us to look
at. The debased man of whom he speaks is not merely
represented as "demersed"—in this there would not be,
necessarily, any figure—but he adds, "in the deep," which
would be very tame of itself; but when he adds, "he
never bubbles to the surface," the picture is spirited and
complete.

The passage from Curtius is most worthy of special
attention. Had this writer simply said, "nimia facultate
mergi," it would have been a merely prosaic statement
expressive of the controlling influence of excessive wealth;

but by the addition, "in voluptates," he converts it into
figure, and shows that he does not mean merely to speak
of influence, but of influence exerted in a certain direction, and to indicate that specific form he introduces a
figurative element, namely, "pleasures."

It is very rarely that the accusative, representing the
element, is thus introduced either in the Greek or in the
Latin. The reason, I suppose, is, because in the secondary
use there is no design to speak in figure; and because the
character of the influence can be gathered, usually, with
sufficient accuracy from the subject-matter of discourse.
Still, it is manifest that the greatest possible precision is
given by the use of this form of speech, and, sometimes,
(as in referring to an influence wholly new or imperfectly
understood) it might be essentially necessary to employ it.

Had one stood on the banks of the Tiber while purification was sought by mersing the head, and thrice sprinkling
its waters, and proclaimed the insufficiency of purification
so secured; and the necessity of mersion by repentance;
some vague idea, and only a vague idea, might have been
received as to the effect of a Repentance Mersion compared
with a Tiber Mersion; but if mersion by repentance *into
the remission of sins* is proclaimed, then the thought is stated
with absolute definiteness, and becomes flooded with light.
So, "mersion by wealth" is an indefinite statement; while
"mersion by wealth *into pleasures*" gives form and feature
to the thought. The former phrase is sufficient for things
with whose nature and influential effects we are familiar;
the latter is necessary in speaking of things unfamiliar and
for rhetorical effect.

In the last two passages, the use of "fluctibus" and
"undis" determines the picture character of the thought
in the minds of the writers. And it may be well to say,
particularly, that these words, although representing a
fluid element, do not represent the element in which, but
the means by which the mersion takes place. This is conclusively shown by the passage of Ovid, which expressly
declares that it was "pondere et ictu" of the wave that

the vessel was mersed "*in ima.*" So in "nimia facultate in voluptates," the instrumental means is represented by its appropriate case. And, in general, it should be understood that the ablative, in all cases of influence-mersion, represents the agency by which, and not the element in which, the mersion takes place.

SECONDARY USE.

INFLUENCE WITHOUT INTUSPOSITION.

Sed me fata me . . . . . his mersere malis. . . *Æneid.*
  The fates have mersed me by these evils.

Abstulit atra dies, et funere mersit acerbo. . . *Æneid.*
  Death has snatched away, and mersed with a bitter end.

Aut quæ forma viros fortunave mersit. . . *Æneid.*
  What form or fortune has mersed the men ?

Et mersis fer opem mitissima rebus. . . . *Ovid.*
  O most Benign! bring help to our mersed affairs.

Ab Jove mersa suo Stygias penitrarit in undas. . *Ovid.*
  Mersed by her Jove shall go down to the Stygian waters.

Affer opem, mersæque precor feritate paternâ. . *Ovid.*
  Help! and receive me mersed by paternal cruelty.

Rerum copia mersat. . . . . . *Lucretius.*
  Abundance of things merses.

Qui peritissime censum domini mergit. . . *Pliny.*
  Who most cunningly merses the estate of his master.

Mersus foro. . . . . *Plautus.*
  Mersed by debt.

Mersus rebus secundis, Alexander. . . . *Livy.*
  Alexander mersed by prosperity.

Mersus vino, somnoque. . . . . . *Livy.*
  Mersed by wine and sleep.

Potatio quæ mergit. . . . . . *Seneca.*
  The drink which merses.

Virum gravem, moderatum, sed mersum vino, et madentem.
Seneca.
A man grave, moderate, but mersed and wet with wine.

Mergere aliquem ad Styga.   .   .   .   .   .   *Seneca.*
Merse any one to the Styx.

Et Cosmi toto mergatur abeno.   .   .   .   .   *Juvenal.*
Mersed by the whole unguent vase of Cosmus.

Mergit longa, atque insignis honorum pagina. .   .   *Juvenal.*
A long and eminent record of honors merses.

Ut mediocris jacturæ te mergat onus.   .   .   .   *Juvenal.*
That the burden of a moderate loss should merse thee.

Seu rore pudico
Castaliæ flavos amor est tibi mergere crines.   *Statius, Thebais.*
To merse thy yellow locks in the pure dew of Castalia.

It is unnecessary to comment on each of these passages. The point to be established is, that *mergo* (placing originally its object in a position where it is exposed to physical influence in the fullest degree) comes to represent a condition which is the result of some controlling influence *independent of position.*

Two or three clear cases will sufficiently illustrate this point.

" O, most Benign! bring help to our mersed affairs."

This is the prayer of Deucalion and Pyrrha, after the subsidence of the general deluge, addressed to Themis: " Declare, O Themis! by what means the ruin of our race may be repaired, and bring help, most Benign! to our mersed affairs."

The prayer was not for a rescue of human affairs under deluge waters; that condition had been, but was now passed away. Human affairs are in a "ruined" condition, which is expressed by "mersed," and from this condition deliverance is solicited.

The meaning of "rebus mersis" in this passage admits of but one possible interpretation in the connection in which it stands. But not indicating any specific form of influence, only controlling influence of some kind, there

15

would oftentimes be a necessity for the introduction of some expounding words. Thus, "ære paterno ac rebus mersis in ventrem fœnoris."—*Juvenal*, xi, 40. "Patrimony and property mersed into the gulf of usury." "Rebus mersis," here needed some explaining word, and it is furnished by "in ventrem fœnoris."

"Mersed by debt"—"that the burden of a moderate loss should merse you." Such phrases express, directly, a ruinous influence. To reach this by a voyage at sea and the foundering of a ship, is, at the best, sailing round the world to arrive at a point one pace behind you.

"Mersed to the Styx," is a phrase perfectly explicit, although the word is used absolutely, because the mention of "the Styx" makes but one interpretation possible. Mergo, here, expresses a condition of death effected by some controlling influence not mentioned, and which may be from anything, and in any form competent to cause death.

This is shown by a parallel passage quoted.

"Mersed by her Jove shall go down to the Stygian waters."

Some, not particularly conversant with the facts of the case, might fancy to translate, "She shall go down *into* the waters of Styx and be immersed by her friend Jove." And this translation might be very manfully defended by triumphantly asking: 1. "Was not 'the Styx' a river, and is there not water enough in a river for *immersion?* 2. Does not 'penetro' mean *to penetrate, to go into*, and what would any one go into a river for except to be *immersed?* 3. Does not 'in' (above all, 'in' with the accusative of a fluid element) denote movement, and what can 'in undas' mean but *into the water?* 4. And to crown all, does not mergo mean '*to dip*'? Have we not, then, the most express statement of immersion, the denial of which shows, 'not the want of light, but of Christian honesty'? 5. If assurance could go farther, is it not found in the declaration that there was an immerser present to do the work?

What, then, is lacking in this overwhelming, concentrated evidence—'River'—'entering'—'into'—'immersed'—'immerser?' Surely nothing; the case is made out."

Now, I frankly confess that if I knew no more about the actual facts of this case than I do about the absolute facts of some other cases from which this reasoning is a transcript, I could say nothing more to disturb the complacent convictions expressed respecting the "immersion" of Semele into the Styx by her special friend, than I could in such other cases.   I must in all honesty confess to the Styx being "a river;" to *penetro* meaning "to enter;" to *in* meaning "into;" to *mergo* meaning "to merse;" and to *Jove* being quite competent to act as "immerser;" but, after all, there is still one difficulty in the way of Semele's immersion in the river by her friend, and that is just this,—*he did no such thing, but killed her by his thunderbolts!* And, now, with this historical help we review our translations, and find that the Styx may remain a river still, without anybody being dipped into it; that "penetro" may carry down very far, indeed, without carrying into the water; that "in" may mean *to* even with "undas;" that "mergo" may express a condition of death by a thunderbolt, as well as a condition of death by drowning; and both, as well as a simple intusposition without any deadly consequence following; and that Jove may be an "immerser" without dipping into water.   I do not know that this case will cause any misgiving as to the reasoning so earnestly urged by Baptist brethren in other cases; but if it should, I have no doubt of there being quite enough of "Christian honesty" on their part (whatever may be true of others) to make all due acknowledgment.   Very sure am I, that whenever the historical facts in those cases shall be fully revealed, that they will show that the actual baptism conferred in those rivers was no more like that immersion in water contended for, than was the actual thunderbolt immersion of Semele like to her, *translation-proved*, immersion into the Styx!   In the *Æneid*, iv, 25, is a parallel passage, the "thunderbolt" expressed, and the

mersion implied—"Vel Pater omnipotens adigat me ful-
mine ad umbras."

"A long and eminent record of honors merses."

How far removed from a water mersion is a statement
like this.

"Mergo" does not necessarily express a condition resultant from a destructive influence, but this is the ordinary result of physical mersion; therefore, when applied,
without qualification, to cases where physics are not involved, we must understand that a destructive influence
is designed.

This is the case here. Juvenal declares that, under certain circumstances, "honors merse"—*bring ruin.* They
do so by awakening envy, jealousy, and hate on the part
of others, or by begetting self-esteem, pride, and ambition,
on the part of the possessor; thus a condition of shame,
suffering, and ruin is induced, well described as a mersion
by influence, but poorly expounded by insisting on a design to picture an intusposition *in water.*

> Potatio quæ mergit.   .   .   .   . *Seneca.*
> *The drink which merses.*
> Mersus vino somnoque. .   .   .   . *Livy.*
> *Mersed by wine and sleep.*

These passages are closely parallel, and afford a good
opportunity to speak of the importance of discriminating,
in cases of mersion, between the agency effecting the
mersion and the element in which the mersion actually,
or (in figure) supposedly, takes place; as, also, of the advanced usage which first obliterates figure and shadow,
establishing a general, secondary meaning, and then, by
frequent use, a specific meaning.

The passage from Seneca presents the agency in the
nominative, and so precludes all question as to its character. I ought to state that I have not seen this passage in
its connection, and cannot vouch for its literal correctness;

but whether there, or elsewhere, the phrase serves equally well for comment.*

The "potation," or drink, is declared to be causative of the mersion. Now, it is a physical impossibility that anything drunk should produce a physical mersion of the drinker. Such a result is, then, out of the question. But mersion by figure is no less out of question, so far as the drink is sought to be made the element in which the mersion is figuratively to take place. If the mersion, by figure, of "a lake into the blood of a mouse," is an intolerable perversion of taste, how much better is that which would figure a man mersed into the fluid which fills his mouth or stomach? If some other sort of figure is sought for, as "into drunkenness," "into insensibility," I admit that such figure may be used for the sake of definiteness of thought, or for giving special force to the expression; but deny the necessity for, or the propriety of, any such thing in the case before us. 1. There is no need for "definiteness." No one who reads this phrase but what understands, at once, that an *intoxicating* drink is intended. 2. There is no need for force. The phrase is one of concentrated energy. There is a power of fact in the utterance which tramples figure under foot, and goes straight forward to its end. It declares something which "potation" does substantially, not figures shadowly. And what does "potation" of an intoxicating liquor do? Why, *it makes drunk.* Then that is what Seneca declares, throwing aside physical intusposition, and figurative intusposition, and passing beyond general controlling influence, he gives individuality, body, and shape to that influence in the nerv-

---

* On examination I find the following passage: " Aliquando vectatio itérque, et mutata regio, vigorem dabunt, convictusque et liberalior *potio;* nonnunquam et usque ad ebrietatem veniendum, non ut *mergat nos* sed ut deprimat." *De tranquilitate animi.* This is the passage, I presume, which is intended to be presented, in a condensed form, in " *Potatio quæ mergit.*" "Not that it may merse us, but depress cares." Has depress, express, impress, oppress, suppress, no secondary meaning? Seneca says: " Bacchus is called Liber because he liberates the mind from the slavery of cares."

ous statement—" *The Drink which makes drunk.*" "Potatio" necessitates such coloring to the thought. We have, then, a mersion by a fluid without being in that fluid, or in any other, but effected by drinking a pint or a quart, thus exercising over the drinker a controlling, *intoxicating* power. Seneca elsewhere says: "Ubi possedit animum *nimia vis vini*, quicquid mali latebat *emergit.*" This shows that wine mersion is not, with Seneca, a dipping or sinking, but a *nimia vis vini*—a controlling influence of wine.

In the passage from Livy, as the ablative is used in expressing the agency, occasion has been taken to convert the agency of the mersion into the element of mersion.

Does any one doubt that "wine and sleep" were the agencies in this mersion? Does any one doubt the essential difference between the agency effecting a mersion, and the element in which the mersion of the object takes place? If these things are beyond controversy, why, then, confound the agency and the element by contending for a "mersion *in* wine and sleep?" How is such mersion conceivable? Are "wine and sleep" to be conceived of as mingled together, and so constituting a joint bath? Or, is there to be a mersion, first into the one, and then into the other? These questions must be met. Difficulties must not be covered up by vague talk of figure.

Interpret according to the facts, making "wine and sleep" agencies, and all runs smoothly. They, by their conjoint influence, exercise a controlling influence of accumulated power, which is described in the strongest language by terming it a *mersive* influence.

Those who contend for figure here, and to effect it turn "wine and sleep" into a nondescript element, appeal for support to *Æneid* ii, 265: "*Invadunt urbem somno vinoque sepultam.*" The appeal brings no valuable aid. "Sepelio" is modified in its usage just as mergo and scores of other words are. We say of an unsuccessful politician, "he is dead and buried;" do we mean by this to picture a graveyard, pit, coffin, and shrouded corpse, with incasted earth? Or, do we mean to express simply that his hopes and efforts for advancement are utterly futile? Besides, how can a city be "buried in *both* sleep and wine?" Is not one entombment sufficient? Virgil utters no such figurative absurdity. He expresses no figure in which tombs, intituled "wine," "sleep," filled with the corpses of a city, are pictured. He does declare that the conjoined influence of sleep and wine induces such profound stupor that all the noise of an invading army cannot break it.

Virgil speaks of another burial, *Æneid*, vi, 424, "*Occupat Æneas aditum custode sepulto.*" How was this "burial" effected? A medicated cake is thrown to the dog Cerberus, under the soporific influence of which he comes by *eating*, and is "buried;" as the Trojans came under the intoxicating influence of wine by *drinking*, and were "buried." But how was he "buried"? Why, by being *poured out* on the ground ("*fusus* humi"), if we may credit those interpreters who insist on "one meaning through an entire language." An odd sort of burial, to be sure; yet, this was all the burial that the three-headed sentinel received.

Suppose, now, we stood by the side of Æneas, and looked down upon that monster, stretched out through the whole length of the cave; how much of a "burial" would we suppose to be in "sepultus," or even in "sepultus in somno," as applied to that unentombed object?

Take another case: *Æneid*, iii, 630, "*Nam simul expletus dapibus, vinoque sepultus.*" "Burial in wine" is a strange sort of a figure. Wine is "the drink which merses"— buries; not the element *in which* mersion or burial takes place. Picture-figure here fails. Influence is the only and most sufficient source of explanation. If confirmation were needed, it is found in another parallel passage: "*Rutuli somno vinoque soluti,*" ix, 236.

Now, suppose we press on this language, as is done in the other cases, and insist that as "solvo" means to dissolve, so, "sleep and wine" are figured as liquids *in which* the Rutuli are placed to be "dissolved"! There is as much good sense in this as making "sleep and wine," in the other cases, *sepulchres*. But few will urge such picture-figure; but if they cannot in the one case, they may not in the other. In all such cases, *mergo, sepelio, solvo,* are used to exhibit the development of strong influence; each one with its peculiar shade of thought. "Sleep and wine," both, induce great relaxation of the muscular system, and therein is the ground of the use of "solvo;" and a relaxed body "stretched at great length on the ground," is like water "poured along;" therefore, the application of "fusus" to Cerberus. "Wine and sleep" are influential *agencies* in relaxing the limbs of the Rutuli, and not a mixture *in which* they are "dissolved."

I only add, that the translation "*in* wine and sleep," does not secure a figurative mersion or burial. Picturing is still excluded, and influence remains sovereign. We say a man drunk is "in liquor;" do we mean to utter figure, or to express influence?

Pope describes one of his Dunciad heroes thus:

> "Where Bentley late tempestuous wont to sport
> In troubled waters, but now sleeps *in Port.*"

His annotator remarks: "A certain wine called Port, from Oporto, a city of Portugal, of which this Professor invited him to drink abundantly."

Now, shall we be told that the poet does, here, "by an elegant figure," put Mr. Bentley to sleep "*in*" a cask of Port wine? Does—"*in* troubled waters"—merse or bury *in* water? What shall be said of criticism which tears words out of organic phrases, and by them conjures up such "elegant figures"? Stones, in a heap, may be handled and treated disjunctly; but when builded into an arch, they can only be treated in their relations to each other, unless our purpose be destruction. Words, in combination, have a common life, which perishes when they are torn asunder.

While Livy and Virgil speak of the controlling influence, conjointly exercised, of wine and sleep, Seneca speaks of the specific power of wine to intoxicate.

CONCLUSIONS FROM USAGE.

1. Mergo represents no definite form of action; is, alike, indifferent to the movement of the object or the element; is equally competent to take a world or a grain of sand for its object; makes no limit of time; puts no bounds to force; establishes no modes of action; claims intusposition for its object, and securing that has performed its duty, and ceases its functions in primary relations.

2. *Secondarily:* Mergo represents a condition which is the result of some controlling influence; the nature of the condition being limited and determined, only, by the nature of the influence, extending through the wide range of purification by sprinkled water-drops, to death by flaming thunderbolts.

3. *Absolutely:* Mergo represents influence destructive in character.

4. *Appropriation:* Mergo means *to drown, to make drunk.* Facts, in this direction, were of constant occurrence, and daily use would stamp specific meaning. Fitness to express the meaning *to purify* is equally good; but evidence for such usage, in fact, is not so strong.

5. With peculiarities of usage, such as must occur, the general features of usage in mergo and immerse are in the most perfect harmony, rather are identical.

6. The characteristics of mergo are in strongest contrast with those of βάπτω, tingo, and dip. If a defiled man seeking purification is commanded to merse his head for this purpose in purifying water, and, its influence having been secured, takes it out again, mergo makes no complaint because he did not keep it there until *another* influence of the water, *drowning,* was secured. If any one should be pleased to say, because of this mode of securing the controlling influence of purifying water, that mergo and dip mean the same thing, he must hold controversy, not with me, but with common sense, with the old Romans, and with the masters in English.

ΒΑΠΤΙΖΩ.

WHAT DOES IT MEAN?

WE pursue our inquiry, guided by, and submissive to, the Horatian law,

"Usus
Quem penès arbitrium est, et jus, et norma loquendi."

In doing this, I stand before the same tribunal with Dr. Carson, who says: "I have appealed to a higher tribunal than the authority of all critics—*to use itself*."

"Truth is on every man's side." Then, this utterance, faithfully interpreted, will not be adverse to any of us, whatever it may be.

May we seek, with all docility, the guidance of the Spirit of Truth, that we may be "led by Him into all truth" necessary for our good, and promotive of the glory of His Name!

Whatever of time or labor may have been demanded to pass over the preceding discussion, few, I hope, will consider the one or the other wastefully expended in view of the vantage-ground which has been thus, and could only thus have been, secured for a discriminating and authoritative determination of this long-debated word.

The words examined clearly belong to two distinct classes. Each class has its own deeply marked and broadly distinguishing characteristics. And may we not affirm, as a point beyond controversy, that *no word can belong to both these classes?*

If, now, the word which we are about to examine belongs to either class, its usage cannot be ambiguous, nor leave a shadow of doubt as to the class to which it must be attached. Its classification having been determined, its development, under the exigencies of language, must be assumed to be in harmony with its original nature.

USAGE OF ΒΑΠΤΙΖΩ.

INTUSPOSITION WITHOUT INFLUENCE.

PRIMARY USE.

1. Ὄυς ὅταν μὲν ἄμπωτις ᾖ μὴ βαπτίζεσθαι.
   Aristotle, *Wonderful Reports.*
2. Ἀβάπτιστόν τε καθ' ὕδωρ φελλόν. *Archias, Epigr.* x.
3. Ἐβάπτισ' εἰς τὸν οἶνον. *Julian, Egypt. Cupid,* p. 223.
4. Οὖν ἰδόντες οὐ βαπτιζομένους. *Lucian, True History,* ii, 4.
5. Ἐς Ὠκεανοῖο ῥόον βαπτίζετο Τιτήν. *Orphei, Argonautica,* 512.
6. Ἐμβαπτισμένας ταῖς τέλμασιν. *Plutarch, Sylla,* xxi.
7. Ἀσκος βαπτίζῃ. *Plutarch, Theseus,* xxiv.
8. Ἕως τῶν μαστῶν οἱ πεζοὶ βαπτιζόμενοι. *Polybius,* iii, 72, 4.
9. Βαπτιζομένου τοῦ δρυΐνου βάρει. *Polybius,* xxxiv, 3, 7.
10. Βαπτίζεται μέχρι κεφαλῆς. *Porphyry, Abstinence,* p. 282.
11. Ὥστε μόλις βαπτίζεσθαι. *Strabo,* xii, 2, 4.
12. Μέχρι ὀμφαλοῦ βαπτιζομένων. *Strabo,* xiv, 3, 9.

MERSION WITHOUT INFLUENCE.

PRIMARY USE.

1. Which when it is ebb tide are not mersed—(sea-coast).
2. And cork unmersed by water—(fishing-net).
3. I mersed him into the wine—(Cupid).
4. Seeing them not mersed—(men with cork feet).
5. The sun mersed himself into the ocean flood.
6. Mersed in the marshes—(armor).
7. A bladder, thou mayest be mersed; but there is no decree for thee to sink.
8. The infantry being mersed up to the breasts.
9. The oak (fishing-spear) being mersed by the weight.
10. He is mersed to the head.
11. So that it is hardly mersed—(dart).
12. Being mersed to the waist.

GENERAL REMARKS.

1. Such cases of usage present a favorable opportunity for determining the meaning, inasmuch as there are no complications arising from influence exerted by the mersion over the object. I have given all the cases of this class with which I have met.

2. There is no semblance, in any one of these cases, of the meaning *to dip*. Cupid is put into the wine without being taken out. He is swallowed by the drinker.

3. There is as little semblance of any other modal act being the exponent of the Greek word, since a variety of modal acts, entirely distinct in character—flowing, sinking, in-putting, falling, throwing, walking—do equally well, and with equal authority perform the baptism.

4. No exposition can meet the facts of the case which does not remove βαπτίζω from the class of verbs expressive of modality in action (whether general or particular), and place it among those which, immediately, demand condition, leaving the form and character of the act securing that condition unexpressed and uncared for.

5. Βαπτίζω has no alliance with βάπτω, *tingo*, and *dip*. It is in most intimate accord with *mergo* and *merse*.

PARTICULAR CASES.

"1." "They say that the Phœnicians inhabiting the region called Gadira, sailing beyond the Pillars of Hercules, with an easterly wind, four days, reach to certain desert places full of rush and seaweed; which when it is ebb tide are not mersed; but when it is full tide are flooded."

ARISTOTLE.

The tidal movement of the Atlantic may have furnished a theme for " Wonderful Report " to the Greeks of Aristotle's day, but it has long since ceased to be classed among "wonders."

The baptism which took place under the operation of the tidal wave, we understand, in all its features, as well as if we had formed a portion of the Phœnician party. The modus of the baptism, as to the act done, is settled beyond controversy. This is of the first importance. Whenever the mode of baptism is not expressly stated, our Baptist friends place their back against the word, and make battle, *à l'outrance*, for "one meaning through all Greek literature," and that meaning—"dip, and nothing but dip." And even here, where it is admitted that the modal act, as declared, is the very antipodal of *dip*, the great controversialist strenuously affirms that it is only, after all, a more beautiful way of saying *dip!* But while Carson is bold enough to vindicate the Baptist dogma by the audacious transmutation of water flowing over an object, into the dipping of an object into water, others, who love the Baptist system as dearly as himself, are unwilling to follow where they see common sense so hopelessly wrecked. Still, even these decline to acknowledge that they have misunderstood the force of the word, and evade the force of the staggering blow, received by their system, by slipping in a word to which is assigned, in exigencies, a double rôle; and pass on from the sea-coast to other scenes of baptism, where "dip" can once more, with some greater show of plausibility, be brought to the foreground.

It will be instructive to look with some particularity at the manner in which leading Baptist writers treat this baptism, all of whose elements are thoroughly understood, and without question from any quarter, seeing that it does, on its face, crush the Baptist doctrine as to the meaning of βαπτίζω.

(1.) The following shows the deep impression, half accepted, half rejected, made by the case on Dr. Gale: " Βαπτί-ζεσθαι being used, here, to sighify the land was under water, by the water's coming in upon it, and not by its being put into the water, some, perhaps, may think it a considerable objection; but it will be found of no advantage to our adversaries, if it be observed, that it here necessarily and unavoidably imports to be under water, or to be overwhelmed or covered with water; and this being the plain sense of this place, 'tis natural enough to say, as it were, or in a manner, or some such expression is to be understood. Besides, the word βαπτίζω, perhaps, does not so necessarily express the action of putting under water, as, in general, a thing's being in that condition, no matter how it comes so, whether it is put into the water, or the water comes over it; tho' indeed to put into water is the most natural way and the most common, and is, therefore, usually and pretty constantly, but it may be not necessarily required."—pp. 116, 117.

If this tidal wave did not carry the learned Gale high up on the shores of truth, it certainly did bring him very near to its " coasts," and he has, thence, brought back a very " Wonderful Report" to his Baptist brethren. He tells them, that the " sea-coasts, west of the Pillars of Hercules, have quite unsettled his notion as to the meaning of βαπτίζω. It sometimes, certainly, means one thing, and, perhaps, pretty constantly, means something quite the contrary, but what it does really mean he will not undertake to say."

In this " report" there is much of honesty, and no little of *naiveté*.

(2.) Dr. Carson has visited this same spot to inquire into this famous classical baptism; let us hear what he has to say in relation to it.

" Now, though the water comes over the land, and there is no actual exemplification of the mode expressed by this word, yet it still expresses that mode; and the word has been employed for the very purpose of expressing it. The peculiar beauty of the expression consists in figuring the object, which is successively bare and buried under water, as being dipped when it is covered, and as emerging when it is bare."

This is a very imperial, not to say a very empirical, mode of disposing of Aristotle's contradiction of the Baptist exposition of a Greek word. Dr. Gale modestly confesses that Aristotle's use of the word, so different from his own understanding of it, clouds the meaning. Dr. Carson says, it illuminates the meaning with all the effulgence of poetry and rhetoric. Dr. Gale once ventured to sport with figure and rhetoric, on a large scale, and " dipped a lake into the blood of a frog." For this he was roundly chidden by Carson, who declared that " there never was such a figure," and pronounced it to be " a paradox in rhetoric." It is now Gale's turn to rehearse in his teacher's ear the lesson which he received, and to inquire, " on what page of Rhetoric, or of the beauties of Poetry, we are to look for an indorsement of ' the peculiar beauty in figuring' the sea-coast as picked up and dipped into the rising tide?" Without waiting for an answer to this inquiry, I would remark, that " the peculiar beauty" of this figure is sadly marred by its being " lame of a leg." " Dip" requires both that its object should be put into and taken out of the water, or, to use the Doctor's language, be " buried and bare;" but unfortunately this was not Aristotle's notion of the meaning of $\beta\alpha\pi\tau i\zeta\omega$, as he has employed it to express one of these conditions only, and used another word to express the other. Dr. Carson, therefore, in converting this very prosaic narrative into poetry, and making $\beta\alpha\pi\tau i\zeta\omega$ officiate as a dipper, can furnish him with but one leg to stand upon.

The transformation of " flowing over" into *dipping into*, is farther vindicated, thus: " Common conversation exemplifies this mode of expression every day; and mere children understand its import. When a person has been drenched with rain, he will say that he has got a *dipping*. Here dipping does not lose its modal import, but immediately suggests it to the mind, and intends to suggest it. But were the English language one of the dead languages, and this expression subjected to learned criticism, it would be alleged that the word *dipping* does not denote mode, but wetting without reference to mode."

Dr. Carson is not more happy in expounding the secondary use of *dip* (supposing it to have such use as he indicates), than in pointing out the rhetorical beauty of *dipping* the sea-coast by the rise and fall of the tide.

The word "dipping" I have never heard used in the connection stated; but *ducking* (an equivalent word), I have. "He was caught in the rain and got a ducking," is a phrase in familiar use. But it is amusing to hear Dr. Carson say that the children (whether of smaller or larger growth) who use such language "design" to give utterance to highly wrought rhetorical figure, "the peculiar beauty of which consists in figuring the object as successively bare and buried under water." Is it not marvellous that any one should think of affirming that a child who speaks of "having got a *ducking* in a shower," means to flash before his playmates' imagination a picture in which he is seen to go under and come out of the water of a mill-pond, or the like! There is, now, before my eye an account of some boys who held one of their companions under the pump, while others "ducked" him by *pumping water upon him.* Is this, too, an elegantly rhetorical use of language representing the object as successively "bare and buried"? In the sea-coast baptism there is a "bare and buried;" but where is it found in the shower *dipping,* or the pump *ducking?* And in the coast baptism there is no basis for such figure, because the twain are not one; but each is designated by an independent word.

Before "the English language is numbered with the dead" and given over to "learned criticism," I wish to say, that both "dipping" and "ducking," as thus popularly used, do mean, and can mean, nothing else, than simply *wetting* without reference to mode. When Walter Scott says, "the boat received the *shower* of brine which the animal spouted aloft, and Triptolemus had *a full share* of the immersion," the use of "shower," and "full share," precludes the idea of "design" to express "one mode of action by another mode of action" in employing "immersion." There is no "mode of action" in immerse, and the word is used to emphasize "the full share of" *wetting.*

But Carson is unwilling that any one should believe that Aristotle writes Greek after a fashion which overturns the Baptist system; he, therefore, presses the point thus: "In the same style we might say, that, at the flood, God immersed the mountains in the waters, though the waters came over them." "Might say this"? Why not say it? Is it not as proper to say that an object is "immersed" when "water comes over it," as when it is "put into the water"? What has "the immersion" to do with the one mode or the other mode? Here is laid bare the vicious element which runs through Baptist writings, to wit, the making "immerse" a verb of modal action; confounding it with dip; as, also, βαπτίζω is confounded with βάπτω. And worse than this is the use, as exigency requires, of immerse, also, as an *immodal* word, with no intimation of the double, groundless, and contradictory sense. God did "immerse the mountains in the waters of the flood;" but no one since the flood, except the very eminent controversialist of Tubbermore, ever thought of saying that in this statement "immersed" is used with the design of expressing, with great beauty of rhetoric, the lifting up of the mountains and *dipping* them into the flood!

It is still farther urged: "The thing here supposed to be baptized was wholly *buried* under water. Can any child, then, be at a loss to learn from this that baptism means *to lay under water ?* Who, then, can be at a loss to know the meaning of the word baptism?"

Then, after all, there was no baptism of the sea-coast. It was only a "supposed" baptism! Observe how uncompromisingly Carson holds on to the idea that a baptism is *a dipping*, and nothing else is. He stands by the dogma of Baptists in opposition to Aristotle; because he knows that to abandon it is to abandon the citadel of his denomination, and to lower the controversial banner under which

16

they have so long and so manfully done battle. Carson, "the man whose like will not arise for a thousand years," felt that this was the point which Baptists had undertaken to defend against the world; he believed it to be true with all his heart, and because he believed it he cast in his lot with them; and he felt that he could not give it up even with Aristotle against him, for with it went, as he believed, everything. Now, when we see other Baptist writers compelled to give up, what Carson felt was giving up all, what shall we think? Must they not change their judgment of their great Leader, or surrender?

(3.) Dr. Fuller treats this passage thus: "A fourth case cited by Pœdobaptist authors is from Aristotle. It is produced to show that Baptizo does not always mean the act of plunging. My position is that Baptizo means *to immerse*. It matters not how the immersion is effected. And the passage is conclusive against those who adduce it."

This passage presents a very neat specimen of controversial tactics. It is confessed that the passage is cited against *plunge, dip, et id omne genus*, as the legitimate representatives of βαπτίζω. Does Dr. Fuller deny that it crushingly proves the point for which it is cited? He is dumb with silence. He has not a syllable to utter in defence of those cherished terms. How, then, does it happen that the passage is conclusive "against those who adduce it?" But why was the passage cited? Because Baptists for a century had proclaimed that "the word meant, always, *to dip, to plunge.*" Does Dr. Fuller deny this? And why does he say, "My position is that Baptizo means *to immerse*"? Why, because he is unwilling to go down in the Baptist boat sinking with its load of *modalism*, and he leaps overboard and swims to the shore, to lift up, not the old Baptist standard, but *Dr. Fuller's*—to wit, "*My* position is that Baptizo means immerse. It matters not how the immersion is effected."

If the passage cited has wrought with such tremendous effect, how is it "conclusive against those who adduce it"?

Does Dr. Fuller say: "But you believe in baptism by sprinkling, and this is not such baptism." I answer: When we adduce this passage to prove baptism by sprinkling, it will be time enough to say, it makes against us; until then it will be sufficient for the Doctor to note the sweeping execution which it makes in the direction for which it was cited.

In the new legend under which Dr. Fuller rallies, solitary and alone, we must not fail sharply to notice the absolute antagonism between the use of "immerse," and the same word as used by Carson. The latter uses "immerse" as the equivalent of *dip;* the former repudiates all such affinity, and declares that there is no necessary connection between them, and "it matters not how the immersion is effected." It is because of facts like these, in different writers, and in the same writer, that I complain of the "duplicity" which characterizes the use of this word. Carson builds his system on the use of dip and immerse as interchangeable equivalents. Fuller makes the corner-stone of "my position" the repudiation of this doctrine, and builds on "immerse" divorced from modalism.

The argument of Carson is pronounced by his friend to be a failure. What fate awaits that which is proposed as a substitute remains to be seen. The Doctor has a very cheering confidence in his success: "I have established, beyond all controversy, what is the only meaning of Baptizo" (p. 20). Having secured such a prize, one would suppose that he would hold it fast. But it seems not to be prized over highly. Witness the following: "You may be immersed in any manner you choose; but sprinkling and pouring are not modes of immersion" (p. 15). This is true only: 1. By abandoning "my position"— "immersion may be effected in any manner." Or, 2. By falling back on the *duplex* use of immersion, and giving it a modal character. For it is beyond denial that the *condition* of "immersion" may be effected by both sprinkling and pouring. Indeed he himself says: "Suppose a man should lie in the baptistery while it is filling. The pouring of the water would not be immersion, yet an immersion would take place if he remained long enough." "If the liquid is poured in such abundance that a baptism (immersion) follows, they cry out, There, how plain it is that to pour and to baptize is the same thing." Not too fast. One thing at a time. 1. We have here the confession that immersion may be effected by pouring, over against the denial that sprinkling and pouring are modes of immersion. 2. As to "the cry" made in view of this fact, we prefer making it ourselves, and in doing so declare, not that "to pour and to baptize are the same thing;" but that pouring is a mode by which baptism may be effected; and add to our cry this farther,—no well-informed person will say that "*to dip* and to baptize are the same thing." Thus Fuller lowers the time-worn standard—"dipping is baptizing, and baptizing is dipping,"—"a definite act,"— "mode, and nothing but mode,"—and unfurls in its stead the heretical motto—"immersion by pouring."

(4.) Dr. Conant translates, without comment, "immersed;" and Professor Ripley translates both $\beta\alpha\pi\tau\iota\zeta\omega$ and $\varkappa\alpha\tau\alpha\varkappa\lambda\dot{\upsilon}\zeta\omega$ by "*overflow;*" with the remark, that "these two words are equivalents." It may, certainly, be so used. But I would ask Professor Ripley if he ever knew $\beta\dot{\alpha}\pi\tau\omega$ and $\varkappa\alpha\tau\alpha\varkappa\lambda\dot{\upsilon}\zeta\omega$ to be used as equivalents?

Baptist writers have been allowed to speak freely on this passage; and we have seen the faith of Gale in modalism sadly shaken by the baptizing billows; while that of Fuller is wholly swept away. Carson, with unflinching courage, holds on to modality in its severest forms, and, with a boldness above that of England's king, plants his system by the sea-shore, and as the ocean billows dash over him and it, proclaims, from out the flood, "that it is only a supposed baptism, and the Prince of Philosophers only means to declare him *beautifully dipped.*"

Alexander Carson, LL.D., is a true representative man. He is the last of the giants among old-fashioned modal Baptists. No other such man will ever say—"to baptize is to dip, and to dip is to baptize." He claims the record, "If *dipping* could have been defended by any right hand, it would have been defended by this."

"3." "I found Cupid among the roses, and holding him by the wings I mersed him into the wine, and took and drank him." JULIAN, EGYPT.

"5." But when the Sun had mersed himself into the Ocean flood. ORPHEUS.

The use of εἰς in these passages does not prove that βαπτίζω expresses *motion*. All languages employ verbs expressive simply of position or condition in connection with prepositions which imply the existence of movement. In such cases the most commonly received interpretation is that which supplies a verb of motion.

Kühner gives the following examples: ἐφάνη λὶς εἰς ὁδόν—στὰς ἐς μέσον—παρῆσαν εἰς Σάρδεις—ἐς τὴν Σαλαμῖνα ὑπέκειται.

Virgil exhibits similar usage: *Sol quoque, et exoriens, et quum se condit in undas.* Ovid: *Mergit in ima ratem.* Seneca: *Mergere ad Styga.* The verb of motion involved in this latter phrase is expressed in a parallel passage by Ovid: *Mersa, Stygias penetrarit in undas.*

The same usage obtains in English: *He buried the ball into the wood. They landed the troops into Fort Pickens.*

"To appear," "to stand," "to be," "to lie," &c., do not express movement, yet they are conjoined with prepositions which require movement. In all the above cases such a verb must be supplied. The same is true with regard to βαπτίζω when it is used with εἰς, which usage is not frequent, and contrasts, in this respect, with that of βάπτω. This interpretation is sustained by the use of the word in such cases as that of "the coast baptism," and in all cases where the nature of the act affecting the condition is such as no one thinks of assigning to βαπτίζω.

The mersion of Cupid is not a dipping, for he remains

mersed in the wine until he is swallowed down by the drinker, within whom his "titillating wings" are soon felt.

" 2." And fishing-rod triply stretched, and cork un-mersed by water. ARCHIAS.

" 4." We wondered, therefore, seeing them not mersed, but sustained above the waves. LUCIAN.

" 7." A bladder, thou mayest be mersed; but there is no decree for thee to sink. PLUTARCH.

No modality of act can be gathered from these passages. The first two are negative, exhibiting their objects in an unmersed *condition;* and thus sustain the view that a baptized object is one which is brought into a definite *condition,* and not one which is made the subject of a definite action.

The third passage is an oracular response in reference to the fate of Athens. The interpretation of the passage turns on the nature of a skin filled with air. This may, by force, be placed in a state of mersion; but its nature is such that it makes constant resistance to a continuance in that state; and whenever the mersing power is removed, it will rise again to the surface unharmed, for a state of mersion is not destructive to a bladder. "To sink" is not a distinctive translation of δύνω, nor is it easy to furnish one; it is used as an equivalent of βαπτίζω; the idea being, that while the bladder might be mersed, for an indefinite time, it was not to continue in a state of mersion. The city might be subjected temporarily to foreign influences, but would recover from them.

Carson translates: " Thou mayest be dipped, O bladder, but thou art not fated to sink." On which Dr. Halley makes the following criticism : "And is it not surprising, if anything could surprise us, in the impetuous movements of theological controversy, that Dr. Carson should, in so many other places, render βαπτίζω *to sink,* or at least sur-

reptitiously introduce that word as its representative, but
here should make this self-same sink, his most obsequious
servant, come out the antagonist of baptize, and in opposition to the characteristic meaning of that word? Observe the tactics of the great defender of the Baptists.
What is to baptize? Something contrasted with sinking,
for so he expounds the oracle, and yet something identified
with sinking; for that word he often employs as its representative, as baptized in debt is, according to him, sunk
in debt. What is the difference between βαπτίζω and δύνω?
The former is only to dip, the latter to sink, according to
p. 61. To sink serves both for the synonyme and for the
opposite of baptize, as it may be needed, and therefore we
say, expurgate the book from that treacherous word, with
which it is so easy to play fast and loose throughout the
controversy" (p. 85).

This "surreptitious" use of sink and other words (among
which should be named, with emphasis, *immerse*) utterly
vitiates Carson's argument. Without the lawless interchange of words, widely removed in meaning, no plausibility could be given to the position, "βαπτίζω always means
to dip."

"6." And dying they filled the lake with dead bodies;
so that to the present many barbaric arrows, and helmets,
and pieces of iron breastplates and swords, mersed-in the
marshes, are found.   PLUTARCH.

Here is a condition of mersion in which these weapons
and pieces of armor are found after the lapse of a long
series of years. It will require Carson to rise from the
dead to pronounce this a case of *dipping*. His mantle has
fallen on no living man. All these bows, helmets, breastplates, swords, were equally mersed. Who will say that
they were mersed by the same modal act? If by acts of
diverse modality, who will say that βαπτίζω represents acts
contrariant in character? Who can believe that it makes

the slightest difference to this word how these articles got into this mersed condition? And does not the long repose of these relics in a state of mersion cast shame on any theory which takes βαπτίζω for its corner-stone, and carves on it in capitals—"TO DIP, AND NOTHING BUT DIP"?

The Greek word is compounded, in this passage, with ἐν, and is translated by Dr. Conant "im-merse." Thus no difference is made between the compound and the uncompounded word. And, farther, the preposition is local, and whether translated merse-in or immerse, the preposition only gives position to the articles mersed. This is always the force of the compound im-merse. The local preposition, or the element in which without a preposition, is rarely expressed. The word itself, as expressive of condition, carries (in primary use) locality with it, and the subject-matter shows the element. It is more necessary to state the mersing agency; and when the simple dative is used, it is employed to express such agency.

The passage exhibits, very fairly, the meaning of the contested word. And there is no point of sympathy with the Baptist theory. "But it makes against those who adduce it," says Dr. Fuller. May-be not. At any rate, we shall have a plea to enter, in good time, so that judgment will not go against us by default.

"12." Alexander falling upon the stormy season, and trusting, commonly, to fortune, pressed on before the flood went out, and through the entire day the army marched mersed up to the waist.   STRABO.

"8." They marched through with difficulty, the infantry being mersed up to the breasts.   POLYBIUS.

Carson (p. 58) says: "Polybius applies it to soldiers *wading* through deep water. Does not this decisively determine the meaning of baptizo? *They were* not, indeed, plunged overhead. That only was baptized which was buried. The soldiers in passing through the water were dipped as far as the breast."

Was there ever such a medley of words! Baptized by *wading*, baptized by *plunging*, baptized by *burying*, baptized by *dipping!* What a commentary on "the one meaning through all Greek literature," and that meaning, "mode, and nothing but mode." Some think the good people of Ireland a little disloyal; but I did not know that the charge covered such disloyal use of the King's or Queen's English as to say that, men walking through the water all day were *dipped!* Such confusion of terms and ideas gives indubitable proof of fundamental error in the conception of the meaning of the word.

The only act causative of this mersed condition of the soldiers is that of "wading" (Carson), "passing through" (Conant), or, technically, marching. Now, does the Greek word mean to wade, to pass through, to march? Yes, if it expresses the act which produces the mersion. No, if it expresses the condition resultant from any form of act competent to effect it. Which view does common sense and the laws of language sustain? Besides, we have the act producing the mersion stated by another word, ($\delta\iota\alpha$-$\beta\alpha\acute{\iota}\nu\omega$). "Going through" neither dips nor plunges. It does merse.

Speaking of the first of the above quotations, Carson says: "Dr. Gale gives some striking examples from Strabo;" and, then, he and Gale join in translating $\beta\alpha\pi\tau\acute{\iota}\zeta\omega$ by "sink," "sink or dipped." Then Carson adds: "Now, in these several passages, the modal meaning of the word is confirmed in so clear, express, and decisive a manner, that obstinacy itself cannot find a plausible objection."

It may be that no objection can be found against the testimony of such passages when adduced to prove that "$\beta\alpha\pi\tau\acute{\iota}\zeta\omega$ means to dip, always, and never expresses anything but mode;" for an objection implies general truth, or some truth, or, at least, an appearance of truth, while the offer of the testimony of such passages to prove a modal dipping is simply the baldest absurdity.

If Dr. Carson were to take the passage from Aristotle— "The berry, being pressed, MOISTENS (βάπτει) and colors the hand," and translate it—"The berry, being pressed, *dips* (βάπτει) and dyes the hand,"—then urge it as proving "the modal meaning of dip, in so clear, express, and decisive a manner, that obstinacy itself cannot find an objection," his assumption, that his readers have not intelligence above idiocy, would not be more manifest than, when, he adduces such passages as that from Strabo as proof of the modal act of dipping.

As the ocean tide *flows* over the Baptist theory, and merses it beyond redemption, so, every heel of the MARCH-ING armies of Strabo and Polybius tramples on it, and leaves it drowned beneath the waters.

"10." Being innocent, he advances, unhesitatingly, hav-ing the water to the knees; but when guilty, proceeding a short distance he is mersed up to the head.   PORPHYRY.

This transaction is represented as occurring at a lake in India, which, according to the Brahmins, has the power of revealing character.

This is another case of baptism by walking. Or, will any one say that the walking into the water and the bap-tizing were two distinct acts; that after "walking into the water up to his knees," he was then dipped "up to his head;" that mersion by walking is no baptism, while mer-sion by dipping is baptism? Will Professor Ripley say this? He does say (as we have seen), "No one believes that the going down into the water is the baptism; these two things are perfectly distinct: the baptism takes place after the descent into the water; it is expressed by another word." Well, Polybius, and Porphyry, and Strabo, had a different notion of baptism from the Professor. They thought that the action of walking was quite competent to effect a baptism without the help of any other word. If these sinners were dipped or plunged, we should, indeed, need another word; but Porphyry manages the baptism by the sole aid of προβαίνω. Surely, this passage brings neither aid nor comfort to the upholders of the dogma, "Baptizing is dipping, and dipping is baptizing." Porphyry, certainly, was a stranger to the doctrine. But, "the passage makes against those who adduce it." Is this the only wine and oil which can be found to alleviate the deadly wounds of Baptist theory? Remember, "a wise man does not determine a matter before he heareth it." Wait and hear.

" 9." Although the spear should fall out into the sea, it is not lost; for it is constructed out of both oak and pine, so that the oaken part being mersed by the weight, the rest is floating and easily recovered.   POLYBIUS.

The modal act in this baptism is *sinking*. So much of the spear as is mersed, is mersed by the act of sinking in consequence of greater specific gravity. Now, shall we on this account say, βαπτίζω expresses the modal act of sinking?

There is no dipping in the passage. The axe which fell into the Jordan and sank, was not dipped. The fish-spear which fell out of the vessel and sank, so far as it became mersed, was not dipped. Whether it was recovered immediately, or whether it be unrecovered to this hour, does not affect the nature of the transaction. The action of falling and sinking cannot be converted into the action of dipping. Nor can the condition of mersion, the result of the action of falling and sinking, undergo the metamorphosis of passing out of condition into this twofold, or any other form of action.

The weight, causing the mersion, is expressed by the

dative without a preposition; which is the common mode
of indicating the baptizing power.

"11." To one throwing down a javelin, from above,
into the channel, the force of the water resists so much
that it is hardly mersed.   STRABO.

This is the case of a stream flowing rapidly through
a contracted channel.   The act of baptism is "throwing
down."   This is as good a modal act for baptizing as any
other, of some scores, that might be mentioned.   Shall we
append it to the list of meanings expressed by that marvellous Greek word?   Or, wearied with such havoc made
of the laws of language, shall we exclaim — *Ohe! jam
satis est.*

RESULTS.

All the cases of primary use, in which the mersed object
remains uninfluenced by the mersion, have, now, been
examined.   Most persons will accept the following results:

1. The confounding together of such widely separated
words as βάπτω and βαπτίζω is as surprising as it is unwarranted.

These words have spheres of their own, and as they do
not, in truth, trench on each other, so they should not, by
our error, be made to do so.

Bapting is not Baptizing, neither is Baptizing Bapting.

2. To represent βαπτίζω by *dip* is wholly destitute of
authority from Greek writers.

3. The corner-stone of the Baptist system—"Dipping
is Baptizing, and Baptizing is Dipping," is pure error.
While the attempt to sustain that system by the admix-
ture of dip and immerse is a mixing together of iron and
clay, which truth will break in pieces.

4. Any attempt to make βαπτίζω express, immediately, form of action and not condition, must prove abortive, because unfounded in truth.

5. The demand of βαπτίζω is for intusposition. To secure this it lays equal claim upon any act, or upon any number of acts, which may be competent and needful to meet the demand.

6. While some objects remain unaffected by intusposition within a fluid, or other closely investing element, it is obvious, that such a condition gives fullest opportunity for the exercise of the peculiar influence of the investing element over the enveloped object.

7. Βαπτίζω is without limitation of power, object, or duration. Limitations, in these respects, must come outside of itself.

We now proceed to consider that class of baptisms which influences the object baptized.

INTUSPOSITION WITH INFLUENCE.

1. Ὅπως τὸ μὲν βαπτιζόμενον τῆς νηὸς ἀνακουφίσαιμεν.

                     Achilles Tat. iii, 1.

2. Καὶ μικροῦ βαπτίζεται τὸ σκάφος.   "   "   iii, 1.

3. Βαπτίζει τοῦ λογισμοῦ τὴν ἀναπνοήν.   "   "   iv, 10.

4. Τῆς νεὼς κινδυνευούσης βαπτίζεσθαι. *Æsop, Shepherd and the Sea.*

5. Τὴν ψυχὴν ἄγαν βεβαπτισμένην τῷ σώματι. *Alex. Aphrod.* i, 28.

6. Βεβαπτισμένην ἐν τῷ βάθει τοῦ σώματος.   "   "   ii, 38.

7. Ἀθρόως καταβαπτίζει καὶ σβέννυσι.   "   "   i, 16.

8. Περιληφθέντα διαφθείρεται βάπτιζόμενα.   *Diod. Sic.* i, 36.

9. Τῆς δὲ νεὼς βαπτισθείσης, ταραχὴ κατέσχε.   "   "   xi, 18.

10. Καταφερόμενος πολλοὺς ἐβάπτιζε.   "   xvi, 80.

11. Τά τε πλοῖα. . . . ναυλοχοῦντα βαπτισθῆναι.

              Dion. Cass. Rom. Hist. xxxvii, 58.

12. Ὅι δὲ καὶ. . . . ΄ ὑπὸ τοῦ βάρους αὐτῶν βαπτισθέντες.

              Dion. Cass. Rom. Hist. xli, 42.

13. Ὅι μὲν ὑπὸ τοῦ πνεύματος. . . . . ἐβαπτίζοντο.

              Dion. Cass. Rom. Hist. lxxiv, 13.

14. Ὃς νῦν τετάρτην ἡμέραν βαπτίζεται.   *Eubulus, Nausicaa.*

15. Ἐν νηὶ μεγάλη. . . . . πλέων βαπτίζεσθαι.   *Epictet. Mor. Dis.* xi.

16. Ἤδη δὲ βαπτιζομένων καὶ καταδῦναι μικρὸν. *Heliod. Æthiop.* v, 28.

17. Τὴν νῆα πολλοῖσι φορτίοισι βαπτίσαντα.   *Hippocrates,* iii, 809.

18. Καὶ ἀνέπνεεν ὡς ἐκ τοῦ βεβαπτίσθαι.   "   iii, 571.

19. Ὡς βαπτισθέντος. . . . ὥς τε θερμανθῆναι. *Homer, Life of;* ii, 26.

20. Καὶ ἔτι ἐν τῷ σώματι βεβαπτισμένη.   *Plotinus, Ennead.* i, 8, 13.

21. Ἀπερίτρεπτον καὶ ἀβάπτιστον.   *Plutarch, Animals,* xxxv.

22. Ὑπ' αὐτῶν βαπτιζόμενοι καὶ καταδύνοντες. *Polybius, Hist.* v, 47.

23. Οὐδὲ γὰρ τοῖς ἀκολύμβοις βαπτίζεσθαι συμβαίνει. *Strabo,* vi, 2, 9.

24. Μηδὲ βαπτίζεσθαι τὸν ἐμβάντα.   "   xiv, 2, 42.

25. Ἐβαπτίζοντο ὑπὸ τῆς πανοπλίας.   *Suidas, Lexicon.*

BAPTISM WITH INFLUENCE.

1. That we might raise up the mersed part of the ship.
2. And the ship is nearly mersed.
3. Merses the breathing of the intellect.
4. The ship in hazard of being mersed.
5. The soul being mersed very much by the body.
6. Mersed in the depth of the body.
7. Suddenly demerses and quenches the vital warmth.
8. Many inclosed by the river perish, being mersed.
9. His ship having been mersed, confusion seized the fleet.
10. Carrying down many, mersed and destroyed them.
11. And ships anchored were mersed.
12. And others perished, mersed, by their own weight, in the very vessels.
13. Some were mersed by the wind, using it immoderately.
14. Who is mersed, now, the fourth day.
15. To be mersed sailing in a large and elegant vessel.
16. Mersed and ready to go down.
17. Mersed the ship by much freight.
18. And breathed as one out of a state of mersion.
19. So mersed as to be warmed.
20. Mersed, still, in the body.
21. Not liable to be overturned and un-mersible.
22. Mersed by themselves and sinking in the marshes.
23. It does not happen to those unable to swim to be mersed.
24. Nor is one entering it mersed, but lifted out.
25. They were mersed by the full armor.

PARTICULAR CASES EXAMINED.

BAPTISM BY STORM.

1. "We all, therefore, changed our position to the higher parts of the ship, that we might raise up the mersed part of the vessel."   Achilles Tatius.

2. "The wind changes suddenly to the other side of the ship, and it is nearly mersed."   Achilles Tatius.

4. "A severe storm occurring, and the ship in hazard of being mersed, throwing out all the cargo into the sea, he was hardly saved by the empty ship."   Æsop.

9. "The commander was slain, and his ship being mersed, confusion seized the fleet of the barbarians."   Diodorus Siculus.

11. "The vessels which were in the Tiber, and anchored at the city and at its mouth, were mersed."   Dion Cassius.

15. "As you would not wish, sailing in a large and elegant and gilded ship, to be mersed."   Epictetus.

16. "Already being mersed and wanting little of going down, some of the pirates, at first, attempted to pass into their own boat."   Heliodorus.

17. "Shall I not ridicule one mersing his ship by much freight, the blaming the sea for sinking it full."   Hippocrates.

21. "Of many models, the only one not to be overturned and unmersible."   Plutarch.

(1.) All these cases, except the last, refer to the loss of vessels at sea by storm or otherwise. Such cases are too fully self-explicative to need detailed remarks. *Βάπτω* is never used in such cases, and, thus, is separated from βαπτίζω.

(2.) *To sink* is the final act of mersion in all these cases, yet Baptists never bring this word into the foreground as their meaning, although "dip" has no claims in comparison with it. It is, not unfrequently, slipped in as a necessity.

(3.) Conant commonly translates such cases by "submerged." Why *sub*-merged rather than *im*-merged or im-*mersed*, if all mean the same thing? And, why these prepositions and diversities when the Greek word has none, and remains the same?

(4.) He also translates, in the third passage, "Saved *in* the empty ship." In itself considered, this is of no moment: yet, as the dative case claims an important position among the determining elements of this inquiry, we should study accuracy and uniformity in all such cases.

This dative is without a preposition, and is not locative. It is, indeed, true that the shepherd was saved in the ship, but this is not the fact designed to be stated. He was in the ship, loaded or empty, and, of course, he was to be saved in the ship; but we are told that he could not be saved by a *loaded* ship, and, therefore, he tried to save himself *by* an empty ship, and was successful. The point of the statement is, that by a loaded ship he would be lost, while by an empty ship he would be saved.

The importance of the passage is not in the sentiment, but in securing the proper treatment of the case.

(5.) All these cases exhibit the mersion as attended with influence in the highest degree. It is destructive in its nature.

In all the usage of βάπτω there is nothing which approaches this, either in measure or kind.

(6.) The duration of the mersion, in connection with these facts, has not yet run out; although, in some cases,

17

it has already lasted two thousand years. It will continue until "the seas give up their dead." Mersion is not, necessarily, of prolonged duration; but it is without any self-limitation. It is permanent, except made otherwise by some extraneous influence.

Does this look like a dipping?

(7.) It is the indefinitely long continuance of mersion which qualifies it to exert a controlling influence over objects physically mersed, and which makes it the representative word for any controlling influence (not associated with physical mersion), however that influence be induced.

INTUSPOSITION WITH INFLUENCE.

BAPTISM BY WEIGHT.

12. "Crowds of them fleeing perished; some in embarking upon the boats, thrown down by the press; others, even in the boats mersed by their own weight."

Dion Cassius.

13. "Attempting to escape, some way or other, some of them were mersed by the wind, using it immoderately; others were destroyed, being overtaken by the enemy."

Dion Cassius.

22. "But mersed by themselves, and sinking in the marshes, were all useless, and many of them were destroyed."

Polybius.

23. "Pools near Agrigentum have the taste of salt water, but a different nature; for it does not happen to the unskilled in swimming to be mersed." Strabo.

24. "Then floating, through the nature of the water, according to which, we have said, to swim was not necessary; nor is one entering it mersed, but lifted out."

Strabo.

25. "They were mersed by the full armor." SUIDAS.

In all these cases of mersion "the act of baptism" is sink, and nothing but sink. Yet I do not know of any Baptist writer who gives this act as the act of baptism. Recognized it has to be; but it is an acquaitance to which they have no partiality; in whose presence they do not feel comfortable, and from whom they part as soon as possible.

There is, of course, a reason for this. What it is, it is not difficult to discover. There is too wide a gulf between dip and sink for the patrons of the former to extend their countenance to the latter. Sink is a very explicit and homely English word, that everybody can understand, and to say that the " one meaning running through all Greek literature" is *sink*, would be to sink the cause; therefore, it is toned down into the Latinism—" sub-merged."

It would hardly answer to insist on a divine command " to sink men in water;" but if a modal act must be assigned to the Greek word, none has a better claim than sink. The truth, however, is, that such is not its meaning; and to look for its meaning in any such direction is fruitful only in disappointment. Sink, like a cloud of other words, puts its object in a state of mersion; but neither it nor they can claim to be expressed, distinctively, by βαπτίζω.

The influence of this mersion is destructive.

BAPTISM BY FLOWING OR UPRISING.

2. " The blood boiling up, through great force, often overflows the veins, and flowing round the head within, merses the breathing (passage) of the intellect."

ACHILLES TATIUS.

6. " Why do some, being alarmed, die? Because the physical power fleeing, overmuch, into the depth, with the blood, all at once sub-merses and quenches the natural and vital warmth which is at the heart, and causes death."

ALEXANDER APHRODISIAS.

7. " Many of the land animals, surrounded by the river, perish, being mersed; but some, fleeing to the high places, are saved." DIODORUS SICULUS.

9. " The river, with a stronger current, rolling down, mersed many, and, swimming through with their arms, destroyed them." DIODORUS SICULUS

Very brief comment will suffice for these passages.

" 2." This is the case of a person who has fallen down, in a state of unconsciousness.

" Whelm" (*Conant*). This translation ignores "the act of baptism." That act was " flowing round " (περικλύζω), which is materially different from dip. Such cases show how vain is the attempt to fasten on to βαπτίζω the form of any act, whatever, by which an object is put into a fluid element; and, no less, any attempt to stamp it with the form of any movement by which a fluid is brought upon its object. It is only surprising that such an attempt should ever have been made. Should it be persevered in, I nominate, as a worthy candidate, for "the one modal meaning through all Greek literature"—*flowing round!*

" 6." The act of baptism is the same with the preceding,—flowing of the blood.

" Whelm" (*Conant*). Whelm neither immerses nor immerges (in the sense put into); nor submerges (in the sense put, moving the object, under); nor dips, nor plunges, nor imbathes (in the sense bathing by putting into). If this be a just and distinctive translation, what becomes of dip and plunge as distinctive translations?

But the point of special interest, in this passage, is the unanswerable proof which it furnishes, that a heated body may be " quenched" by pouring, or, in any other way, bringing water over a heated mass. The vital warmth

was baptized and quenched by blood pouring over it.
Baptist writers have ever insisted, most uncompromisingly, that there was but one way in which heated metals
could be quenched by baptism, and that was by dipping
them into water. This error is, here, made patent. The
mode which is orthodox for baptizing the vital warmth, is
equally orthodox for baptizing heated metal.

" 7." The inundation of the Nile is the subject of description.

It seems hardly credible that Carson should offer this as
a case of modal dipping, and yet it is even so. It is well
to have a writer who uses a pen which leaves a mark so
bold in character, that he who runs may read, as otherwise
it would soon be questioned that such extravagant views
were ever held, or that it was ever said, that "βαπτίζω meant
dip and nothing else." This is his language: " The whole
land, overwhelmed, might be said to be modally dipped,
by catachresis, and that the animals would at first swim,
and then sink, and be entirely immersed. The sinking
of animals is here called baptism. What, then, is baptism
but immersion?"

Here is a *mélange* of words which exhibits a remarkable
rhetorical and logical monstrosity. Egypt might, by the
Nile's inundation, " be said to be *modally dipped*." Undoubtedly it might be so said; but not outside of a lunatic
asylum. But if Egypt, or any part of it, might be said to
be " modally dipped," Diodorus says nothing about the
land being dipped or baptized, but the animals only.
Might it, also, be said that these drowned animals were
" modally dipped by catachresis"? Such catachrestic dippings would not answer in Tubbermore baptisms. But
" the animals swim, then sink, then are immersed." Can
there be the shadow of a doubt as to the sense in which
" immersed" is, here, used? Is there any possibility for
its meaning *to dip*, even " by catachresis"? Does it not
represent the condition of the animals after sinking, and

as a consequence of the act of sinking? Is there not, therefore, an elimination of the expression of act on its own part? And this is the true and only proper use of the word. But Dr. Carson tells us, in the opening of his book, that the modal act dip, and immerse, are equivalents; while, here, he uses it stripped of all modal act, and expressive of condition resultant from the act of sinking. Such is the duplicity of use (not of intention) which marks this word. "The sinking of animals is here called baptism." This is error. It is neither here said, nor can it be said, that sinking is baptism. The one word expresses an act, and the other a condition. They cannot, with any propriety, be interchanged. Sink, on this occasion, as flow, fall, throw, walk, &c., &c., &c., on other occasions, expresses the form of the act by which the drowning-baptism took place.

"What, then, is baptism but immersion?" Logic would reply: "If the sinking of animals is called baptism," then "baptism must be *sinking*." But this would not answer Baptist need, nor "the one meaning throughout Greek literature;" therefore, the duplicity-word—immersion— must be slipped in, and in a sense which gives it mode. For if sinking is baptism and baptism is immersion, then immersion is the modal act,—*sinking;* which is not true. The passage reminds us, very forcibly, of "nodding Homer." Indeed, Dr. Carson's book of half a thousand pages, so far as intended to prove that "βαπτίζω means to dip and nothing but dip," is one long nod.

Dr. Fuller expounding the passage says, "the violent current sank many." The Doctor forgets that the sea-coast Baptism made him flee from a modal act to immodal immerse—exclaiming, with conscious relief, "*My* position is that βαπτίζω means to immerse." Why has that position been abandoned for this *sinking* position? Are immerse and sink the same? The sea-coast was admitted to be neither dipped nor plunged; was it "sunk"?

Baptist writers (seeing that the suggestion of difficulty in the translation of this word is all "a pretence," and that it has but one meaning, of which they are the perfect masters) present themselves, in their writings, in a rather remarkable aspect by such colliding translations.

"9." This is a death baptism by a strong river current.

These baptisms are a sort of dipping hardly contemplated in "Baptizing is dipping, and dipping is baptizing." They exhibit an influence exerted over their object such as no Greek ever used βάπτω to express, and to which no one, in a sane mind, would apply *dip*.

BAPTISM THROUGH FOUR DAYS—"DROWNED"—"DRUNK."

"12." "Who is mersed, now the fourth day, wearing away the life of a miserable, starveling mullet."
EUBULUS.

"Immerged" (*Conant*). Why, rather than immersed, dipped, plunged, I do not know. He says: "It is spoken with comic extravagance of one whose vessel is wrecked in a storm, and a prey to the ingulfing floods." A translation from the Athenæus of Schweighauser is given:

"Qui nunc quartum in diem undis mergitur
Jejunam miseri mugilis terens vitam."

A similar translation is given in *Athenæi Deipnosophistarum*, Lugduni, 1612:

"Quartum jam diem, in aqua, mergitur
Misellique Nestios Cestrei vitam agit."

Dr. Fuller takes a different view of the passage: "Athenæus quotes an ancient author, who says of a drunken man: He is drowned or sunk (baptized) now the fourth day, leading the life of a miserable mullet."

The limited examination which I have been able to give the passages, in a library some distance from my home, does not warrant my acting as umpire between these parties. Whether this unfortunate man was "immerged," or

" drowned," or " sunk," or " made drunk," his case is a much more serious one than it could have been under any condition of *dipping*.

" Four days " is a long time to pass through the process of dipping.

———————

" 16." " For, indeed, hereby he shows greater emphasis, as if the sword were so mersed as to be warmed."

HOMER'S LIFE AND POETRY.

" Imbathed " (*Conant*). Who refers to Iliad, xxi, 476 (xx, 476, it should be), and xvi, 333, for the passages which induce the comment.

I see nothing in Homer which implies that the entire sword was within the body in either case. Nor does the comment require that the critic supposed any such thing. He only says that the sword was *so* baptized as to be heated. Warm blood covering a sword, more or less, might heat the entire blade, or be poetically supposed to do so.

Im-bathe has no right to represent βαπτίζω. The sword was warmed *by* blood and not *in* it. The sword was so baptized with blood as to be warmed by it.

The baptism was one of decided influence.

BAPTISM OF THE SOUL.

" 4." " They have the soul very much mersed by the body, and therefore the seminal element partaking in the highest degree of the rational and physical power, makes its offspring more intelligent." ALEXANDER APHRODISIAS.

" 5." " Because they have their nature and perceptive power mersed in the depth of the body." ALEX. APHROD.

" 17." " She dies, therefore, as the soul may die; and death to her, even yet mersed in the body, is to sink in matter, and to be filled of it." PLOTINUS.

(1.) We, naturally, notice first, that the investing element is not a fluid but a corporal body. It is similar to the use of *mergo* with a cavern, and to that of immerse with inclosure in a dungeon.

(2.) The first and second of these passages do not present their mersions under the same aspect. In the second (which refers to brutes) it is simply intusposition, which is, directly, stated. The preposition is used with the dative (ἐν τῷ βάθει τοῦ σώματος). The implication of influence is found in ἐν τῷ βάθει.

In the first passage, the position of the soul is made subordinate to the influence exerted over it by the body, in consequence of that position. Consequently, we have the dative without the local preposition (βεβαπτισμένην τῷ σώματί). Accordant with this is the qualifying ἄγαν, "very much." This is perfectly suited to qualify influence, but not position. The body acts upon the soul, in unusual degree, and represses its development, while the soul reacts upon the body, mersing it, interpenetrating it, with those powers which are not allowed to have outward development.

(3.) The third passage combines both those features. It gives the soul intusposition *in* the body (ἐν τῷ σώματι βεβάπτισμένη), and, then, describes the excessive and improper influence exerted over it, through the body, as death to the soul, while the body lives.

(4.) How the soul is mersed *by* the body, we may understand, measurably. By what process the soul becomes mersed *in* the body is not said. Βαπτίζω does not throw one scintilla of light on this point. Dr. Halley says: "The Platonists evidently meant, by their baptism, the becoming inclosed in the body, whether, as they sometimes speak, the soul enters the body, or, as at other times, the matter concretes around the soul" (p. 362).

(5.) All these baptisms are marked by powerful influence. Dipping is unknown to them.

INTUSPOSITION FOR INFLUENCE.

1. Βαπτίζων αὐτὸν ἀπέκτεινεν. . . . *Æsop, Ape and Dolph.*

2. Καὶ βάπτίζειν τὰ ἀγγεῖα. . . . " *Mule.*

3. Σὲ κύμασι πόντου βαπτίζων, ὀλέσω. . *Alcibiades on Eupolis.*

4. Κοντὸν οὖν εἰς τὸ ὕδωρ βαπτίζουσι. . *Achilles Tatius,* ii, 14.

5. Βαπτίζεσθαι τὸν σίδηρον κατὰ τοῦ σώματος. " " iii, 21.

6. Καὶ κοίλην βαπτίσας καὶ πλησάμενος ὕδατος. " " iv, 18.

7. Ὑπ᾽αὐτοῦ τοῦ πλήθους τῶν κωπῶν βαπτισθείη. *Dion Cassius,* L. 18.

8. Τρωθέντον ἂν σφίσι τῶν σκαφῶν ἐβαπτίζοντο. " " L. 32.

9. Καὶ πέτραις καὶ μηχανήμασι βαπτίζοντες. " " L. 32.

10. Παιόμενοι ὑπὸ τῶν ἐναντίων ἐβαπτίζοντο. " " L. 35.

11. Τοὺς δὲ εἰς τὴν λίμνην . . . βαπτιζόντων. *Heliodorus, Æth.,* i, 30.

12. Διὰ χειρῶν τὸν Περσῶν στόλον βαπτίζοντα. *Heimerius,* x, 2.

13. Καὶ βαπτίζειν πάλιν ἐς γάλα γυναικός. . *Hippocrates,* ii, 710.

14. Ὠθεῖν καὶ τούτον ἐπὶ κεφαλὴν βαπτίζοντα. *Lucian, Timon,* 44.

15. Πολέας ἐμβάπτισον ἅλμῃ. . . . *Nicander, Geo.,* ii.

16. Ὁ Φίλιππος μέχρι τοσούτου διαβαπτιζόμενος. *Polyænus,* iv, 2, 6.

17. Ὀρθὰς ἐπὶ πρύμναν ἐβάπτιζον. . . *Plutarch, Marcell.,* xv.

18. Καλῶς ἑαυτὸν βαπτίζων εἰς τὴν Κωπαΐδα λίμνην. " *Gryllus,* vii.

19. Καὶ εἰς τὸ αἷμα τὴν χεῖρα βαπτίσας. *Plutarch, Par. Gr. & Rom.,* iii.

20. Καὶ πολλὰ τῶν σκαφῶν ἐβάπτιζον. . *Polybius, Hist.,* i, 51, 6.

21. Βαπτιζόμενα, πλήρη θαλάττης ἐγίγνετο. . " " viii, 8, 4.

22. Βαπτιζομένην ὑπὸ νεὼς πολεμίας. . . " " xvi, 6, 2.

23. Περιπήττεται ῥαδίως τὸ ὕδωρ παντὶ τῷ βαπτισθέντι.

Strabo, xii, 5, 4.

24. Ἐν τῳ πλῷ ὃν καὶ βαπτίσαι ἄμεινον ἦν. . *Themistius, Orat.,* iv.

BAPTISM FOR INFLUENCE.

1. And the dolphin, displeased at such a falsehood mersing, killed him. . . . . . *Æsop.*
2. Always, passing through the river, he let himself down and mersed the panniers. . . *Æsop.*
3. But I, mersing you by sea-waves, will destroy with bitterer billows. . . . . . *Alcibiades.*
4. They merse, therefore, a pole into the water. *Achil. Tat.*
5. They think that the sword is mersed down the body.

   Achil. Tat.
6. Mersing and filling it, hollowed, of water. " "
7. Would be mersed by the very multitude of the rowers.

   Dion Cassius.
8. Their vessels, being pierced by them, were mersed.

   Dion Cassius.
9. Mersing them both by stones and engines. " "
10. Struck by the enemy they were mersed. " '
11. Mersing . . . . others into the lake. . *Heliodorus.*
12. Mersing with his hands the fleet of the Persians.

    Heimerius.
13. Merse it again into woman's milk. . *Hippocrates.*
14. Thrust such a one upon the head, mersing him. *Lucian.*
15. Many, merse-in strong brine. . . *Nicander.*
16. Philip was so long thorough-mersing. . *Polyœnus.*
17. Lifting up, by the prow, erect upon the stern, they mersed them. . . . . . . *Plutarch.*
18. Nobly mersing himself into the lake Copais. "
19. Mersing his hand into the blood. . . "
20. They mersed many of the vessels. . *Polybius.*
21. Mersed, they became full of the sea. . "
22. Mersed by a hostile vessel. . . . "
23. The water is incrusted so easily about everything mersed into it. . . . . . . *Strabo.*
24. One saved in the voyage whom it were better to merse.

    Themistius.

PARTICULAR CASES EXAMINED.

DROWNING BAPTISM.

1. "And the dolphin, displeased at such a falsehood, 'mersing, killed him."   Æsop.

3. "But, mersing you by sea-waves, I will destroy you by bitterer billows."   Alcibiades.

10. "Struck by the enemy, were mersed."

Dion Cassius.

11. "Mersing others into the lake."   Heliodorus.

14. "Thrust such a one upon the head, mersing him."

Lucian.

18. "Nobly mersing himself into the lake Copais."

Plutarch.

24. "One saved in the voyage, whom it were better to merse."   Themistius.

(1.) These are cases of drowning. The drowning was by mersion, and was the influence designed to be secured over the mersed objects.

Mersion does not necessarily drown, because something may intervene to arrest this consummation; but where there is no such intervention, all living animals are drowned by mersion.

(2.) In many of these cases the mersed object was already in the water, and only the head remaining above; yet the putting under the head merely, causing death, is called mersion (baptism) of the person.

This is of interest to those who claim to baptize by walking into the water and then dipping the head. *Dipping* the head would have been quite another affair to the ape, or to Eupolis, from the baptism which they are reported to have received.

(3.) Βάπτω, *tingo*, *dip*, are never used to express any case of drowning. Their power and nature unfit them for any such use.

(4.) " The act of baptism," as a uniform modal act, has no shadow of existence. The form of the act, through which the mersion is secured, does not enter into the meaning of the word. Such acts are multitudinous and endlessly diverse.

(5.) We see from such usage how readily βαπτίζω might (does?) advance, from the idea of mersion, to express directly that of drowning.

In such use as in 24,—" the pilot does not know whether he saves in the voyage one whom it were better to merse," —we are shut up to the meaning, *to drown.*

VARIOUS INFLUENCES.

SATURATION, INCRUSTATION, ETC.

2. " Always, passing through the river, he let himself down and mersed the panniers." Æsop.

4. " They merse a pole into the water prepared with pitch." Achil. Tat.

6. " He lets down his hand into the water, and mersing and filling it, hollowed, with water, darts the drink towards his mouth, and hits the mark." Achil. Tat.

13. " Then dipping into oil, rose or Egyptian, apply it through the day, and, as soon as it stings, take it away, and merse it, again, into woman's milk." Hippocrates.

15. " Merse many in strong brine, after dipping in boiling water." Nicander.

16. " Philip was so long thorough-mersing with the Pancratiast and sprinkling the face, that he did not give up, until the soldiers, wearied, scattered." Polyænus.

19. "He gathered the shields of the slain foe, and, having mersed his hand into the blood, he reared a trophy and wrote upon it."   PLUTARCH.

23. "The water is incrusted so easily about everything mersed into it, that they draw up crowns of salt, when they let down a rush circle."   STRABO.

It is not necessary to enter minutely into each case. Some of the more important features will be noticed.

(1.) TRANSLATION.—Dr. Conant translates " 2." " immerse;" " 4." "plunge;" " 6." " dip." Why, this varying translation is inexplicable either on the merits of the case or on Baptist principles. The word remains the same in every case, while the translation is different in every case. Baptists say there is but one meaning to the word throughout the entire Greek language; while here, in three passages, we have three distinct meanings.

Dip, plunge, and immerse differ, essentially, in meaning, and cannot possibly be, true, critical, translations of the same word.

Besides, in two of these passages (2 and 6), the act of baptism is expressly stated. In the first by ὑφιέναι, in the second by καθῆκε; neither of which, distinctively, means to immerse, to plunge, or to dip; as neither of them is capable of expounding βαπτίζω, although capable, in particular cases, to answer its demands. Whenever the translator represents the Greek word by a modal act, it is, always, of his own will, and without warrant from βαπτίζω.

(2.) DIP.—Passages marked 6, 13, 16, 19, afford altogether the best foundation on which Baptist writers can stand to make a plea for their *dip*. Besides these passages, there are but three others (out of more than one hundred) which Dr. Conant translates by *dip*. That any Baptist writer, thoroughly committed to dipping, should be unable to introduce the word, on which his system hangs, in more than one passage in twenty, is a fact which,

of itself, throws the gravest doubt about the justness of
such translation in any case.

Of the three passages (not given here, they will be hereafter) which are translated by dip, one is stated with the
acknowledgment, that such translation is embarrassed by
the construction; another is accompanied with a doubt as
to the nature of the transaction; and, the third makes the
dipping take place in an element, represented by the dative
without a preposition, contrary to current usage.

In the first of the above cases, dip, clearly, has nothing
to do with βαπτίζω. You might as well translate πλησάμενος
by dip as βαπτίσας. They both exhibit results, and not acts,
consequent on the act expressed by the phrase, τὴν δὲ χεῖρα
ἐις τὸ ὕδωρ καθῆκε. If dip could be introduced, anywhere, it
must be as a *substitute* for καθῆκε. This is the only word expressive of the act done, and this was the act of baptism
and of filling. But dip, and "let down," are forms of act
which work themselves out very diversely. They do so
here. It is one thing "to let the hand down into the
water" for the sake of "mersing and filling it," and, after-
ward, "darting the water thus secured into the mouth;"
and, it is another thing to dip the hand into water. The
process of letting down, mersing, filling, darting, may be
a very rapid one, and a little complicated, and some may
think that dip may, as well as not, be thrown in, some-
where; but the short answer to this is, Plutarch did not
think so. When he put βαπτίζω there, he selected a word
which can never be displaced by βάπτω, without Greek
usage uttering an indignant protest, from a hundred
mouths, against such violation of her sovereignty.

To introduce dip, as representing βαπτίζω, is out of all
question. To introduce it as expressive of the act by
which the baptism is effected, and as much disconnected
from it as καθῆκε, is, equally, inadmissible.

These words are separated by the Greeks, in their vocabulary, and that separation is maintained, I confidently
believe, throughout all Greek usage. To say that βαπτίζω
may be controlled by βάπτω, and that a baptism may be

produced by a bapting, is to say what the language will be searched, in vain, to sustain.

There is a sort of mersion connected with the modal act to dip, full of limitations, which, because of this very *quasi* character, is unfitted to represent the true and unlimited mersion of the Greeks. Dipping-mersion belongs to itself; has a mission and history of its own; and never, in the hands of a Greek, intermeddles with the mersion of intus-position and controlling influence. The accidental accord between a dipping and an intusposition, in rare instances, in brevity of duration, will never be made the ground, by any thoughtful person, of their confusion or their interchange.

It should, also, be observed, that the introduction of an act, effecting baptism, into the office of a representative of βαπτίζω, is a liberty which, while Baptists indulge in most licentiously so far as comports with their own views, they will not tolerate in contradiction of their views.

Dr. Fuller will not accept the act *overflow* (which confessedly effects the baptism), in the case of the sea-coast. Then, " my position is," it expresses no form of act at all, but only " immerse." When he admits that pour is an act competent to effect a baptism in the baptistery, he smiles at the witlessness which can confound the act inducing the baptism with the resultant, covered condition, in which, only, the baptism is to be found. But when he feels compelled to admit that an object is declared, by a Greek writer, to be baptized, *on which water had been poured*, without its lying in a baptistery, and *without its being covered*, then, baptize means—what, pour? By no manner of means. The act must not be put for the resultant condition. " Immerse," is it? Why, no. Unfortunately, there was no immersion effected; but the object was made *very wet!* And cannot a child understand that βαπτίζω is here used, by a fine stroke of rhetoric, to mean "TO DRENCH"? Perhaps so; at least, if he do not, he lacks Dr. Fuller's facility in changing " position," and coolness, under embarrassing circumstances, in finding an accommodating interpretation. Baptist writers should remember that within the domain of philology there is an equality of rights.

Carson translates and comments on the passage marked "13," thus: "Dip it again; the first dipping is expressed by βάψας. This shows that, in the radical signification of dipping, these words are perfectly of the same import."

If such argumentation had been addressed to Dr. Carson, by an opponent, he would have met it with that peculiar treatment which his eulogist delicately terms— "Attic salt."

The reasoning assumes that βάπτω and βαπτίζω are of "perfectly the same import." The assumption is groundless, and the argument based upon it falls. Had it been said, "dip it in oil and then soak it in milk," what would have been thought of the reasoning which would make dip and soak "of perfectly the same import"? Are they not words of contrasted intensity, rather than of agreement? Dip expresses an act introducing its object momentarily into "the oil;" soak expresses no form of act, but brings its object under the unlimited influence of "the milk." Such is the distinction between the Greek words. Their use by Hippocrates, instead of proving that both have the same power, proves the reverse. •When the feebleness of βάπτω has failed to mollify the application sufficiently, then the greater power of βαπτίζω is to be resorted to. The same conclusion is established by the contrasted use of these words in the Epigram on Eupolis: "You have *bapted* (whether washed, dyed, dipped, or any other possible thing) me; but I will *baptize* (killing) you." "Any child can see" that the latter word is used because it has a power which whelms the former.

The same contrast is developed in quotation "15." To make a pickle the article is first to be "*dipped* in boiling water," and then to be "*baptized* in strong brine." The sea-coast baptism is not better understood than is this domestic process. The "dipping" is not for the purpose of securing the full influence of the boiling water, but the

18

reverse; while the baptism into the brine is to secure its full power. Hippocrates affords no countenance to the theory which would confound these words.

In "16," βαπτίζω is evidently used because a dipping could not express the idea. The point of the contest was to vanquish an opponent by depriving him of the power of breathing, whether the water was thrown into the face, or whether the head was held under water. The vanquished, on yielding, was released by his opponent from farther assault. This is quite a different affair from a simple dipping. Hippocrates speaks of the effect upon the breathing when one has been kept under water some time—*καὶ ἀνέπνεεν ὡς ἐκ βεβαπτίσθαι*—*breathes as one out of a state of mersion.* Such a passage ought to be sufficient to show that a bapting and a baptism, even when they are brought into the nearest possible contact, are two very different things. The breathing is not affected by a dipping; it may be to any extent by a baptism. Therefore, Hippocrates, like a true Greek, rejects βάπτω and employs βαπτίζω.

The passage marked "19" is the last which makes special claim to a dipping, and no passage makes it with more plausible, though superficial, pretensions. A Roman soldier, wounded, is left on the battle-field, who spends his failing strength in gathering the armor of his slain enemies to erect a trophy. In order that he may write an explanatory and dedicatory inscription, "he merses his hand into the blood." It is claimed, that baptize, merse, in this statement, means "*to dip.*"

We ask for the grounds on which such claim rests. Is it the current usage of the word? We reply, there is no such usage as requires or warrants any such meaning. If anything in language can be proved, it has been proved that βαπτίζω does not express any definite form of act, and, therefore, does not express the definite act to dip.

Is it said: This particular passage requires this meaning. I answer: Such declaration is founded in error. But if any act of dipping were present, such act could

not be made the utterance of this word any more than the
act of overflowing, pouring, sinking, walking, and a score
of others, present in other cases of baptism. But there is
no necessity for its presence. The hand may be introduced into a pool of blood in other ways than by a dipping.
The idea of a dipping is facilitated by the mention of
writing, as though the statement were the same with dipping a pen in ink to write with it. A closer examination
of the phraseology will show that such idea is not well
founded. It is said, " the *hand* was mersed into blood."
Now this, according to Baptist views (substantially, if not
absolutely correct), requires that the entire hand should be
covered in blood; but we cannot write with the entire
hand, and it is simply absurd to suppose that the whole
hand was covered in blood for the purpose of writing
with the finger's point. The attempt to ally this phraseology with pen-dipping, therefore, falls to the ground.
It is not said that he wrote with the same hand that was
mersed. Indeed it is quite possible, not to say probable,
that the blood was taken up in the mersed hand, and from
it the blood was taken, by dipping the finger of the other
hand into it, and, thus, writing the inscription. If the
statement were made, " He scooped up blood with his
hand and wrote with it;" would "scoop" mean to dip?
If it were said, " He buried his hand into the blood and
wrote with it;" would bury mean to dip? It is as indefensible to convert baptize into dip, as it is to convert
bury into dip.

If any Baptist writer thinks that to dip would answer,
in such case, just as well as to merse, that is a matter to
be settled with Plutarch. I do not pretend to correct or
to rewrite (in imagined equivalent phrases) this old Greek;
but merely to interpret what he has written. And he has
written that the hand was mersed and not dipped, baptized
and not bapted. I presume it will have to stand so.

All the passages most favorable to dipping have now
been examined, and I very cheerfully submit, whether the
result is such as should overturn that meaning so well

established " through all Greek literature," and sustained by correspondent usage in other languages.

" 5." " But they who look on think the sword to be mersed down the body, but it runs up into the hollow of the handle."   ACHILLES TATIUS.

" Plunged " (*Conant*). This is another example of a substitutionary translation. This introduction of definite acts to displace βαπτίζω is a mere matter of will or imagination on the part of the translator. It is not in the text. A description is given of a juggler's trick. In the first member of the sentence the condition of the sword, supposed to be sheathed in the body, is stated without expressing the form of action by which it reaches that condition. In the latter member of the sentence, the mode of statement is reversed. The form of action is given, but not the condition resultant from that action.

An ellipsis, in both members, might be supplied thus: " They who look on think the sword to be mersed, *running* down into the body; but it is *mersed* running up into the hollow of the handle." Or, you may substitute act and condition in the one case or the other—" They who look on think the sword to be *run* down the body; but it is mersed into the hollow of the handle." But we must not give substitution for translation, whether it be dip, or plunge, or run up, or run down.

The sword is not influenced by mersion into the body, but the body is. The body is mersed by the sword run into it, just as Semele was mersed by the thunderbolts of Jove. And in such case no intusposition exists, real or imaginary; but the simple and direct import of mersion, as so used, is that of death-producing influence. The intusposition of one thing within another is equally favorable to the communication, as well as the reception of influence.

VESSELS MERSED IN ORDER TO THEIR DESTRUCTION.

" 7." " And if any vessel came near, how could it be that it would not be mersed by the very multitude of the oars?" DION CASSIUS.

" 8." " If they succeeded, they came off the better; but if they failed, their own vessels, being crushed, were mersed." DION CASSIUS.

" 9." " The others, mersing the attacking ships by stones and engines from above." DION CASSIUS.

" 12." " I will show you, also, my soldiers, one fighting, most naturally, even in a painting; and another, by his hands, mersing the fleet of the Persians." DION CASSIUS.

" 17." " Some, by a weight fastened above, pressing down they sank into the deep; others, by iron hands or mouths like cranes, drawing up by the prow, upright upon the stern, they mersed." PLUTARCH.

" 20." " They made incessant attacks, and mersed many of the ships." POLYBIUS.

" 21." " But the most, the prow being let drop from on high, were mersed, and became full of the sea and confusion." POLYBIUS.

" 22." " Pierced and mersed by a hostile vessel." POLYBIUS.

The features of these baptisms are too obvious to call for exposition. The act effecting the baptism is widely various; the farthest possible removed from dip. The dative without a preposition, and the genitive, express the agency. The duration of the baptism has no limit. The baptism is sought for its destructive influence. The ships were baptized, were left in a state of baptism, and have continued in it for two thousand years.

INFLUENCE WITH RHETORICAL FIGURE.

1. *Καίτοι γὰρ βαπτιζόμενος ὑπὸ τῆς ἐπιθυμίας . . . καθάπερ δὲ ἐκ κύματος ἀνέκυπτε, λέγων.* . . . . *Chariton Aphrod.*, ii, 4.

2. *Διονύσιος δὲ, . . . κατείληπτο μὲν ὑπὸ χειμῶνος καὶ τὴν ψυχὴν ἐβαπτίζετο.*
   Chariton Aphrod., iii, 2.

3. *Πλοῖον . . . ἰδίου χειμῶνος γέμον, καὶ βαπτιζόμενον ἐν γαλήνῃ.*
   Chariton Aphrod., iii, 4.

4. *Οὐδὲν τῶν χειμαζομένων διαφέρουσιν, . . . κἂν ἄρα τι καὶ τὸ βραχύτατον σφαλῶσι, παντελῶς βαπτίζονται.* . *Dion Cass.*, xxxviii, 27.

5. *Καὶ αὐτός εἰμι τῶν βεβαπτισμένων ὑπὸ τοῦ μεγάλου κύματος, ἐκείνου.*
   Libanius, Epist., xxv.

6. *Ἀβάπτιστός εἰμι, φελλὸς ὣς ὑπὲρ ἔρκος, ἅλμας.* *Pindar*, ii.

INFLUENCE COMPARED TO AN OVERFLOWING WAVE.

1. Then appeared the conflict of reason and passion. For, although mersed (*baptized*) by the passion, the noble man attempted to resist; and rose up, as out of a wave.
   Char. Aph.

2. But Dionysius . . . was seized by a storm, and mersed (*baptized*) as to his soul; but yet he strove to rise above the passion, as out of a great wave. . . *Char. Aph.*

3. I saw a vessel wandering in pleasant weather, full of its own storm, and mersed (*baptized*) in a calm. *Char. Aph.*

4. Carried along in troubled and unsettled affairs, they differ little or nothing from those tempest tossed; and should they commit any, even the least, mistake they are wholly mersed (*baptized*). . . . . . *Dion Cass.*

5. And I am of those mersed (*baptized*) by that great wave.
   Libanius.

6. I am unmersed (*un-baptized*), like a cork upon a net, of the brine. . . . . *Pindar.*

(1.) In no one of these quotations is there the shadow of a dipping.

(2.) In most cases, it is the element which moves to reach its object. A sea-wave is irresistible. So is baptism.

(3.) The point of the figure, in no case, is either act or covered condition; but turns wholly on influence, powerful influence. To work out a parallelism beyond this, would speedily carry us to the point where would be practically exemplified the truth, that "there is but one step from the sublime to the ridiculous."

FIGURE WORN OUT BY CONSTANT USE.

These passages receive vividness and force from rhetorical embellishment. For this purpose, appeal is made to those physical facts which give origin to the word in its literal use, and which serve to illuminate its tropical use.

The number of such passages is not large. Words which pass from a primary to a secondary use, and are in daily employ, lay aside their rhetorical character, and become purely prosaic in their import. The secondary meaning becomes as simple, direct, stripped of ornament, and unfigurative as in the primary use. A designed and obvious rhetorical use of words (which have been turned aside from the expression of physical to denote logical relations), in ordinary conversation or writing, would be eminently ridiculous. Words which are simply tropical, which are in everyday use and have secured a well-defined meaning of their own, cannot, with any propriety, be termed figurative. They are as truly literal, in this acquired secondary use, as in their original, primary, and physical application. Observe the following definitions.

"A figure of language, then, I define to be a *distinguished* mode of speech, which expresses a thought, mostly with some additional idea, and always more to the purpose of a writer or speaker than ordinary language, and which naturally results from a state of mind suitable to itself."

CARSON, *Interp. of the Scrip. Figures of Speech.*

"Simple expression just makes our idea known to

others; but Figurative Language, over and above, bestows
a particular dress upon that idea; a dress, which makes it
both to be remarked and adorns it. . . . No language is
so copious as to have a separate word for every separate
idea. Men made one word, which they had already appropriated to a certain idea or object, stand also for some
other idea or object; between which and the primary one
they found, or fancied, some relation. Thus the preposition *in* was invented to express the circumstance of place:
'The man was killed *in* the wood.' In progress of time,
words were wanted to express men's being connected with
certain conditions of fortune, or certain situations of mind;
and some resemblance, or analogy, being fancied between
these and the place of bodies, the word *in* was employed
to express men's being so circumstanced; as one's being
in health or *in* sickness, *in* prosperity or *in* adversity, *in*
joy or *in* grief, *in* doubt or *in* danger, or *in* safety. Here
we see this preposition *in* plainly assuming a tropical signification, or *carried* off from its *original meaning, to signify
something else*, which relates to or resembles it.

"Tropes of this kind abound in all languages. We say,
inflamed by anger, *warmed* by love, *swelled* with pride, *melted*
into grief; and these are almost the only significant words
which we have for such ideas. . . . . In every language,
too, there are a multitude of words, which, though they
were figurative in their first application to certain objects,
yet, *by long use, lose that figurative power wholly*, and come to
be considered as simple and literal expressions."

DR. BLAIR, *Fig. Lang.*, xiv.

In accord with this last statement, Dr. Carson says:
"Very many of the words of every language have received a metaphorical application; *but when custom has as
signed this as their appropriate meaning, they are not to be considered as figures of speech.* The grammarian, as Dr. Camp-
bell observes, will find many metaphorical words which
will not be recognized as such by the rhetorician. In
explaining the word *enlighten*, for instance, the grammarian

will say, that it signifies to instruct, in a metaphorical
sense, from the resemblance between the effects of light
and information. But this term being as much appropriated, now, in the above sense, as the proper term itself,
the rhetorician does not consider it as belonging to his
department." *Fig. of Speech*, p. 278.

" A figure of speech is a certain conformation of speech,
removed from the common form, and that which first presents
itself." *Quintillian.*

All these statements and definitions justify the position,
that any word which, in secondary use, has secured a well-
defined meaning of daily, long-continued use, and with
great breadth of application, loses, wholly, its figurative
character, and must be considered simple and literal in its
expression.

This is true, in all respects, of βαπτίζω. We find this
word used through a thousand years, commonly, variedly,
and independently, as expressing a definite meaning of its
own, clearly growing out of, yet wholly distinct from, its
original, primary, physical use.

It is a noticeable fact that this Greek word, according
to Baptist writers, presents a figurative use as frequently,
if not more frequently, recurring than the literal use. Is
not this extraordinary? But this fact becomes more noticeable when we turn to βάπτω, and find scarcely a single
instance of figurative use in its primary meaning. Can
any explanation be given of this very diverse usage of
these two words, which, we are told, are of entirely the
same value? There is an explanation, and one full of
meaning. There was a time when Baptist writers gave as
long a list of cases of the figurative use of βάπτω as they
now give of βαπτίζω. How has that great cloud of figures
been dissipated? Why, by the admission that they had
made a mistake in denying to βάπτω a secondary meaning;
and, thus, had been compelled to resort to figure to expound difficulties, which, even by all the help of figure,
Carson says, and says most justly, were " very clumsily

got over." This history is repeating itself. By denying a secondary use to βαπτίζω, a necessity has been induced for resorting to figure as often as to fact; seeking for help to get over difficulties, which, after all, are not got over, and the failure brings out the clumsiness of the attempt into the boldest relief. When βαπτίζω is acknowledged to have a secondary use, it will be found to have but little more figure about it than has βάπτω.

To show the difference between figurative and simple statement, Dr. Blair gives the following: "A good man enjoys comfort in the midst of adversity." This, he says, "expresses thought in the simplest manner possible." But Baptist writers say no; this is figure. It represents a good man "*in the midst* of a tempest—*adverse* winds, *adverse* waves, *adverse* skies, dark, glittering with lightnings, and shaking with thunderings, in all which he has peace and comfort"! Whither has simplicity of expression fled? Again: "'It is impossible, by any search we can make, to explore the divine nature fully,' is to make a simple proposition," says Dr. Blair. Baptist interpretation says, not so: "Search," "explore," demonstrate figure, and represent the divine nature as *a dark cavern*, whose recesses are not fully penetrable!

Yet again: "The simple style of Scripture, 'He spake and it was done; he commanded, and it stood fast.'" But Dr. Blair is sadly at fault according to Baptist interpretation. This is not the sublimity of simplicity. This is highly wrought figure. The elements of chaos are represented as endued with intelligence, hearing and obeying the voice of Omnipotence!

Remember such cases when confronted by figures, conjured up by our Baptist friends, out of elements less propitious than those furnished by either of the above cases. Almost any sentence, of the most purposed simplicity, may be clothed in figurative habiliments until no longer recognizable by its author.

We, now, come to consider baptism as a controlling influence, changing condition, *without any mersion.*

CONTROLLING INFLUENCE—GENERAL.

WITHOUT INTUSPOSITION IN FACT OR IN FIGURE.

SECONDARY USE.

1. Ἐκπλήσσει τὴν ψυχήν. . . . . καὶ κατεβάπτισε.
   Achilles Tatius, Leucippe and Clit., 1. 3.
2. Τοσούτῳ πλήθει βαπτισθῆναι κακῶν.   "   "   " iii, 10.
3. Ὁ δὲ τῷ θυμῷ βεβαπτισμένος καταδύεται.   "   " vi, 19.
4. Ἐμπίπτουσαι δὲ αἱ τύχαι βαπτίζουσι ἡμᾶς.   "   " vii, 2.
5. Καὶ στυπεῖον ἐλαίῳ βαπτίσας.   .   .   Æsop, Man and Fox.
6. Καταβαπτισθήσεταί μοι τὸ ζῆν. .   .   Alciphron, Epist., ii, 3.
7. Τὸ πλῆθος τοῦ οἴνου. . . . καταβαπτίζει.
   Alexander Aphrodisias, i, 16.
8. Οὗτοι μὲν γὰρ ἐπίστανται τούτῳ διαβαπτίζεσθαι.
   Demosthenes, Aristogeiton, 1. 5.
9. Μὴ παντελῶς βεβαπτίσθαι ἀλλ' ἀνέχειν.   Demetrius Cydon., xiv, 4.
10. Τοὺς δὲ ἰδιώτας . . . οὐ βαπτίζουσι ταῖς εἰσφοραῖς.
    Diodorus Siculus, i, 73.
11. Καὶ τῇ συμφορᾷ βεβαπτισμένον.   Heliodorus Æthiopics, ii, 3.
12. Μέσαι νύκτες ὕπνῳ τὴν πόλιν ἐβάπτιζον.   "   " iv, 17.
13. Μὴ συμβαπτιζώμεθα τῷ τούτου πάθει.   "   " iv, 20.
14. Ἐπειδή σε τὰ συμβεβηκότα ἐβάπτιζεν.   "   " v, 16.
15. Ἐβάπτισε γὰρ ὅλην ἐκεῖ τὴν Ἀσίαν μαχόμενος. Heimerius, xv, 3.
16. ᾧ ἂν εὐθὺς ἐβαπτίζετο τὸ ἄστυ. . Libanius, Life.
17. Ἡ Σαλαμὶς περὶ ἥν τὴν Ἀσίαν ἐβάπτισας.   "   Declamat., xx.
18. Ὑπὸ μικρᾶς ἂν βαπτισθείη προσθήκης.   "   Epistle, 310.
19. Ὁ βαπτιζόμενον εὑρὼν τὸν ἄθλιον Κίμωνα.   "   " 962.
20. Ἡ λύπη βαπτίζουσα μὲν τὴν ψυχήν.   "   Emp. Julian, 148.
21. Τὸ δὲ ὑπολελειμμένον ὀλίγον ὄν ἐβαπτίζετο. "   "   " 71.
22. Βαπτιζομένου τοῦ πράγματος.   .   "   Oration, xliii.
23. Οὐκ ἄγεις σχολὴν, ἀλλὰ βαπτίζῃ.   .   "   Memorial.
24. Βαπτισθεὶς ἤ νόσοις ἤ μάγων τέχναις. Plotinus, Ennead., 1, 4, 9.
25. Ὅτι τοὺς ταμίας ἐβάπτισεν.   .   Plutarch, Aristoph. and Men.
26. Ἡμᾶς βαπτιζομένους ὑπὸ τῶν πραγμάτων.   "   Socrates.
27. Πεντακισχιλίων μυριάδων ὀφλήμασι βεβαπτισμένον.
    Plutarch, Galba, xxi.
28. Τοῖς δὲ ὑπερβάλλουσι βαπτίζεται.   .   "   Education, xiii.
29. Βεβαπτισμένος πολλῷ φρυάγματι.   .   Proclus, Chrestom., xvi.
30. Βαπτιζόμενον τε ὑπὸ τῆς ὀδύνης, καὶ. . Themistius, Oration, xx.

CONTROLLING INFLUENCE—GENERAL.

WITHOUT MERSION, IN FACT OR IN FIGURE.

SECONDARY USE.

1. Astounds the soul, befalling it unawares; and de-mersed (*de-baptized*) it. . . . . . *Achilles Tatius.*
2. As in a few days to be mersed (*baptized*) by such a multitude of evils. . . . . . *Achilles Tatius.*
3. But he, mersed (*baptized*) by anger, sinks.   "   "
4. Misfortunes befalling merse (*baptize*) us.   "   "
5. And mersing (*baptizing*) the tow with oil. *Æsop.*
6. My life will be de-mersed (*de-baptized*). . *Alciphron.*
7. The quantity of wine de-merses (*de-baptizes*) the physical and vital power. . . . . . *Alex. Aphrod.*
8. For these know how to thorough-merse (*thorough-baptize*) with him. . . . . . . *Demosthenes.*
9. Not wholly mersed (*baptized*), but bears up. *Demetrius.*
10. They do not merse (*baptize*) the people by taxes.
    Diod. Sicul.
11. And mersed (*baptized*) by the calamity. . *Heliodorus.*
12. When midnight mersed (*baptized*) the city with sleep.
    Heliodorus.
13. But let us not be co-mersed (*co-baptized*) by this grief of his.
    Heliodorus.
14. Because the events still mersed (*baptized*) you.   "
15. For there fighting he mersed (*baptized*) all Asia.
    Heimerius.
16. By which the city would, immediately, have been mersed (*baptized*). . . . . . . *Libanius.*
17. Salamis, where thou didst merse (*baptize*) Asia.   "
18. Would be mersed (*baptized*) by a small addition.   "
19. Who finding the unhappy Simon mersed (*baptized*).
    Libanius.
20. Grief mersing (*baptizing*) the soul and darkening the judgment. . . . . *Libanius.*
21. But the remaining part being small, was mersed (*baptized*). . . . . *Libanius.*
22. But now, as you see, the duty being mersed (*baptized*).
    Libanius.

23. You have no spare time, but are mersed (*baptized*).

Libanius.

24. Mersed (*baptized*) either by diseases or arts of the wizards.

Plotinus.

25. Because he mersed (*baptized*) the stewards. . *Plutarch.*

26. That we, mersed (*baptized*) by the affairs of life. "

27. Mersed (*baptized*) by debts of fifty millions. "

28. But is mersed (*baptized*) by those which are excessive

Plutarch.

29. Mersed (*baptized*) with much wantonness. . *Proclus.*

30. Both mersed (*baptized*) by grief. . . . *Themistius.*

Although a word may have attained to a secondary meaning, it is still possible, with more or less facility, and with more or less apparent fitness, to treat it merely as tropical, and refer it back for exposition to its primary use. Dr. Carson says that "enlighten" has a secondary meaning. If so, it should be expounded directly by that meaning, and not by resorting, every time it is encountered, to the roundabout process of a reference to light and its effects in revealing the true position, character, worth, and relation of things. There is, however, scarcely any case in which this word is used, but that any one, who chooses to deny or to disregard its secondary meaning, may deny its acquired rights, and make out a case (in his own judgment a triumphant case), by appealing to light, and darkness, and mental analogies. Whether such persons can be better answered than by being let alone, I do not know.

If in those cases which illustrate the secondary meaning of βαπτίζω, many of them can be robbed of their simple statement and acquired character by dressing them up, with more or less of violence, in the elements of figure, and dipping, or plunging, or sinking, or overflowing with water, no one need be surprised. The same can be done with the secondary meaning of almost any word, *mutatis mutandis*. This was done through long years, by Baptists, with the secondary meaning of βάπτω, resolving every case of *dyeing*, into a *dipping*, unmindful of the havoc they

made of rhetoric or common sense. The same blind per-
sistency in maintaining an erroneous idea is shown in Dr.
Carson when he sets up the astonishing error, that " βαπτίζω
means dip and nothing but dip, expressing mode always;"
and then, to make good his false position, brings in "catachresis" *to dip* the shore by the flowing tide, and the land
of Egypt by the *overflowing* of the Nile.

This position of Dr. Carson is too grossly erroneous,
and its defence too utterly indefensible, for some of his
admirers longer to maintain; but with inconsistency, which
has not yet settled down, they admit variety of modal action. They refuse, however, with one voice, still to admit
any secondary meaning; and with no less violence to the
laws of language development than in the case of βάπτω,
turn every case of the secondary meaning of βαπτίζω into a
dipping, or plunging, or sinking, or overflowing with water.

SECONDARY MEANING.

TO EXERCISE A CONTROLLING INFLUENCE CHANGING CONDITION.

1. "For what is sudden, all at once and unexpected,
astounds the soul, falling on it unawares, and de-merses it."
ACHILLES TATIUS.

What is there, on the face of this statement, suggestive
of water? Certainly, dipping, and plunging, and sinking,
are out of all question. The only thing that could be,
with any consistency, introduced, here, would be a wave,
and from that Baptists shrink, because it moves the element and not the object. But to take "the soul" out to
sea, and then conjure up a wave "suddenly," "all at
once," "unexpectedly," "to fall upon" it, is a piece of
extravagance in the way of taste which will commend
itself to but few. How simply, clearly, and fully is the
case met by attaching to the word the secondary meaning,
to exercise a controlling influence, changing the condition.

The notion that the soul is put under water, in any way,

or intended to be so represented, is simply absurd. It is influence only which is at issue.

---

2. "What crime have we committed, so great, as in a few days, to be mersed by such a multitude of evils?"

ACHILLES TATIUS.

It would require some ingenuity to work up "a few days," and "a multitude of evils," and a mersion, so as to form a billow, or a dipping, out of them. But supposing some imagination to be sufficiently inventive and constructive, better save it for a better purpose, and take, what is on the face of the record, *the exercise of a controlling influence.* The agency is expressed by the dative without a preposition.

---

3. "But he, mersed by anger, is subdued; and wishing to escape into his own domain is no longer free, but is forced to hate the object loved."

ACHILLES TATIUS.

"Speaking of love, contending with and subdued by anger, in the same bosom" (*Conant*). I do not know how "love and anger" are to be got into the water, unless it be in a "dipping match" after the fashion of Philip and the Pancratiast. But this will hardly answer; for love, it would seem, is kept under the water, unable "to escape." A wave, or a sinking ship, will not answer. Until a better solution is found, therefore, we will accept, what every letter of the passage proclaims, *controlling influence.* Anger exercises a controlling influence over love; holds it in subjection; will not let it escape.

The agency is marked by the simple dative.

---

4. "Misfortunes befalling us merse us."

ACHILLES TATIUS.

I take this to be a very direct and prosaic statement

announcing the homely truth—Misfortunes exercise a controlling influence over us. The introduction of "falling" waves or wrecked ship going to the bottom is a freak of the imagination not to be laid to the charge of Achilles Tatius. So Virgil—" Mersed by these evils."

---

5. " And mersing the tow with oil, binding it to her tail, he set it on fire."　　　　　　　　　　ÆSOP.

This is told of a fox that had been caught, and was thus punished for mischief done. " Dipping tow in oil," is Dr. Conant's translation. It is objectionable:

1. Because " dipping" is no translation of βαπτίζω.

2. The proper form for expressing the element, in which, by the dative, requires the preposition. Its use may not, necessarily, indicate the element; but it lays the burden of proof, to the contrary, heavily, on the objector.

3. In every clear case, where the inclosing element is associated with the dative, the preposition, by itself or in composition with the verb, is used.

4. The dative, without the preposition, ordinarily, indicates instrumentality. It does so in all clear cases (in common with the genitive) with which we have to do. If such is not accepted as its import, in any particular case, proof to the contrary must be adduced.

5. No proof can be found in βαπτίζω. Once this word was deemed sufficient to prove this point. The best Baptist scholars believe this no longer. Dr. Fuller escapes from the plunging fire of facts directed against the old position, confessing that any mode, " pouring," will answer, *provided the object is covered*. A heavy gun is turned against this new position, and it, too, is abandoned, with the admission that pour will answer, *even if it does not cover*, provided it wets very thoroughly, and there is a good deal

of water all around! Dr. Carson is very indignant at either of these admissions. Until Baptist doctors come to some agreement among themselves we may be excused from accepting the dogma of either party.

6. It is beyond all rational controversy that this tow *could* be baptized as properly by pouring oil upon it as in any other way. Vessels in which oil is kept are best adapted for pouring. It is improbable that a mass of tow would be mersed in a large vessel of oil. We claim that tow brought, thoroughly, under the influence of oil, in any way, is baptized, saturated, mersed, of changed condition.

7. The translation should be, mersing the tow *with* oil; the dative being without the preposition.

---

6. "If I purpose to see all the rivers, my life will be demersed, not seeing Glycera." ALCIPHRON.

An invitation to visit Egypt, and see "the beautiful Nile," was declined, on the ground that equal reason might be urged for visiting the Euphrates, the Danube, the Tigris, &c., to do which would consume his life and deprive of fellowship with Glycera. Is there anything in this form of expression, or the nature of the sentiment, which shadows forth water and a dipping? Is there not the clearest statement, that to enter upon the course indicated would exercise a controlling influence over his life?

---

7. "Why do many, made drunk with wine, die? Because the quantity of the wine de-merses the physical and the vital power and warmth." ALEXANDER APHRODISIAS.

Wine drank neither dips, plunges, nor sinks; not even by "catachresis." Nor does it, in this case, "cover" by

19

pouring down the throat; for it is a physical impossibility thus to cover over "the physical and vital power and warmth." For another reason. If wine, as a fluid, effects this mischief, then as much water would do the same. But this is not true. Therefore, it is a case of controlling influence; not exerted by wine as a fluid, but by its peculiar, influential qualities as a drink. Life is mersed by it on the same principle that the life of Semele was "mersed" by the thunderbolts of Jove. Each has its peculiar power to influence controllingly, changing condition.

---

8. "Not the speakers, for these know how to thorough-merse with him, but private citizens and the inexperienced."   Demosthenes.

"Showing what kind of persons Aristogeiton was accustomed to harass by false accusation and extortion. In this case the compound word is used metaphorically, and the sense is: For these know how to match him in foul language—in the game of sousing one another." (*Conant.*) Supposing this use to be derived from the contest in "thorough-mersing," it shows the very varied and facile application of the word. The orator employs the word to show the mastery which practised speakers have over their opponents; being able to confound them by their skill and power in the use of language, and thus bring them under their controlling influence.

---

9. "For the soul has control over the body, and *entering into it is not wholly mersed by it*, but rises above it; and the body, apart from her, can do nothing."   Demetrius.

We are, certainly, exempt from the intrusion of water here. And we are, certainly, brought face to face with controlling influence. Will any one say, the soul "entering into the body"—δῦσαν εἰς αὐτὸ—is not "wholly covered by the body"? This would be a very nondescript sort of figure. For the soul "to enter the body, yet not be wholly" *under the controlling influence* "of the body," is a very intelligible statement; very conformable with facts, and very much like what the writer declares. The soul " controls the body," and is not controlled by it.

---

10. " On account of the abundant revenue from these sources, they do not merse the people with taxes."

Diodorus Siculus.

The following exposition is given by Dr. Carson : " In this figure, the rulers are supposed to immerse the people through the instrumentality of oppressive taxes. Mr. Ewing very well translates, ' on account of the abundant supply from these sources, they do not oppress the common people with taxes.' The literal translation is : 'They do not immerse the common people with taxes.' The people, in the case of oppressive taxation, are not supposed in such figures either to have the taxes *poured upon* them, nor themselves to be *immersed in* the taxes; but to sink by being weighed down with taxes. The taxes are not the element in which they sink, but are the instrumental baptizers. They cause the people to sink by their weight. This suits the words; this suits the figure; this suits the sense ; this suits every example which refers to debt; this suits the analogy of all other languages. We say, ourselves, dipped in debt, drowned in debt, sunk by debt, or sunk in debt. To sink in debt figures the debt as that in which we sink. It is a deep water in which we sink. *To sink by debt* figures the debt as a load on our shoulders, while we are in deep water. In this view, it is not the drowning element, but the baptizer or drowner. To be dipped in debt, supposes that we owe something considerable in proportion to our means. But we may be *dipped* without being *drowned.* The last cannot be adequately represented by baptize except when circumstances render the meaning definite."

This exposition would answer better as the basis for a caricature in the "London Punch," than as a simple interpretation of the historian. Is it to be imagined, for a moment, that Diodorus means, by a word, to touch some secret spring in the imagination of his readers, whose movement would expose to their view the land of the Nile flooded, through all its borders, while its inhabitants were seen, with packs on their backs, struggling and sinking in deep waters? Is this the import of the phrase, "mersed by taxes"? Dr. Carson commits a marvellous error in the transmutation of mersion *by taxes* into such a water scene. What have "taxes" to do with water, shallow or deep? Do taxes dip people, or sink people, or drown people, *in water?* "But *mersion* has something to do with water." Mersion had something to do with water, once; but when it entered into fellowship with "taxes" it came to live on dry land, and if it did not wholly lay aside the character of a baptizer, it certainly did bid farewell to all baptisms *into water.* If any one, through curiosity or any other motive, has a fancy for tracing back the relations of this word, after passing through all watery depths, they can bring back nothing germane to the case in hand but the simple idea of *ruin.* Dipping, plunging, sinking of the Egyptians in water is pure impertinence. The dipping, plunging, or sinking of anything else is equally so, in all respects, save only as to the one point of *destructive influence.* Hence proceeds, for those who need it, a flash of light which illumines the passage. But the passage needs no such help. It is self-luminous. It proclaims with its own tongue the ruinous character of excessive taxation. This merses not into *water,* but into *a stinted wardrobe,* into *a pinched table,* into *the sale of a cow, a horse, a plough, a farm;* into *unrequited toil and bitter penury!* If the historian must be made to write in figures, this is his figure,—*heavy taxes merse the people into financial ruin.* But he uses no figure at all. He employs a word which was used every day to develop, in the fullest measure, the influence of its adjunct.

Greek literature shows this secondary use and meaning

to be as true, as broad, and as self-sustaining as is the primary use and meaning. So self-evidencing is this use, that if every primary use were blotted out from the Greek language, and the remembrance of its existence obliterated from the minds of men, still this secondary use would live unharmed, "having life within itself," to vindicate its unborrowed rights and claim a controlling influence over its objects. Can this be denied? Can this be admitted, and a secondary sense be denied? The dative is without a preposition. Carson rejects the translation *in* taxes and adopts *by* taxes without any reason given, and without any capable of being given harmoniously with his principles or practice. If the form ὁυ βαπτίζουσι ταῖς εἰσφοραῖς does not, of itself, determine that "the taxes" occupy the position of agency, whence the influence proceeds which effects this baptism, then, I know of nothing else which can confer such character upon it. According to Carson's own showing, there is nothing to prevent "taxes" from occupying the position of *element* in baptism. He says, sink *in* debt and sink *by* debt is equally proper; and as he, here, "surreptitiously" introduces sink for baptize, of course, it is equally proper to say baptize *in* taxes or baptize *by* taxes. But it is by no means a matter of indifference whether we assign to the dative, thus used, the office of agency or of element; nor is it reasonable to believe that we are left, at will, to select the one or the other; yet this must be so, unless the form of the phrase is taken as an authoritative guide.

The translation of Dr. Carson is right, and the reason is, the grammatical form, and the elements of thought which enter into it, require it. The mersion is, purely, one of influence, and the source whence that influence proceeds, and which gives character to the mersion, is stated. This completes the thought—mersion by taxes—such controlling influence as excessive taxation universally begets, changing the condition of those subject to it.

11. " Cnemon, perceiving that he was deeply grieved and mersed by the calamity, and fearing lest he may do himself some injury, removes the sword privately."

HELIODORUS.

Is there anything, here, suggestive of a cold bath? Is there not the clearest statement of controlling influence? Does not the introduction of figure, "water floods, or inundations, swollen torrents, or shipwrecks," dislocate everything? " Whelmed *by* the calamity" (*Conant*). Calamity is the *agency*, source of influence, and is represented by the simple dative.

---

12. " When midnight had mersed the city by sleep."

HELIODORUS.

When midnight had *plunged* the city *in* sleep (*Conant*). An object may be physically baptized by plunging; but to plunge is not the meaning of the word. Why "plunge" should be chosen to introduce to a quiet night's rest is hard to tell. I do not remember ever before to have seen plunge and sleep associated together. The ideas of force and violence are out of place. Sometimes it is said—" he took an opiate and *fell* into a sweet sleep." But in such case to suggest that figure is, here, used, and the sleeper is represented as standing on the edge of a precipice, or the bank of a river, and "falling" thence into a running stream, is too irrational even to be laughed at. "To fall," thus used, expresses, merely and directly, the idea of *passing quickly* from a state of wakefulness into a state of slumber. "To *plunge* into sleep," is phraseology difficult to vindicate under any circumstances, and cannot be vindicated, here, either as the translation of the Greek word, or as the work of midnight. The probable use of this word was to secure the introduction of *in.* "Whelm" is the, almost, invariable translation of the many passages which Dr. Conant calls figurative. But "whelmed *in*" would not answer well; neither would a *dipping* in sleep answer; therefore, to save *in*, the rude term "plunge" is adopted. But according to Baptist interpretation, "plunge in" brings up a water scene. Sleep is figured as a flood large enough for a city to be plunged into it. Did any poet or orator ever venture to state, in words, any such figure? Rhyme and rhetoric carry license, oftentimes, into licentiousness; but I do not remember that either has ever taken the liberty of putting a city to sleep, figuratively, by plunging it into water! The communication of the gentle influence of sleep, when represented by figure, proceeds on a wholly different basis.

It has been already shown that "Invadunt urbem vino somnoque sepultam"—"Expletus dapibus vinoque sepultus"—"Rutuli somno vinoque soluti"—as well as "Sleeps in Port"—have nothing to do with graveyards, dissolution of the body *in* sleep and wine as a menstruum, or with the inside of a wine-cask as a bedchamber; but that the influence of wine and sleep, only, are indicated.

I may now add that the same is true of other passages where a narrow interpretation would much more plausibly find *water :*

> " Unfit he was for any worldly thing,
>   And eke unable once to stirre òr go;
> Not meet to be of counsel to a king,
>   Whose mind *in meate* and drinke was *drowned* so:
> Such one was Gluttony."   *Faerie Queene,* p. 36.

> " There did the warlike maid herself repose,
>   Under the wings of Isis all that night;
> And with sweet rest her heavy eyes did close,
>   After that long daies toile and wearie plight;
> Where whilst her earthly parts with soft delight
> Of senseless sleepe did deeply *drowned* lie."
>   *Faerie Queene,* p. 505.

To represent any one as plunged amid "*meats* and drinks" for the sake of "drowning" them, is a kind of figure distinguished neither by elegance nor congruity. It is but little better, in the same sentence, to make one " sleep all night under the wings of Isis," and, also, lie " drowned" at the bottom of a pool.

Edmund Spenser is not responsible for these beauties of poesy. He uses "drown," simply, to give strong development to the influence of its adjuncts, without any regard to cold water, just as Virgil uses "buried," for the same purpose, without any design of introducing his readers to a graveyard.

That sleep is not a vast lake, or sea, in which cities may be plunged, is farther shown by its distinct representation as an *agency*, and by the methods of its procurement.

Ovid says : " Before the doors of the dwelling of the God Somnus rich poppies grow, and countless herbs, from the juice of which humid night gathers soporifics, and *sprinkles* (*spargit*) them over the darkened earth."

There is no plunging or water-pool here. The *sprinkling* of poppy-juice upon the eyelid is sufficient to " merse a city with sleep," or *to drown* the darkened earth in deep repose. Elsewhere he speaks of sleep as agent in relaxing the bodies of men, *homines solverat alta quies.* He, also, represents it as an agent, bringing Iris, standing in the chamber of Somnus, under its power: " She could no longer endure the power of drowsiness; and as she felt sleep to glide into her limbs (*labi in artus*), she fled." Virgil says: "Venus diffuses (*irrigat*) gentle sleep through the limbs of Ascanius."

I know of no representation of sleep which differs, essentially, from these in any accredited writer. " To *plunge* a city in sleep" does essentially differ, and, I must think, is both an error of translation and of adaptation to the fitness of things. Spenser is quite in harmony with these classical writers in making sleep a gentle agency :

> " And then by it his wearie limbes display,
> Whiles *creeping* slomber made him to forget
> His former payne, and wypt away his toilsome sweat."

Will any one put his finger on " creeping," and cry out, Figure! Shall we be treated to the picture of an *animal* stealthily approaching its prey with a collar around its neck labelled—"Sleep"?

Spenser thought that there was another and a better method for putting sleep into full possession of its object. He thus describes it:

> "By this she had him lulled fast asleepe,
>   That of no worldly thing he care did take;
>   Then she, *with liquors strong his eies did steepe*,
>   That nothing should him hastily awake."

I have dwelt upon this passage, and endeavored to illustrate its true character; because it is all-important to show, that this and kindred passages are exhausted, under a just interpretation, by showing the agency, clothed by its associate βαπτίζω, with a plenary influence over its object; and that no element for dipping, or plunging, or sinking, in fact or in figure, belongs to the exposition. From the original, physical use the idea of controlling influence has been eliminated; and we have no need any longer to recur, in word or in thought, to such physical use.

And now, in view of the fact that Heliodorus declares "the city baptized by sleep"—without giving any mode of baptism; and in view of the fact that Ovid declares the mode by which "night brings all in this darkened earth into a somnolent condition" is by "sprinkling;" it follows, incontrovertibly, that a mode of effecting sleep-baptism is *by sprinkling*.

Let no Baptist friend be solicitous lest I should forget the difference, or should surreptitiously confound, sleep-baptism and water baptism. I will ever try to distinguish between things that differ, and am, for the present, quite satisfied with the point reached—the unchallengable position—*Sleep-baptism may be by sprinkling*.

Dr. C. puts the passage under consideration with others, under the explanatory heading—"To plunge, to immerse, to whelm (as in ingulfing floods) . . . . . in sleep," etc. Dr. Conant does not tell us the point of resemblance between a city asleep at midnight and "a man *plunged in ingulfing floods*." Until he does, I rather think that the world must remain in ignorance on the point. Whatever exposition ne may give, it is quite probable that some second Carson will enumerate it as among those cases which were " clumsily got over by the help of figure."

Hear a criticism of Carson of Tubbermore: " 'Steep me in poverty to the very lips.' It is here supposed that there is a likeness between being in great poverty, and being steeped in water. We cannot say that the likeness is faint, for there is no likeness at all."—(*Figures of Speech*, p. 286.) But if no resemblance in such a case, how much less in one where gentle sleep confronts *plunging into floods.*

---

13. "But let us not be co-mersed by this grief of his, nor be, unobservantly, carried away by his tears, as by torrents." HELIODORUS.

If any one should think that the mention of "torrents." in close connection with mersion, is indicative of an allusion to primary use, I would care but little to debate the matter. Such rare references would rather strengthen the general position, that where there is nothing of the kind mentioned, no allusion is intended. But, in the present case, "torrents" are not connected with the mersion, but with the "tears." And in determining the relation between torrents, we must guard against the extravagance of supposing tears to be converted into torrents. Such is not the point. The resemblance is between the moral effect of tears and the physical effect of torrents. The influence of tears changes our feelings and purposes, as the influence of torrents changes the position of objects encountered. The man who is influenced by tears is not supposed to be carried away by torrents; but is like, so far as change of moral position is concerned, to one who is carried away by torrents, so far as physical position is concerned.

The mersion is by grief, and is indicative of profound influence.

In this case, and in all similar cases, mersion, or baptism, represents a complete change of condition.

14. " The relation of your wanderings, often post-
poned, as you know, because the casualties still mersed
you, you could not keep for a better opportunity than the
present. HELIODORUS.

Could any statement be farther removed from a dipping
or plunging into water? There cannot be a reference to
an act, for the statement turns on a continuous condition.
How devoid of all reason would be the idea of a long-continued mersion in water of a living man! That remarkable events and casualties of life should exercise, for a
long time, a controlling influence over our feelings, so that
we should feel a reluctance to speak of them, is a matter
of daily experience. This, and not plunging or lying
drowned in water, is the statement made by Heliodorus.

---

15. " Great at Salamis; for there, fighting, he mersed
all Asia." HEIMERIUS.

17. " Salamis was the pinnacle of exploits; where thou
didst merse Asia." LIBANIUS.

However bravely the attempt may be made to put " all
Asia" into the waters of the gulf Argolis, the attempt will
issue in both a physical and rhetorical failure. Why
should "all Asia" be dipped, or plunged, or sunk into the
gulf? All the fleet was not. The mersion of Asia did
not turn on the mersion of the ships. If not one vessel
had been sunk, but every vessel captured and brought
into port, Asia would have been, equally, mersed. Had
the battle been fought on the land, in a sandy desert, with
like issue, Asia would, still, have been mersed. It was
the triumphant victory, which gave Greece a power competent to sway a controlling influence over, to merse, Asia.
Gale would dip a lake into the blood of a frog, because
he would not acknowledge a secondary meaning to βάπτω.
Carson exclaims: " Monstrous perversion of taste!" And

all from a denial of the truth,—βάπτω has a secondary meaning. Its admission obliterates all idea of a dipping, and establishes an *effect* in the stead of an *act*.

When will a second Carson arise, and, with imperial utterance, constrain his friends to confess βαπτίζω, too, has a secondary meaning, putting to flight shadowy figures and "monstrous perversions of taste"?

Asia was mersed by "fighting," not by dipping. Controlling influence changed her condition.

---

16. "He exhorts the class of bread-makers to be more just, but he did not think it proper to use compulsion, fearing the running away of the mass; by which the city would, immediately, be mersed, just as a ship, the sailors having deserted it." LIBANIUS.

Two mersions are, here, distinctly stated. The one of a city, and the other of a ship. The one by the desertion of food-makers, the other by the desertion of the navigators. Mersion in the one case is said to be just as certain as in the other. That the one mersion is like the other is a folly not stated. That the one mersion is likened to the other, as a dipping, or plunging, or sinking in water, is a crude conceit nowhere intimated. There is a point in which the two widely different mersions are like; not a likeness dimly seen through the haze of figure, but an absolute likeness. The likeness is that of *certain ruin.* A city abandoned by its food-producers will be ruined by tumult and famine. A ship abandoned by its navigators will be ruined by winds and waves. The nature of the baptism in the one case and in the other, is indicated by its proximate cause.

It would be difficult to find a clearer proof passage of the existence of the secondary meaning contended for. Agreements and differences are best seen when the objects involved can be placed side by side. This is done here. And we find that the baptism of an abandoned city, and the baptism of an abandoned ship, have nothing in common, save *the being subject to controlling influences issuing in destruction.* This is the point of likeness stated by Libanius. It is the true, only, and all-sufficient point of contact between the primary and secondary meaning.

All attempts to trace resemblances between dippings, plungings, and sinkings in water, is as unprofitable as ploughing the sand. Bread-makers would baptize the city.

---

18. "He who hardly bears the things which he is, already, bearing, would be mersed by a small addition."

LIBANIUS.

Where is the person, here, spoken of? On the land or in the water? What are the things which he is already bearing? Blocks of granite, or masses of pig-iron? If he is travelling, or swimming in the water, and bearing a hundred weight, a small addition may put him under the water; but if he is on the land, and his burden consists of intellectual or moral responsibilities and solicitudes, then, a very large addition will not transport him to a flood, or merse him under its surface; however much it might exercise a controlling influence over him.

No comparison is instituted with an overburdened vessel, but the statement has the most absolute limitation to the man and his circumstances. It is their influence, an influence to be determined by their nature, which is spoken of. A "small addition" may change his condition.

---

19. "This is he who having found the miserable Cimon mersed and forsaken did not overlook him." LIBANIUS.

Does the writer intend to picture Cimon as found lying under the water, drowned and forsaken?

A man who is in distress, beyond what courage and hope can contend with, is a mersed man; and would be so if there were not a drop of water on our planet.

20. " Grief for him mersing the soul and darkening the understanding, brings a certain mistiness over the eyes."

LIBANIUS.

This is a passage taken from a funeral discourse on the Emperor Julian. "*Whelms* the soul" (*Conant*). Against this translation we must enter our protest. Not on the ground of merit, but as a Baptist translation. We call attention to this translation, because, as used, it is full of meaning and an efficient argument for our cause. Dr. Conant gives sixty-four quotations, under the head of "Tropical or Figurative Sense." *Fifty-one* of these he translates by "whelm." Such a translation is contrary to Baptist views, long advocated, and is repudiated by Dr. Carson. This fact becomes the more remarkable, when it is added, that of eighty-six passages, under the caption, "Literal, Physical Sense," there is but a solitary case which receives this translation.

Dr. Conant's work has been too laboriously, and too artistically constructed, to permit us to suppose that no strong reason underlies these facts. Let me suggest: 1. *Whelm* does not answer Baptist views, because they have insisted upon an act, a definite act, an act which moves the object into the water. But whelm has not these characteristics. It expresses a condition; the result of the element coming over its object with uncontrollable power. Whelm is, therefore, eschewed by Baptists as representing the "Literal, Physical Sense," and im-merse, im-merge, sub-merge, dip, plunge, are pressed into the service. 2. These terms, which are made to express, as far as possible, forms of action, will not answer for the tropical or secondary use; because it exhibits merely controlling influence, eliminated from the primary, physical use, and resort is had to *whelm*, which does, in like manner, carry into tropical or secondary use the same idea of controlling influence. Dr. Conant, therefore, in rejecting im-merse, im-merge, sub-merge, plunge, dip, in the tropical use (these words not carrying with them the idea of

controlling influence), and by adopting the before discarded term, *whelm* (which does carry with it this idea),
furnishes the most conclusive testimony to the point, that
βαπτίζω, when turned from its primary use, does carry with
it, and directly express, the secondary meaning of *controlling influence*. Thus, "grief" is said, in the passage before us, to exercise "a controlling influence over the soul,
darkening the understanding," &c. A physical, whelmed
condition is induced by other forms of movement than
flowing. A falling avalanche whelms. Whatever comes
upon and rises over constitutes a whelming. Nor is it
matter in masses, or fluids in streams, only, that whelms.
Flakes of snow, particles of sand, drops of water, may
whelm. The traveller may be whelmed by snow-flakes;
the caravan may be whelmed by sand particles; and the
globe may be whelmed by rain-drops.

Whelm in secondary use rejects, 1. All forms of action;
2. All varieties of physical material; 3. All physical covering; and adopts, and carries with it into its new domain,
controlling influence, which is, always, present in every
case of physical whelming.

It is because of this truth that Dr. Conant abandons his
translations in the physical use, and adopts another in
what he terms figurative use. In so far forth as controlling influence is concerned, baptize and whelm do, very
completely, measure each other. The nature of this influence is determined by its adjunct terms. It may be of
joy or sorrow, virtue or vice, life or death. Whatever can
influence its object controllingly—be it great or small,
much or little; be it applied to the lips as wine, to the
eyes as poppy-juice, to the ears in perplexing questions,
to the heart through joy or grief—whelms, baptizes,
merses, changes, completely, the condition.

---

21. "But the remainder (of the city councils) being
small, was mersed."   LIBANIUS.

This refers to the opposite courses, selfish and unselfish,

pursued by the members of the councils in the cities, and
the issue to the honest few. They were mersed; and
fidelity to their trust ended in beggary.

The absolute use of the word, joins, with all other considerations, to demand a direct and essential value to be
given to it. The influence brought to bear upon them
was beyond their control.

22. "But now, as you see, the matter (of instruction,
Libanius was a teacher) being mersed, and all the winds
put in motion against it."   LIBANIUS.

As the context speaks of "sailing," &c., we may suppose, from the rhetorical embellishment, that the origin
of the word was present to the writer's mind. There is,
however, a strong and exclusive forth-putting of the idea
of controlling influence.

23. "But you do not announce this want of leisure to
those giving splendid feasts; but if asked your decision
concerning any more important matters, you have no
leisure, but are mersed."   LIBANIUS.

Such free and absolute use of the word is highly indicative of its being not merely a satellite in the world of
letters, shining only with borrowed light, but a fixed star,
having light of its own. If we are unable to affix a specific
character to the general import of the word, as thus absolutely used (and some question might arise here), still, we
know, beyond controversy, that some controlling influence
is referred to.

24. "But when he does not so continue, being mersed
by diseases and by arts of wizards."   PLOTINUS.

"Whelmed either with diseases or with arts of ma-

gians" (*Conant*). Why not *in* diseases and *in* magical arts
as well as "*in* sleep"? The former is as suitable to represent the *element* of mersion as the latter. But neither of
them should do so. It is the *agency*, the source of influence, only, that is spoken of. And what appearance
of water is there in this statement? How shall it be introduced? What part belongs to "diseases and wizard arts"
in the picture? Does the unhappy man lie down on the
sea-shore while diseases and incantations, converted into
billows, roll over him? Or, is the sufferer to be metamorphosed into a ship, and the scene a naval battle, where he,
as a ship, goes down under the hostile assaults of disease
and magic, in the shape of "stones and machines"? The
picture must be filled up in some such way, if we have a
picture at all.

But Dr. Carson says, that "whelming" is no baptism in
fact, but only *è gratia*, because whelming is not dipping.
If Dr. Carson be right, then Dr. Conant bases a figure on
a figure, which is a very baseless basis. But if Dr. Carson
be wrong, then his "millenary" honors become imperilled
among his friends, while they deny his "complete demonstration" that "βαπτίζω means nothing but dip."

I will not say that this very remarkable language of
Plotinus cannot, by ingenuity or violence, be made to take
the aspect of figure; for, with "ample verge and room,"
this can be done to almost any language. When Marcus
Antoninus speaks of a man δικαιοσύνη βεβαμμένον, Dr. Gale says
he speaks in figure, and βάπτω has its primary meaning.
The man is "*dipped in* justice." Dr. Carson protests
against this, declaring that βάπτω has here a secondary
meaning, and is used literally, meaning to *dye with*. Again,
Dr. Carson says: the sea-coast is baptized, not literally,
but only by the help of figure; while Prof. Ripley says,
there is no figure about it, but βαπτίζω means *to overflow*.

Now, until these most estimable Doctors can agree as
to what is primary and secondary use, what is literality
and figure, in the case of these words, they should not
press their opponents too hardly with the dogmatic asser-

tion, that the case before us is figure, and that "diseases and wizard arts" represent ocean billows.

---

25. "He is praised because he mersed the stewards; being not stewards but sharks." PLUTARCH.

I do not know the nature of this baptism. I cannot say that water had not something to do with it, or everything, because I have no certain knowledge. The passage, as it stands (I am indebted for it to Dr. Conant), does not throw a ray of light upon the nature of the baptism. It is impossible to tell whether it is primary or secondary, literal or figurative. The stewards might have been *drowned*, might have been *put to sleep* by an opiate, might have been *made drunk*, might have been *confounded* by an *exposé* of their administration, or a dozen other things, and the language would apply equally well in either case. They would all, alike, be mersions, baptisms. How delusive is the position,—"One meaning, clear, precise, definite, through all Greek literature." Any such word could expound itself. But this word cannot. Completeness of condition is its essential demand.

---

26. "Mersed by worldly affairs—we should struggle out and try to save ourselves, and reach the harbor."
PLUTARCH.

Rhetorical figure carries the mind back to the circumstances out of which the secondary use sprang. Therefore, to insist on introducing shipwreck, struggling, swimming, reaching a harbor, into every conversational use of the word, would be as stilted and as mistaken as to put on a state dress to go out and do a day's ploughing.

---

27. "Knowing him to be licentious and extravagant, and mersed by debts of fifty millions." PLUTARCH.

" Whelmed with debts amounting to fifty millions"
(*Conant*). " Oppressed with a debt of five thousand myr-
iads" (*Carson*).

Conant figures the debts as a mass falling on the debtor,
or as flowing waters rolling over him. It is entirely wrong,
according to Carson, to expound βαπτίζω as bringing the
element over the object. The word demands that the
object be put into the element. Hence the figure which
he pictures, out of these same materials, is that of a man
sinking, in still waters, with a millstone around his neck.
" This debt was not poured upon him, nor poured into
him; but oppressed by it, as a load, he *sunk*, or became
insolvent." " The figure does not represent the mode of
putting the debt on him, for in this there is no likeness.
It represents the debt, when on him, as causing him to
sink."

Carson forgets that he should make the debt *to dip* the
man, not *to sink* him. But we get used to this slipping
one word into the place of another, in reading this writer.
I would, also, call attention to the confusion and error
arising from the use of "oppress" as the equivalent of
press. To press and to oppress are very different words.
The same amount of pressure may cause oppression to
one man and not to another. Debt or load may press on
a man, and his ability to bear the one or the other be
entirely adequate. Debt or load which oppresses a man
has reached a measure exhaustive of his ability. When,
therefore, Dr. Carson translates by " oppress," he vindicates (in like manner as Conant by his translation,
" whelm") the point we advocate—namely, a secondary
use expressive of *controlling* influence.

Carson has, heretofore, remarked: " To be dipped in
debt, supposes that we owe something considerable in
proportion to our means." In this he is professedly speaking of the Greek βαπτίζω, while, really, he is expounding
the English *dip*. Dipped, in connection with debt, in English, implies but a slight indebtedness compared with the
means to pay; baptized, in the same connection, was used

by the Greeks to express indebtedness beyond all means to pay. "We may be dipped, in debt, without being drowned. The last cannot be adequately represented by baptizo, except when circumstances render the meaning definite." The reverse of this statement is the truth. A man baptized in water is a *drowned* man, unless there is evidence to the contrary; and a man baptized in debt is a *ruined* man, unless there is evidence to the contrary. It is very doubtful whether the English language can furnish a second book equalling that of Carson in its confusion of important words.

It is not claimed that this mersion is *in* debts; the dative is instrumental, as elsewhere. In every aspect the passage vindicates the idea of controlling influence.

---

28. "Eager that their children excel, quickly, in all things, they impose on them labors beyond measure. . . . For as plants are nourished by water, in measure, but are choked by excess, after the same manner the soul grows by labors, in measure, but is mersed by excess."

PLUTARCH.

It is impossible to figure "mersed" as a dipping in water without making Plutarch one of the saddest of blunderers. "The soul *grows* by limited labors, but is *dipped in water* by unlimited labors." Is that the way in which the preceptor of Trajan harmonized the members of a sentence? Certainly he succeeded better in the attempt immediately preceding—"Plants are *nourished* by water in measure, but are *choked* by excess." We cannot consent to an interpretation of "mersed" which casts shame on this accomplished Greek writer. If he affirms that the influence of moderate labor is healthy growth, then he affirms that the influence of excessive labor is unhealthy decay. Moderate labor is within the power, under the control, and made subordinate by the soul, to its advantage; immoderate labor is beyond the power, not subject to the control of the soul, but subordinates the soul to itself, and injures or destroys it. To express such controlling influence, Plutarch employs the term in question.

Carson thus comments: " Mr. Ewing says, ' the reference here to the nourishment of plants indicates *pouring*, only, to be the species of watering alluded to in the term.' But in this figure there is no reference at all to the mode of watering plants. The reference is to the quantity of water. The mode is not mentioned; but even were it mentioned, it would merely be a circumstance to which nothing corresponds in the thing illustrated. What critic would ever think of hunting after such likeness in figurative language? There is, actually, no likeness between the mode of watering plants and the proportioning of labor to the mind of a pupil; and Plutarch is not guilty of such absurdity. To Plutarch's figure it would be quite the same thing, if a pot of plants was dipped into water, instead of having the water poured into it. The pot itself might be dipped into water without any injury to the plants. The plants are injured when the water is suffered to lie about them in too great abundance, in whatever way it has been applied. The choking of the plant corresponds to the suffocation in baptism or immersion. The choking of the powers of the mind is elegantly illustrated by the choking of the vegetable powers when a plant is covered in water. There is a beautiful allusion to the suffocation of an animal under water. Were Plutarch to arise from the dead, with what indignation would he remonstrate against the criticism that makes him to refer to the *mode* of watering plants, in a figure intended to illustrate the bad effects of too much study! How loudly would he disclaim the cold, unnatural thought! Is it not possible to illustrate, figuratively, something by a reference to the mountains buried under the snow, without referring to the *manner* of its falling, and pursuing the resemblance to *the flakes of the feathered snow?* So far from this, I assert, that this manner of explaining figures is *universally improper.* No instance could be more beautifully decisive in our

favor than the above figure of Plutarch. Mr. Ewing
makes him compare the *choking* of one thing to the *overwhelming* of another. But the author himself compares
the *choking of a plant*, or the extinction of vegetable life, to
the *choking or extinction of the mental powers;* and in both
there is an elegant allusion to the choking of an animal
under water."

In this interpretation Carson abandons dip, all act, and
makes the solution turn on *effect*, a doctrine which he
reprobated in Gale and Cox. This effect results from
"water lying about" the plants. But can "dip" produce
any such effect? Besides, it is not the "lying about,"
whether by pouring or any other way, with which the
sentiment has to do; but the consequent result, the influence proceeding from such a condition. It is that destructive influence, and not a mersed condition, any more
than the form of the act, inducing such condition, of which
Plutarch speaks. Carson cannot interpret the passage
without an utter abandonment of that meaning, of which,
he says, he has made a "complete demonstration."

Compare the views here announced with those on the
baptism of taxes. "In this figure the rulers are supposed
to *immerse* the people. The literal translation is—'they do
not immerse the people with taxes.' The people, in such
figure, *sink* by being weighed down with taxes. They
cause the people to *sink* by their weight. It is a deep
water in which we *sink*. To sink by debt, figures the
debt as a load on our shoulders, while we are in deep
water. A man struggling for life in deep water, and at
last sinking by exhaustion, is a true picture of an insolvent
debtor."

Thus we see, when Dr. Carson can lay his hands on
immersing, sinking, plunging, or *struggling,* in water, whether
lawfully or unlawfully, he works them into figure with a
will. But when the act is *pour*, why, then, to base interpretation on that, is enough to stir old Plutarch in his
grave, and put a tongue between his crumbling teeth to
cry out in indignation. When the act by which a baptism

takes place is, or is supposed to be, dipping, plunging, sinking, mode is everything, and βαπτίζω denotes modal act; but when the act of baptism is *pour*, then, "it is nought, it is nought," cries the controversialist; and βαπτίζω has nothing to do with the act; everything is concentred in effect, resultant condition, water *lying about* the plants, and consequent choking influence!

When it is claimed that hot iron may be cooled by pouring water upon it, Carson is indignant that "the usual mode" should be disregarded. When it is pleaded that "the usual mode" of watering plants is by pouring, why, then, the pot can be just as well dipped!

The choking or extinction of the mental powers is compared to the "choking of a plant." Plutarch does not say one syllable about the *choking* of the mental powers, and the introduction of the word is a surreptitious abandonment of the claimed figure, dipped in water, for the influence which results from a mersion. And as for the elegant allusion in "the soul mersed by excessive labor" to an "animal suffocating under water," Plutarch will not be indignant at such an allusion being, most gratuitously, attributed to him, for Plutarch, alas, is dead! But Dr. Carson thinks that no likeness can be pointed out between an act and an effect. We are glad to hear him say so. How it happens that he has undertaken to point out the resemblance between *the act* of baptism (mode and nothing but mode) and *the effect* of debt, taxes, grief, sleep, wine drinking, &c., &c., we will not attempt to explain. He says: "Plutarch is not guilty of such absurdity." Put another name for Plutarch, and will the commission of the absurdity be wisdom?

Whether we regard the passage itself, or its attempted exposition by those who would expound it as a water figure, we are shut up to the conclusion that controlling influence proceeding from excessive mental labor, is what is, only and directly, stated.

29. " The Io-Bacchus was sung in feasts and sacrifices of Bacchus, mersed with much wantonness." PROCLUS.

"Im-bathed with much wantonness" (*Conant*). Baptist translators have a remarkable *penchant* for compounding the translation of βαπτίζω as in *im*-merse, *im*-merge, *sub*-merge, *over*-whelm, *im*-bathe, when there is no corresponding feature in the original.

It is, somewhat, remarkable that the power of the dative should assert itself as agency contrary to the tendency of the use of *im*-bathe to convert it into the mersing element. Milton's language, probably, helped to this result. In "imbathe," dipping, plunging, sinking, all disappear. The cherished dogma, "mode, and nothing but mode," has utterly vanished. Im-bathe has not the strength of an infant to put its object in anything. It may, but does not necessarily, envelop its object. It has extremely limited use in application to physical elements, and I do not know that it is found in such use out of poetry. Imbathe and bathe-in are no more equivalent, in use and meaning, than are op-press and press-on. Imbathe and oppress refer, almost exclusively, to things and influences which are un-physical. When Dr. Conant translates by the very unusual word "imbathe," (unusual, I mean, in his translations), he does, again, establish the position that the usage we are examining is declarative of controlling influence.

He quotes Milton : " And the sweet odor of the returning gospel imbathe his soul with the fragrancy of heaven." The soul is not put into this heavenly fragrance, but it comes upon the soul, and communicates to it its delights aboundingly. A passage more parallel in sentiment may be found in Spenser :

> " That nigh his manly hart did melt away,
> Bathed in wanton blis and wicked joy."

Imbathe always implies influence from the element or agency imbathing. Milton gives an illustration :

" Bearing her straight to aged Nereus' hall,
  Who, piteous of her woes, rear'd her lank head,
  And gave her to his daughters to imbathe
  In nectar'd lavers strew'd with asphodel,
  And through the porch and inlet of each sense
  Dropt in ambrosial oils till she revived,
  And underwent a quick immortal change."

Comus, 835–41.

Hence, when Dr. Conant says this is "the corresponding English word," there is much truth in it, so far as this secondary use is concerned; but very little so far as the primary use is concerned; as the facts abundantly show.

----

30. "But when she (Philosophy) sees me mersed by grief and carried away into tears, she is displeased."

THEMISTIUS.

"Whelmed by grief and moved to tears" (*Conant*). In translating εἰς δάκρυα καταφερόμενον—"moved to tears"—is it designed to treat this as figure? Is "tears" to be represented as a town some distance off, to which "move" carries Themistius? Or, is καταφερόμενον a rushing torrent, bearing the mourner for his father into some gulf or bay denoted by "tears"? Does any one say, "this is inexcusable ridicule." I answer, it is just such exposition as this that Carson treats us to when he represents Egypt flooded with water, and its inhabitants sinking in the flood with loads upon their backs labelled "taxes." Or, debtors floundering in deep water, and going down under the burden of unreceipted bills.

If "moved to tears" is an everyday phrase, well understood as directly expressive of a change in feeling under some powerful influence, which it becomes an impertinence to expound, soberly, as figure denoting a change in locality; by what law is it that "mersed by grief" is excluded from the same just method of interpretation?

"Mersed by grief" was as familiar phraseology to the

Greeks, expressive of the controlling influence of sorrow, as is "moved to tears" familiar to us, as expressive of a change of feeling under tender influences. While the origin of both is obvious, frequent use has given to each a direct power of expression which at once carries thought to the mind without any, the least, reversion to a pri mary use.

These phrases justly claim our recognition of them in this their acquired character.

WHAT IS IN PROOF?

Having seen exemplified by numerous passages—(1.) Simple intusposition without influence; (2.) Intusposition accompanied with influence; (3.) Intusposition for the sake of influence—we have, now, very conclusive evidence for, (4.) *Influence* WITHOUT *intusposition.*

That such a change is no novelty in the history of language is evident:

1. From an analogous change in βάπτω. This word, originally, meant to dip. By dipping into coloring matter the object became colored; hence, came the secondary meaning *to dye*, in which the original act, dip, was laid aside, and the resultant influence of the act, color, was retained.

2. By a similar change in *steep*. The primary use of this word requires intusposition within a fluid, for the purpose of giving or receiving thorough influence. In this respect it is quite identical with the third class above mentioned. But steep does, in usage, *lay aside this intusposition*, both as of fact and of figure, retaining only the idea of fulness of influence. Witness the following:

> "The soveraine weede betwixt two marbles plaine
> Shee pownded small, and did in peeces bruze;
> And then atweene her lilly handës twaine
> Into his wound the juice thereof did scruze;
> And round about, as she could well it uze,
> *The flesh therewith she suppled and did steepe.*"

F. Q. iii, 5.

Also this:

> " But faire Priscilla (so that lady hight)
> Still, by her wounded love did watch all night,
> And all the night for bitter anguish weepe,
> *And with her tears his wounds did wash and steepe.*"
>
> *F. Q.* vi, 3.

3. If this usage were originally tropical, it is an uncontroverted point, that tropical use may become literal.

4. It is impossible to make these passages figure simple intusposition. With this they have no shadow of sympathy. Every letter sends forth a ringing cry of influence. It must, then, be intusposition for influence. But if so, then we must rack our invention for an element (for none is stated) appropriate to each case. The idea of making *water* the element into which these varied agencies merse their objects, is sheerest nonsense.

5. There is no escape from influence under any interpretation. We claim it proved that βαπτίζω, absolute or with appropriate case, in unphysical relations, expresses CONTROLLING INFLUENCE *without intusposition.*

CONTROLLING INFLUENCE—SPECIFIC.

WITH OR WITHOUT INTUSPOSITION.

SECONDARY USE.

There are some things which exert over certain objects a definite and unvarying influence. Whenever, therefore, βαπτίζω is employed to denote the relation between such agencies and their objects, it no longer expresses a merely general influence, or one which, while receiving some coloring, still admits a varied application; but gives development, in the completest manner, to that specific influence which belongs to the case in hand. The specific influence exerted by water over a human being put within it, is *to drown*. The specific influence of wine, freely drunk, is *to intoxicate*. The specific influence of an opiate is *to stupefy*. The specific symbol, influence of pure water, or sea water, used in religious rites, is *to purify*.

The rising sun does not more surely, or more necessarily, bring with it light, than does this Greek word, in such relations, bring with it the specific conceptions of induced drowning, drunkenness, stupefaction, and purification. And it would be just as necessary and suitable to call in the help of an old broom to aid the sun in clearing away the mists of night, as to call in the help of figure to illumine a usage which is so perfectly self-resplendent.

This usage justifies, in the fullest manner, the conclusion founded on the preceding passages, and goes beyond them, in that it justifies and enables us to employ specific terms, which definitely embody the influence in question, as the most legitimate translation of the word, used absolutely, or, of a phrase, with which it is in living union.

Some passages justifying this view will, now, be presented.

SPECIFIC INFLUENCE.

1. *Ἦν τῷ αὐτῷ φαρμάκῳ καταβαπτίσας.*
Achilles Tatius, Leuc. and Clit., ii, 31.

2. *Βεβαπτίσθαι τε τῷ ἀκράτῳ . . . δοκεῖτέ.*
Athenæus; Philos. Banq., v, 64.

3. *Εἶτ᾽ ἐλευθέραν ἀφῆκεν βαπτίσας ἐρρωμένως.*
Athenæus; Philos. Banq., ix, 44.

4. *Οἴνω δὲ πολλῷ ᾽Αλέξανδρον βαπτίσασα.* ᾽ *Conon; Narrat.,* L.

5. *Βαπτίζει δ᾽ ὕπνῳ γείτονι τοῦ θανάτου. Evenus Paros; Epigr.,* xv.

6. *Ὕδατι βαπτίζεται . . . ὕδατι κατασβεσθὲν. Homeric Alleg.,* p. 495.

7. *Καρηβαροῦντι καὶ βεβαπτισμένῳ ἔοικε. Lucian; Bacchus,* vii.

8. *᾽Αυτός εἰμὶ τῶν χθὲς βεβαπτισμένων. Plato; Banquet,* iv.

9. *Καὶ ἐγὼ γνοὺς βαπτιζόμενον τὸ μειράκιον. Plato; Euthedemus* vii.

10. *Βαπτίζοντες ἐκ πιθων μεγάλων . . . προέπινον.*
Plutarch; Alexander, lvii.

11. *Κραιπαλῶσι γὰρ ἔτι τὸ χθιζὸν καὶ βεβαπτισμένοις.*
Plutarch; Water and Land Anim., xxiii.

12. *Εὐκρασία σώματος ἀβαπτίστου καὶ ἐλαφροῦ. Plutarch; Banq.,* vi.

13. *Τὸ δὲ σῶμα . . . μήπω βεβαπτισμένον.* " " iii, 8.

14. *Βαπτίζειν τὸν Διόνυσσον πρὸς τὴν θάλατταν.* " *Phys. Ques.,* x.

15. *Καὶ βάπτισον σεαυτὸν ἐις θάλασσαν. Plutarch; Superstition,* iii.

---

1. Whom having de-mersed by the same drug. *Achilles Tatius.*
2. You seem to be mersed by unmixed wine. *Athenæus.*
3. Then, mersing powerfully, he set me free. "
4. Having mersed Alexander by much wine. *Conon.*
5. Merses by a sleep, neighbor of death. . . *Evenus.*
6. Merses by wàter. . . . quenched by water. *Homeric Alleg.*
7. Resembles one heavyheaded and mersed. *Lucian.*
8. I myself am of those mersed yesterday. . *Plato.*
9. I knowing the youth to have been mersed. "
10. Mersing out of great wine-jars, drank to one another.
Plutarch.
11. Crippled and mersed by yesterday's debauch. "
12. A good temperament of the body, unmersed and active.
Plutarch.
13. But the body not yet mersed. . . . . "
14. To merse Bacchus at the sea. . . . . "
15. And merse thyself, (going) to the sea. . "

SPECIFIC INFLUENCE.

STUPEFACTION.

" Satyrus had somewhat left of the drug by which he had put Conops to sleep. Of this, while serving us, he pours, secretly, into the last cup which he brought to Panthia. She, rising, went into her chamber and immediately slept. But Leucippe had another chamber servant, whom, having mersed by the same drug, Satyrus comes to the doorkeeper, at the third door; and him he cast down by the same potion."   ACHILLES TATIUS.

Four cases are here presented, with varying phraseology, in which the work of stupefaction is accomplished by an opiate drug.

Are these cases all spoken of under the form of figure? Are some presented in figurative dress, and some in literal attire? Or, are all spoken of with a simple, prosaic literality?

If all are figure, by what figure are Conops and Panthia put to bed? Does the drug, under figure, perform the office of a chamberlain?

And by what figure is the doorkeeper " cast down " to the ground? Does the drug, here, represent an expert in wrestling, or a bludgeon, or what? And Leucippe's handmaid, by what figure is she " whelmed " (*Conant*), or *dipped*, as Carson would insist? Does this drug, now (chameleon-like), take the shape of a " mountain wave," or " a rushing torrent," or a weighty bale of " 'pothecary stuff," like unto the bales of " taxes " and " debts," &c., which we have seen baptizing, whelming, dipping, sinking so many heretofore?

If this view is not satisfactory, is there a mixture of the literal and figurative? And who is to take the responsibility of this clay-iron style of writing? In the absence of Tatius, I, as his nearest friend, beg that it may be laid at some other door than his.

Most persons will see, in this passage, a very unembel-
lished statement of the controlling influence of this drug;
and as it was soporific in its nature, always producing one
definite effect, they will recognize the propriety of translating the word which represents this influence by the
specific term—*to stupefy.*

DRUNKENNESS.

"You seem to me, O convivialists! to be flooded, beyond expectation, with impetuous words, and to be mersed
by unmixed wine."   ATHENÆUS.

The description of the wine, which causes this mersion,
as "unmixed," determines, in the most absolute manner,
that no physical "whelming" or "dipping" is in the mind
of the writer. As it is of no consequence to a drowned
man whether it is* salt water or fresh water that drowns
him, so it is of no consequence, in a physical mersion,
whether mixed or unmixed wine be used. But when the
influence of wine, as an intoxicating drink, is in question,
then it is a matter of prime importance whether it is the.
one or the other. As Athenæus lays emphasis on the wine
as without any mixture of water, he could only intend to
express its fullest intoxicating power. Unmixed wine,
freely used by convivialists, invariably produces one effect
—*makes drunk*—therefore, the word which embodies such
intoxicating influence may, with the highest propriety, be
translated by the specific word expressive of drunkenness.

"Then mersing, powerfully, he set me free."
                                                        ATHENÆUS.

"The servant girl, describing the effect of a cup of wine,
given by her master, says: 'Then whelming potently he
set me free.'" (*Conant.*)

Dr. Conant, in making βαπτίσας express an "effect," becomes exposed to the charge of treason to the cause, as
brought by Dr. Carson. "Potently" is not a proper quali-

fying term for dipping; nor for whelming, or mersing, or baptizing, in primary use. The agency may be potent, but not the condition. It is, entirely, proper as characterizing the secondary use, expressive of controlling influence.

A specific translation, here, is more than justified.

---

4. " Thebe exhorted to the murder, and having mersed and put to sleep Alexander, by much wine, she dismisses the guards of the bedchamber under pretext of using the bath, and called the brothers to the work."   Conon.

" Having immersed Alexander in wine—that is, having made him drunk with wine" (*Carson*).

This translation shows the intenseness of theory, while it exposes its error.

1. " Immersed." This word is, professedly, used as synonymous with dip. This profession is never carried out in practice, nor can ever be. Here, as in unnumbered other places, dip is slipped out and immerse is slipped in, because the former would not answer the purpose. To " dip any one in wine," for the purpose of representing a state of drunkenness, is figure which no thoughtful person ever employed. (1.) Because of inconsistency. Dipping causes but a trivial effect, while drunkenness is one of power. (2.) Because of want of adaptation. Nothing is made drunk by being put into wine.

But " immerse" is as unsuitable, for other reasons, as dip. No one insists more strongly than Carson that the whole person, in baptism, must go within the element, consequently, Alexander must go, head and ears, within the wine; and when there, he must stay there long enough to imbibe the intoxicating qualities of the element. How long this will take I cannot say; but quite probably before he gets drunk he will have got drowned. Such a case shows the Baptist error of confounding a dipping with a baptism. The qualities of wine cannot be extracted by a dipping, if they may by a baptism. It shows, also, the essential error of a figure which represents drunkenness by *immersing a living being in wine.* A condition which has no tendency to make drunk, but which must drown.

2. "*Much* wine." *Much* is, significantly, omitted in the translation. It has no fitness in announcing a physical mersion. What matters it whether Alexander were physically mersed in "*much* wine" or not? There is no significance in any quantity beyond what will barely suffice. Dr. Carson felt this, and throws it out. But this word is, eminently, significant, if the writer means directly to express a state of intoxication. "*Much* wine" gives emphasis to the influence exerted.

3. "*In* wine." The introduction of *in*, localizing the tyrant of Pheræ within the wine, is an error resulting from the previous error in the form of act attributed to the verb. If dip (or its claimed equivalent, immerse) be associated with a fluid, that fluid necessarily becomes the element, and if no appropriate preposition is furnished, one must be supplied. This Dr. Carson has found it necessary to do. Error begets error. This construction, with its translation, it is important to notice.

In the phrase, ἐβάπτετο δ'αἵματι λίμνη, the translation turns on the meaning assigned to the verb. Take the old Baptist position—βάπτω has but one meaning, *to dip*—and, of necessity, "the lake becomes dipped *in* blood." It is all idle to talk about rhetoric, bad taste, instrumental dative, and such like things, so long as the prime error is sustained. Abandon this error; admit that βάπτω has a secondary meaning in which no form of act appears, and every other error is carried with it. And, then, we have—"the lake DYED *by* blood." What a difference! The rectification of one word works the change. Color takes the place of the form of an act; instrumentality takes the place of locality; and literality takes the place of figure.

We, thus, see what vital issues depend on the right determination of the value of βαπτίζω. Has it "but one

meaning through all Greek literature—mode and nothing
but mode—to dip"? Or, is it devoid of all modal action—
demanding a condition of intusposition? And does it,
with a parallelism to βάπτω, lay aside this primary demand
for intusposition, and substitute for it a demand, only, for
controlling influence, which attends on some phases of intusposition, as *dyeing* on some cases of dipping? Apply
the one view, or the other, to a passage, quite parallel to
that just mentioned—ὕπνῳ τὴν πόλιν ἐβάπτιζον—and "*plunged
the city in* sleep," is the translation promptly offered by
the advocates of the first view. It is all in vain to plead
against the use of a term expressive of violence in connection with sleep. It is vain to speak of the questionable
rhetoric which picks up a city to plunge it into sleep. It
is equally in vain to plead for instrumentality in the dative.
The ear is deaf. It is filled, to repletion, with "one meaning, modal action, dip, plunge." Accept the alternative
view, and—"the city is *thoroughly influenced by* sleep." So
long as the old error in defining βάπτω is fastened on to
βαπτίζω, we must have errors of conception and translation
in the latter word paralleling those, now abandoned, which
mark the history of the former word.

Carson dips, plunges, immerses Alexander *in* wine, instead of allowing him to be "influenced (made drunk) *by*
wine." He might as well have allowed Gale to dip the
lake in blood, and not have insisted on its being influenced
(dyed) by blood.

INTERPRETATION.—After having, most loyally, paid trib-
ute to theory and system by introducing modal act and
figure into his translation, Carson adds—"that is having
made him drunk with wine." With this admission of the
meaning, and with the admission of Conant (in his translation, "*whelmed with wine*"), that there was no dipping,
even in the figure, we may be satisfied that we do not
greatly err in the position that *influence* is directly expressed, and as that influence can take but one form, the
translation is faithful which says, "having made Alexander
drunk by much wine."

This baptism claims attention in other aspects:

1. A physical, fluid element was present in the baptism and causative of it, *while there was no physical mersion* in this physical element. The idea of a figurative mersion in the wine drunk is untenable in every aspect. Carson would not put Otho *in* his debts; why will he put Alexander *in* his cups, or *in* his casks? But enough of figure. No one pretends that "the Tyrant" was physically dipped, mersed, or drowned. And yet a fluid element was present, was operative, and there was no physical mersion in it, or in anything else, although we are told by controversialists, "Alexander was dipped, immersed in much wine."

2. There was a baptism, it was caused by this fluid, yet not by it as a *fluid*.

The causative power of wine to effect this baptism was not its character as a *liquid*, but as possessed of an *intoxicating* quality. The exercise of this quality over the husband of Thebe did, in the estimation and absolute language of the Greeks, baptize him—merse him—as really and truly as if, instead of being laid in his chamber, he had been laid in the lowest cavern of the sea. The nature of the baptisms differs: the reality is equal.

3. The mode of using this baptizing element was by *drinking*.

Thus is its power to baptize developed. The skin is *bapted* by the rays of the sun falling on it. The *intellect* and *the body* are *baptized* by draughts from the wine-cup.

4. Symbol wine baptism may be set forth by *sprinkling* the intoxicating element.

> "Poure out the wine without restraint or stay;
> Poure not by cups, but by the belly full;
> Poure out to all that wall,
> And *sprinkle* all the posts and wals with wine,
> That they may sweat, and *drunken* be withal."
>
> *Spenser, Epithalamion.*

5. " Bacchus—wine—merses by sleep, the neighbor of
death."　　　　　　　　　　　　　　　EVENUS.

" *Plunges in* sleep, neighbor of death" (*Conant*). This
form of translation differs, both remarkably and unaccount-
ably, from the very uniform translation adopted in other
cases, identical in spirit and in grammatical structure. I
give the translation of all the passages from classical
writers, containing the simple dative, under the head,
" Figurative Sense," in Dr. Conant's classification.

1. " *Whereby*" (*i. e.* by which desertion) " the city would
have been whelmed." 2. " Whelmed *by* the calamity." 3.
" Whelmed *with* such a multitude of evils." 4. " Whelmed
by anger." 5. " Whelm the common people *with* taxes."
6. " Whelmed *with* debts." 7. " Overwhelmed *by* such
as are excessive." 8. " Whelmed *with* undiluted wine."
9. " Whelmed *with* much wine." 10. " Imbathed *with*
much wantonness." 11. " Whelmed *with* him in his grief."
12. " When midnight had plunged the city in sleep."

Thus, in every passage (but one, and in that relating to
sleep), the translation is by whelm, and with the prepositions (*by, with*) expressive of instrumentality. " *Plunge in*
sleep" is not only out of harmony with Dr. Conant's translations, but with the facts of nature. Dr. Cox complains
of opponents translating by *plunge*, because that word expresses " suddenness and violence." But neither " midnight" nor " wine" does " suddenly" or " violently"
plunge into sleep. Midnight perfects what earlier hours
of the night have been steadily bringing on. Wine does
not, primarily, induce sleep; that is a secondary result;
therefore, it cannot be characterized as sudden or violent.

It is very clear, both on general views of the meaning
of the word and the special features of the case, that
" plunge" has no right to appear here. Dismissing it,
then we have no difficulty in recovering " sleep" from its
false position as element, and instating it in its true position, as an instrument in the hands of Bacchus.

The alliance of a drunken sleep with death is founded in nature.

> "Ne would he suffer Sleepe once thether-ward
> Approch, albe his drowsy den were next;
> For next to Death is Sleepe to be compared;
> Therefore his house is unto his annext."   *Spenser.*

---

6. "Since, now, a mass of iron, pervaded with fire, drawn out of the furnace, is mersed by water, and the heat, by its own nature quenched by water, ceases."

HOMERIC ALLEGORIES.

"Since the mass of iron, drawn red-hot from the furnace, is *plunged in* water" (*Conant*).

1. It is as certain as anything in philology, that "plunge," distinctively, as expressing a form of action, does not define βαπτίζω. To *overflow*, as expressing a form of action, is as near the contradictory of plunge as it can well be; yet overflow is used by Baptist scholars to define this Greek word. And in such use overflow performs its duty, to say the least, as faithfully as does plunge. But it is a philological axiom, that where two differing forms of action can be employed in the exposition of the same word, such word can be, strictly, defined by neither.

Plunge has no right to appear as the critical representative of βαπτίζω. And in any case of baptism where the form of act is not expressly stated (it can never be learned from the word itself), it is entirely inexcusable for any one to bring forward the form of an act, insist upon its autocratic rights, and fashion the phraseology after its model.

No argument can be grounded on the assumption of a plunging.

2. The simple dative, with βαπτίζω, announces, with authority, the presence of agency and not of element.

There is, therefore, no authority in ὕδατι βαπτίζεται for saying that hot iron is "*plunged in* water." If it is urged,

in defence, that water is capable of receiving hot iron by
plunging; this is freely admitted. If it is urged, "hot
iron is very frequently, in fact, plunged in water," this,
too, is unhesitatingly admitted. And after all else can
be said, the reply is short and crushing—1. Βαπτίζω says
nothing about plunging. 2. Hot iron may be mersed in
other ways than by plunging. 3. The phraseology indicates the agency by which, and not the element in which,
the result is accomplished. Rational discussion must here
end.

Wine is capable of having an object "plunged in it;"
yet Dr. Conant does not say that Alexander was plunged
in it, in fact, but whelmed by it. A *soporific potion* is capable of having an object plunged in it; yet Dr. Conant
does not say that Leucippe's maid was so treated; but
whelmed with it.

3. A FLUID ELEMENT *may be used, as an agency, in baptism,
and accomplish such baptism, without involving the baptized object in a physical mersion.*

This is a vital position, and, if made good, carries everything with it. In support of it, now, I observe: 1. Wine,
a fluid element, has already been seen, as an agency, to
effect a baptism without any physical mersion. "But this
was figurative, and mersion is supposed to be in it." This
is an error. First. There is no sign of any such figure.
Second. The wine is used as agency, and not as element.
Third. The *physically mersing quality* of the fluid has nothing to do with the baptism. It is, exclusively, its *intoxicating quality* and the introduction of its physical quality is
a huge blunder. When Alexander was brought, through
the intoxicating principle, into a *drunken condition*, he was
baptized. Call this figure, if you will; it was baptism by
a fluid element, in which its nature as a fluid had no con-
cern. A distinctive principle, which is itself devoid of
covering qualities, performed the baptism. Wine baptizes
by its intoxicating principle solely; robbed of this it ceases to
baptize. Baptize is applied to the case, not because of

any physical investiture of the object, real or supposed, but because of a controlling influence.

2. An opiate potion, a fluid element, has, also, been seen to effect a baptism without any physical mersion. As in the case of wine, the fluid character of the agency had nothing to do with the baptism. No one has suggested "plunging" the doorkeeper into the potion to put him to sleep; and into the wine to make him drunk. Why not? A man put into the "elixir of opium" would as soon be put to sleep, as one put into a wine-cup, or cask, would be made drunk. And both would be put into that long sleep which "knows no waking." But the physically mersing quality of this drug-potion has nothing to do with the case. It is limited, solely, to the soporific principle. Had the drug been in the form of a pill, it would have baptized equally well. But what, then, would have become of the figure by which the baptized are to be "plunged in" a pill? The somnific quality of a potion drunk exhausts its baptizing power. Fluidity is an accident, a mere vehicle of the controlling influence.

3. Water, by its deintoxicating quality, when mixed with wine, baptizes wine. Does it do so by any physically mersing quality? All such notion, through figure or fact, is put to flight by such a baptism.

4. Dr. Fuller admits a case of baptism by water where the *drenching* qualities of water took the place of physical mersion. I do not enter into the case, because it is outside of classic writers; but I glance at the admitted existence of a case parallel with those in hand, and uniting to prove, that a quality of a fluid developed in a controlling degree over its object, is legitimately termed a baptism. Dr. Fuller retreats from the ruins of his falling system with the cry—"The writer is one of the most impassioned of men!"

5. The passage before us sustains the position. Water has many qualities besides that which adapts it for physical

envelopment. It will *make very wet,* as in Dr. Fuller's case, when poured on profusely; it will *make unintoxicating* when poured in wine; and it will *make cold* when poured on hot iron. And all these cases of controlling influence, apart from physical envelopment, the Greeks called baptisms.

Heraclides Ponticus (if the writer of the passage) gives an allegorical representation of Mars, Vulcan, and Neptune, under the symbols, Iron, Fire, and Water. Mars (iron) is held under the power of Vulcan (fire); but Vulcan being brought under the power of Neptune (water), Mars is set at liberty.

The point involved in this representation is not whether water can physically merse iron, but the relation between *heat* and water. The writer says that heat is of such a nature that it is mastered, mersed, completely controlled by water. This is not true of cold iron. Cold iron may be mersed in water; but this mersion is essentially different from the mersion of hot iron by water. The one is simply a mersion of position. Iron may be mersed a thousand years in water and not be influenced by it. The other is a mersion of influence. This has nothing to do with position. *Hot* iron is mastered, subdued, influentially baptized, robbed of its heat, by water, however brought in contact with it. Let it be remembered that it is the relation of water and heat, and not of water and iron, which is involved. The live chicken of the Roman poet was mersed by wine through mersion in wine, because the influence desired (drowning) could not be secured in any other way. Alexander was mersed by wine, not by mersing in wine; because the influence desired could not be secured in this way. It was not designed to have the physically mersing quality in *drowning;* but its influentially mersing quality in *making drunk.* Therefore, Alexander was not mersed in the wine, but the wine was mersed in Alexander. It was, only, thus that he could be mersed by wine.

Hot iron, when desired to be brought into a state of coldness, may be mersed by water by being mersed in water; or, if the iron be hollow, by mersing the water in the iron; or, if solid, by pouring the water over it; or, by sprinkling the water upon it. It is a matter of the most absolute indifference how the water is applied; βαπτίζω claims no control over it, and is infinitely indifferent to it. Although physical bodies are embraced in the transaction, still, physical mersion is not at issue; but the quality of water *to induce a condition of coldness* in a heated body. No one will say, that to induce this, physical intusposition is necessary. Mersion by water, and mersion in water, are two vastly different statements. Mersion by wine, and mersion in wine, are equally at variance. Mersion by a soporific draught, and mersion in a soporific draught, idiocy, only, could confound.

Heraclides does not say one syllable about a mersion in water. He says, that "*red hot* iron mersed by water"— brought under the cold-inducing quality of water—"the heat is quenched by the water, and ceases."

The use of the word must not be made the occasion of error. Βαπτίζω, second, must neither be deprived of its peculiar rights and privileges, nor made responsible for duties which belong exclusively to βαπτίζω, first. Βαπτίζω, like βάπτω, is geminal. For a very long time the distinct personality of the second was denied, and merged in the first. Whenever the second βάπτω appeared he was made, will or nill, *to dip*, by figure. And, now, the second βαπτίζω is made, rationally or irrationally, *to put under water*, by figure. It often happens that heated iron is of such weight, or form, or in such relations, that it cannot be physically mersed. I have witnessed such cases mersed— brought *out of a hot* state *into a cold* state—by water, both poured and sprinkled.

Spenser seems to have had his eye on the very passage before us when he wrote:

> "And hundred furnaces all burning bright
> To melt the golden metall, ready to be tryde:
> One with great bellowes gathered filling ayre,
> And with forst wind the fewell did inflame;

> Another did the dying bronds repayre
> With yron tongs, and *sprinckled* oft the same
> With liquid waves *fiers Vulcans rage to tame,*
> Who, maystering them, renewd his former heat."

5. COROLLARY.— *Whenever any liquid, possessed of a quality capable of exerting a controlling influence of any kind whatever, is applied to an object so as to develop such influence, it is said, on all classical authority, to baptize that object, without regard to mode of application, and with as little regard to physical position.*

---

7. " When an old man drinks, and Silenus takes possession of him, immediately, he is, for a long time, silent, and resembles one heavy-headed and mersed." LUCIAN.

This passage gives the clearest evidence for a secondary use and sense. Lucian is not speaking of drinking from a wine-cup, but from the fountain of Silenus. He does not describe directly the effect of such drinking, except as to its inducing " silence;" in other respects, he says, the drinker " resembles one heavy-headed and mersed."

In this statement, βαπτίζω is joined with a word which, in its literal, primary meaning, expresses one of the features of wine-influence over the system,—" heavy-headedness." It is incredible that a reference to intoxication would thus mix up together the literal and the figurative. If " heavy-head" is literal, " mersed," also, is literal. Again: We use for illustration things well known, to throw light on things less known. " Heavy-headedness and mersion," therefore, must have. been things well understood, as they are the illustrative explanation of the influence exerted upon those drinking of the Silenic fount. Now, these terms are used by Lucian to express a state of intoxication. They must, therefore, have been in familiar use, with such meaning. The language bears, on its face, evidence of well-worn, every-day use. " Mersed" is used absolutely and as self-explanatory. A coin worn smooth by use, a golden eagle with the bird of Jove worn away by attrition in passing through the hands of the million, does not more fully self-evidence long and familiar use, than does this phraseology prove every-day familiarity to the popular lip and ear.

But again: The idea of figure is precluded, because resemblances are not traceable between facts and figures. Figure cannot be the basis of figure. If Lucian uses the condition of mersion to expound some other condition, then the condition expressed by mersion must be a reality, and not the figure of something else.

We, then, have the case of a man not only baptized by a fluid element, but at a fountain without any mersion in it.

What higher evidence we could have that the Greeks appropriated this word to express a state of drunkenness, I do not know.

---

8. "For I myself, am of those who, yesterday, were mersed." PLATO.

Again, we have the absolute use of the word without the slightest indication of a picture or a comparison. Language could not be used more deeply stamped with the evidence of self-completeness. Yet Dr. Carson says: "When baptizo is applied to drunkenness it is taken figuratively; and the point of resemblance is between a man completely under the influence of wine and an object completely subjected to a liquid in which it is completely immersed" (p. 80). It is an error to say, "a man completely under the influence of wine resembles an object completely immersed in water." Because, 1. There is nothing in the former case to which the envelopment in the latter can be resembled. Wine does not exert its intoxicating influence by the envelopment of its object. 2. Envelopment of an object in water does not necessarily exert an influence over the immersed object. A flint stone, immersed in water, experi-

ences no influence from the enveloping fluid. 3. When
the object is of such a nature as to be influenced by such
position, as a man suffocated by encompassing water, there
can be no resemblance to such *position;* because a drunken
man is in no analogous position. The resemblance must
be confined to the influence, to the exclusion of position
inducing such influence; and in the influence there must
be a farther limitation : its specific character must be disregarded; for there is no resemblance between the specific influence of wine drunk, and the specific influence of
water over a man immersed in it. There is, then, nothing left but the *controlling power* as common to the one
and the other. Wine, in its fully developed influence,
sways *a complete and controlling influence* over the intellect
and body; water sways *a complete and controlling influence*
over a living man immersed in it. There is no resemblance between the mode in which the influence is exerted,
for there is no resemblance between drinking and immersion; there is no resemblance in the specific influence,
for there is no resemblance between drunkenness and suffocation; the resemblance is, and only is, in controlling
power: the wine controls human intellect, the water controls human life.

This is the original ground on which the word became
applied in secondary use; but to say that every use through
a thousand years must carry a designed, or an apprehended, resemblance, is to set at naught endless facts and
clearest principles in the development of language. All
resemblance might be expected to disappear, first, from
the form of utterance; then, from conscious intellectual
apprehension, leaving behind, only, the abstract thought
of controlling influence. The facts of usage show that
such was the case. An advance step would give the word,
by frequent appropriation, a specific character. This seems
to have been done, as in this and other passages, by its
identification with wine-influence. " I was of those, yesterday, mersed—*made drunk.*"

The perfectly analogous development of βάπτω has al-

ready been pointed out. Dr. Conant translates: " I myself am one of those who, yesterday, were overwhelmed."
By this translation he falls under the ban of Carson, who
affirms, " The classical meaning of the word is, in no instance, overwhelm" (p. 311). Whence this contradiction
between the ablest Controversialist and the Scholar without a superior among Baptists, in regard to a word of
" one meaning, easily understood, and to make a difficulty
in translating which is all a pretence"? Carson rejects
" overwhelm," because the word means the definite act,
" dip and nothing but dip, through all Greek literature ;"
a position which will never be maintained again by any scholar
of half the learning of Carson, after looking through the
facts of usage. This is not Conant's position. But what
his position is, is left in obscurity by the commingling of
the inconsistent terms, dip and plunge, severely modal in
form of act, and the use of immerse, immerge, and submerge, equivocal as to form of action; as, also, by the use
of the terms whelm, overwhelm, imbathe, immodal as to
act, but having a secondary use expressive of controlling
influence, while such use is denied.

In the passage before us, as an English word, " overwhelm" can, only, have the meaning of controlling influence. To say that it does, and is designed to figure
" mountain billows, rushing torrents, sweeping inundation, sinking with a millstone weight in deep water," is
preposterous. The meaning of controlling influence is
sustained by the quotation given by Conant: " In this use,
the Greek word corresponds to the English word *drench.*
So, Shakspeare, Macbeth, i, 7, (speaking of the ' spongy
officers' plied 'with wine and wassail,')"

> " When in swinish sleep
> Their drenched nature lies."

In a note, Dr. Conant adds: " Icelandic, *dreckia*, to plunge
in water; Swedish, *draenca*, same sense; also, *to drown.*—
Dict. of Eng. Etymol., Wedgewood." He might have farther
added, Saxon, *drencean*, to soak, to inebriate; Dutch, *dren-*

ken, to water, to soak. Is any support, herein, given to the idea that "overwhelm" means to plunge, or to be swept away by billows and torrents? Is it not established that "drench" has a secondary meaning, and a specific appropriation like βαπτίζω, to express "drowning" and inebriety?

Drench, like βαπτίζω, expresses no form of act, but condition. The condition demanded may be effected by any, competent, form of act; whether it be that of sprinkling, pouring, dipping, plunging, sinking, whelming, or what not. "Drench with water" is a command, not to execute a form of action, but to effect a certain condition; *to wet thoroughly*, to bring completely under the wetting quality of water. "Drench with wine" is a command, not to subject to the wetting quality of wine, but to bring completely under its *intoxicating* quality by drinking. "Drench with rhubarb" is neither to make wet, nor to make drunk, but to bring fully under its *purgative* quality.

Dr. Conant is right in saying "the Greek word corresponds to the English word drench," inasmuch as drench expresses, 1. Condition, and not the form of an act. 2. Completely developed influence. 3. Appropriation to drowning and drunkenness. He, therefore, errs when he translates the Greek word by "overwhelm," using it in any other sense than that of complete influence, unless he will attach to it the Saxon idea "to inebriate," and admit that βαπτίζω has secured to itself the power to express, directly, *a condition of intoxication*.

TO BEWILDER.

9. "I knowing that the youth was mersed, wishing to relieve him."   PLATO.

Cleinias, a young man, in company with some sophists, was hopelessly embarrassed by a series of subtle questions addressed to him. And, on this foundation, shall we sketch a picture of a youth exposed to rolling billows and sweeping torrents? If Gale was justly liable to the charge of a "monstrous perversion of taste," in dipping a lake into a frog's blood, to avoid a secondary meaning to βάπτω; what shall be said of those who will take Cleinias from his entangling questions to drown him in the sea, in order to escape a secondary meaning to βαπτίζω?

If usage like this does not prove an absolute departure from water mersion, both in fact and in figure, what can prove it?

To baptism, thus exhibited, there is but one idea to be attached; it is that of *bewilderment*. And this case shows the greatness of the error, when a figure is attempted, in bringing water envelopment, or any specific influence flowing from it, into the foreground of the picture. What has "bewilderment" to do with immersion in water or with suffocation? Understood to express, generally, controlling influence, it has a facile adaptation to any case, of whatever nature, marked by such influence. One bewildered by questions, or drunk with wine, is, equally, a baptized man. *They are brought into new conditions of being.*

TO MAKE DRUNK.

10. "You would not have seen a shield, or a helmet, or a long pike; but soldiers mersing with bowls and cups and flagons, along the whole way, pledged one another out of large wine-jars and mixing vessels."

"Εἶδες δ᾽ ἂν οὐ πέλτην, οὐ κράνος, οὐ σάρισσαν· ἀλλὰ φιάλαις καὶ ῥυτοῖς, καὶ θηρικλείοις παρὰ τὴν ὁδὸν ἅπασαν οἱ στρατιῶται βαπτίζοντες, ἐκ πίθων μεγάλων καὶ κρατήρων ἀλλήλοις προέπινον." PLUTARCH.

The historian is speaking of the riotous march of Alexander's army, through a region of abundance, after the perils and sufferings of the homeward march from their Eastern conquests.

"The soldiers along the whole way dipping with cups and horns and goblets, from great wine-jars and mixing-bowls, were drinking to one another" (*Conant*).

Dr. Conant mentions a doubt expressed by Du Soul as

to the correctness of the reading, βαπτίζοντες, on the ground of its construction with ἐκ πίθων. He thinks, however, that the difficulty is obviated by the suggestion of Coray, "a part of the action is put for the whole, as one must dip the vessel in order to fill it."

The difficulty arises from, and the explanation proceeds on the assumption, that the word signifies *to dip;* which is a mistake. It is quite possible that the cups, used for drinking, were filled by being dipped into the wine; but Plutarch says nothing about the manner in which they were filled. We must not confound βαπτίζω with βάπτω.

In the edition of Plutarch, before me, there is a comma after βαπτίζοντες; showing that, in the judgment of the editor, there was no immediate logical or grammatical connection between that word and ἐκ πίθων. According to the punctuation of this edition, and without changing the Greek order, it would read, "but with bowls and cups and flagons, along the whole way the soldiers mersing, out of large wine-jars and mixing-vessels, drank to one another;" or, the soldiers drank to one another, out of large wine-jars and mixing-vessels, with bowls and cups and flagons, along the whole way, mersing (making drunk one another). Βαπτίζω, in the sense to make drunk, is entirely familiar to Plutarch. The translation, "dipping," is entirely without authority from use, as has been shown; and as is confirmed by this construction so impracticable on that view. Yet Dr. Fuller translates—"*dipping* with cups . . . . out of large casks;" adding, "dipping wine out of casks is here called baptizing out of casks and urns." *Bapting* out of casks (although this is not said), might be expounded, but "baptizing out of casks" does not admit of exposition. Besides, Dr. Fuller seems to be entirely oblivious, that he had before, right squarely, turned his back on dipping as a sense beyond defence. At the sea-coast baptism the Doctor separated himself from the defeated dippers, and raised a banner for himself, exclaiming—"My position is that baptize means *immerse.*" What has become of that position in this "*dipping* out of casks, called *baptizing* (im-

mersing?) out of casks"? Oh! this slipping one word
into the place of another to meet an exigency! Look at
this translation, by dipping, to escape an immersion, and,
then, at the following statements, made, in triumph, to
escape from, impossible, dipping: "Every candid reader
will, I think, grant that I have ascertained the meaning
of Baptizo. It signifies *to immerse*, and *has no other meaning*" (p. 251). "To any man it ought to be enough that
I have proved *the only meaning of Baptizo to be immerse*"
(p. 58). Well; and if *immerse* has been *proved against dipping*, what about "*dipping* out of casks" "called baptizing"? The Doctor has two strings to his bow. Politi-
cians have a word, "gerrymandering," to denote all
manner of crookednesses. The full power of this word
will be taxed to express the ins and outs of Baptist writers
in jotting down the "one only meaning of βαπτίζω through
all Greek literature."

When Plutarch uses this Greek word, in connection
with the drunken rout described, he undoubtedly uses it,
as he does elsewhere, to express the controlling influence
of the wine, which was flowing like water.

––––––––––

11. "The nobleman being sober, as you see, and prepared, sets upon us debauched and mersed from yesterday."   PLUTARCH.

There is an express contrast made between one in a
state of sobriety and others in a state of inebriety. Drunkenness presents various stages and phases. It is to its later
developments that reference is, here, made.

How dipping into water is to be made, by figure, to
illustrate such a passage, I leave for others to explain.
The contrast of the sober man and the drunken man; the
association of κραιπαλάω with βαπτίζω; and the reference to
"yesterday," would seem to call for some other element
than water.

It is impossible to find resemblance between *the action*

22

of drinking and *the action* of dipping; for there is none.
It is impossible to find resemblance between *the mode* in
which wine (drinking) exerts its influence, and *the mode* in
which water (enveloping its object) exerts its influence;
for there is none. It is impossible to find any resemblance
between *the nature* of wine influence and *the nature* of water
influence; for there is none.

---

12. "A great resource, truly, for a pleasant day is a
good temperament of body un-mersed and unburdened."
PLUTARCH.

This remark is based on the benefit consequent upon an
abstemious mode of living. An unmersed body is one
not under the influence of wine. An unburdened body
is one under the influence of a cheerful spirit.

---

13. "Of those slightly intoxicated only the intellect is
disturbed; but the body is yet able to serve its impulses,
being, not yet, mersed."
PLUTARCH.

"For of the slightly intoxicated only the intellect is disturbed; but the body is able to obey its impulses, being
not yet overwhelmed" (*Conant*).

The word translated "slightly intoxicated," ἀκροθωράκων,
means, literally and primarily, "slightly *armed;*" yet Dr.
Conant does not hesitate to translate it as having, also,
the direct meaning, "slightly *intoxicated.*" Is there any
better reason for giving a secondary meaning to one of
these words rather than to the other? If the former
means "*slightly* intoxicated," must not the latter, of necessity, mean *thoroughly* intoxicated? Does Plutarch say,
the intellect yields, in the first stages of drunkenness,
while the body yields only in the later stages, when it is—
dipped in water?

Dr. Conant quotes another passage entirely parallel with

this, but, if possible, still clearer and more conclusive for our interpretation; but which I do not adduce, because not within the limits of those writers to which I, now, restrict myself. The passage is from Philo, and is translated thus: "And I know some, who, when they become slightly intoxicated" (αχροθώραχες, slightly armed), "before they are completely overwhelmed (baptized), provide by contribution and tickets a carousal for the morrow"— (*Conant*).

Any one who can accept this as saying—"when they become slightly intoxicated, before they become over-whelmed—*as it were dipped in water*—provide for a carousal next day"—need have no difficulty in rejecting the secondary meaning of βάπτω, and accepting the lake dipping in frog's blood.

All others will confess that βαπτίζω has acquired the power to express, directly, the influence of wine to make drunk. The evidence for this is *overwhelming*—not, "as it were, dipped in water, or sunk by a weight, or whelmed by a torrent"—but as adequate to exercise an influence controlling the judgment.

---

14. "Why do they pour in beside the wine sea-water, and say that fishermen received an oracle commanding them to merse Bacchus by the sea?" PLUTARCH.

"Why do they pour sea-water into wine . . . to merse Bacchus in (or at) the sea?" (*Conant*). A note is appended, in which is quoted the statement—"To immerse Bacchus is nothing else than *to temper wine.*"

Here is a baptism commanded by divine (according to their notions) authority. Dr. Conant says, it is a literal, physical (such is the caption) baptism. We are, then, happily, out of the land of figures. How was this oracle-command to baptize Bacchus obeyed?

1. *As to Bacchus.* We learn that Bacchus has no per-

sonality, but only stands as representative for wine. Well, then, the command is *to baptize wine.* How is this done?

2. *As to the sea.* It is to be done "by the sea." Whether this means locality, only, or directly declares, or indirectly suggests, the means of the baptism, all will admit that there is enough of appropriate element at hand for any amount of dipping, or any measure of immersion. How was it used? Wine, in a bottle, skin, or cask, is as capable of being dipped or immersed in the sea, or of being whelmed, "in the literal, physical sense," as any other thing. And such, we are told, is the only mode of literal baptism, and to this only one, all figurative baptisms must be *procrusted.* Was such the style of this Bacchus baptism?

3. *As to baptize.* Dr. Carson says, I will make the word baptize find me water, enough to dip in, amid a sandy desert. The word need not go far, then, when standing on the sandy shore of the sea, to find sufficient for every demand. Does it make use of it for "dipping" Bacchus? Does the fisherman take his wine-vessel, in his boat, out far enough, and honestly dip it, putting in a short distance, and, then, promptly recovering it? Or, as honestly baptize it by putting it under without regard to a recovery? The one way is *bapting,* the other way, unquestionably, is one mode of *baptizing;* and if there be "but one mode," then it is the only mode. Is this the fishermen's mode of baptizing Bacchus? Plutarch says not. He declares that as he was ensconced in the goblet they took water from the sea and poured it over him. "True, they poured the sea-water over him, but pouring is not baptizing; yet, if you pour long enough and cover him all over, there will be a baptism" (*Fuller*). I do not think the pouring was "long enough." I rather think that Bacchus would have resisted the mode as heretical and un-Greekly. Had it been persisted in "long enough," I think that he would have overleaped the goblet's brim, and utterly refused to be "covered over." In plain English, covering over wine,

by pouring water into it, cannot be done. The baptism must be sought in another direction.

Dr. Fuller admits, that an altar on which water was poured, without being "poured long enough to cover it," was, still, said to be baptized; because it was "drenched." Will Dr. Fuller admit that wine is "drenched" by water poured into it, although not "poured long enough to cover it"? Dr. Fuller has progressed from dipping to immersing, and from immersing to pouring long enough to cover, and from pouring long enough to cover, to pouring long enough to drench; will he take one more step in advance (it is all that I care for him to take), and pass on from "pouring long enough to drench," to pouring long enough *to change the quality or condition of an object?*

Let this be granted by Baptist brethren, and the material for controversy on this subject will be exhausted.

Does the case before us necessitate such acknowledgment? I think that it does, most unmistakably.

1. It is a fact, that Bacchus (wine) was commanded to be baptized.

2. It is a fact, that under this command water was poured into wine.

3. It is a fact, that water thus poured into wine exercises a controlling influence over it; "tempers it;" changes its character; takes away its intoxicating quality; removes it *out of the class* of intoxicating liquids *into the class* of unintoxicating liquids; changes its condition.

4. It is a fact that such baptism is in completest harmony with the exposition of the baptism of hot iron by pouring water on it: it controls its peculiar quality of heat; changes its character; makes it cold; brings it into a new condition.

5. It is a fact, that such baptism accords, most fully, with the exposition given of drunken baptism by pouring wine into a man; it controls him; changes his character; makes him irrational; removes him out of sobriety into inebriety.

6. It is a fact, that Dr. Conant places this among "literal, physical" baptisms. We are happy to have his high authority for such a truth. It has our very cordial concurrence. There is no dipping, no plunging, no immersing, but there is a controlling influence exerted over an object; and that, whether it be by putting water into wine, or wine into a man, or water upon hot iron, is true and literal baptism, if the usage of classical Greek writers is of any authority.

Wine made unintoxicating by water poured into it, is baptized wine.

PURIFICATION.

15. " Call the purifying Old Woman, and merse thyself (going) to the sea, and remain all day sitting on the ground."   PLUTARCH.

This baptism differs from all others which have claimed our attention (unless it be the baptism of Bacchus), in that it is a religious baptism. The passage constitutes the counsel given to one who had been disturbed, and was supposed to be defiled, by ill dreams. Sea-water is to be used *for the sake* of its purifying influence.

"Plunge yourself into the sea" (*Conant*). "Baptize yourself into the sea—this baptism, also, must be by immersion" (*Carson*).

1. It will be my endeavor to show that neither of the specific forms of action, " plunging into the sea,"—" dipping into the sea,"—is stated, or of necessity required, by the text.

2. To show that, no specific form of action being stated, it is wholly beyond our power to know (therefore with propriety to affirm) by what form of action this baptism was consummated.

3. To state a possible way in which it may have been done.

1. There is nothing in the passage to indicate the form of the act but βαπτίζω; and that word is incompetent to

perform any such duty, as has been, abundantly, shown. Besides, *plunge*, given by Conant, and *dip*, given by Carson (for " baptize means dip, and only dip"), are words of essentially different character; and baptize is so far from expressing either, that Fuller is compelled, openly, to abandon both for the cloudier term—" im-merse."

It is a point as settled as anything of the kind can be, that the demand for plunging or dipping rests in the fancy of these writers, and not in the Greek word.

" If the specific forms of act claimed are not in the word, yet is not a mersion, stripped of specific forms, to be found in ' the sea' ? " I answer, no; for Bacchus was baptized " by the sea" without mersion by any form *in* the sea.

" But does not the phrase βαπτίζειν εἰς θάλασσαν, necessarily require that the object (without giving to it form) should pass *into the sea?* " I answer, yes; provided there is an immediate relation between these words. That, however, is not necessarily the case in the present instance.

The person to whom these words are addressed is not standing on the sea-shore. If he were, these words would carry him (in some way not defined) into the sea. But he is at a distance from the sea, and, therefore, εἰς θάλασσαν may be exhausted by a relation established with a verb of motion to be supplied.

That this suggestion is not groundless is evident from the fact, that such a verb of motion is supplied in a French translation (1599), met with in the Philadelphia Library. It is true that this translation, still, supposed that there was a passing into the sea; but if this phrase be construed with a supplied verb, it is divorced from βαπτίζω, and has no longer power to interpret that word.

That such separation should take place may be, farther, argued from the unsuitableness of such phraseology to express the use of sea-water for purification. It is such language as is, elsewhere, used for *drowning*, and unless deliverance come from some other quarter than the phrase itself, drowning is inevitable. I do not say that every baptized man must become a drowned man; but I do say

that βαπτίζω never did, and never will take any man out of
the water; and a command to baptize a man in the sea,
or to baptize himself into the sea, is a command (interpreted simply by the force of its terms) to drown a man,
or to commit suicide by drowning, just as surely as that
2 and 2 make 4. For this reason, I say that the weight
of evidence is in favor of another, possible, interpretation.
The translation *may be*, "baptize thyself, going to the sea;"
leaving the way open, after arrival there, for the use of the
water, in any way that fancy, or superstition, or religious
usage may determine.

2. No manner of using the water having been stated,
and βαπτίζω being absolutely dumb with silence on that
point, no human being can throw one ray of certain light
on the mode of practice on this, or on any other occasion, characterized, only, by this single word. This truth
becomes emphasized when, as here, there is no demand for
even a mersed, physical, condition; much less for a definite
act to effect such condition.

If the counsel, given to the Dreamer, require mersion
in the sea, it is obvious that it does so, not as an end, but
as a means, a means to purification; but unless sea-water
cannot purify except mersed objects (which we know is
not true), then, so far as the attainment of this end, we
are not shut up to a mersion in the sea. And the way for
the manner of use opens wider still.

It is important to keep in remembrance that this was a
case of religious defilement; and that the point to be
secured was, to bring the man *out of this condition* of defilement *into a condition* of purity. Now, whatever will accomplish this will render him a baptized man, according to
the principle, "whatever is capable of changing the condition, character, and relations of its object, is capable of
baptizing that object." And, here, allow me to trespass,
once more, by a reference to a writer outside of the classic
circle. In the Stromata, iii, 18, ἐκ σωφροσύνης εἰς πορνείαν
βαπτίζουσι—δογματίζοντες, we have a baptism *out of one* condi-

tion *into another*, " out of purity into impurity," and the baptism is effected by "licentious teaching." This is the most perfect confirmation of the principle deduced from the classics— *Whatever exercises a controlling influence over its object*, BAPTIZES THAT OBJECT, *by transferring it from one state or condition to another*. If sea-water has a controlling influence over superstitiously induced defilement, then, *in whatever way such water may be used* (securing the development of such influence), *it baptizes*, taking out of defilement and putting into purity, with all its rights and privileges, whether by sprinkling or otherwise.

3. This sea-water may have been used by pouring, by sprinkling, by washing the hands, or in any other way in which it was popularly imagined, or religiously required, to secure purification. The word $\beta\alpha\pi\tau i\zeta\omega$ places, absolutely, no limits to the case. If it was supposed that the virtues of sea-water were secured by *drinking*, then such mode of use would be just as legitimate a *mode of baptism* as any other. It would control the condition. The Rev. R. S. Fullerton, missionary to Hindostan, says: " Upon this the dying man is placed, and pieces of gold and silver and coral, *together with some Ganges water* and a tulsi leaf, were placed in his mouth. The tulsi is a plant much worshipped by the Hindoos. All this is done *by way of purifying the man* and preparing him for death." Now, I do not say, as a matter of fact, that Plutarch's dreamer did take sea-water and "put it into his mouth" for purification; but I do say, that if the purifying influence of sea-water was supposed to be thus developed, then, Greek usage would say that such a man was a *baptized* man. And whether, in this passage or not, we should read, "*purify* thyself, going to the sea,'*there is nothing in classic usage to prevent $\beta\alpha\pi\tau i\zeta\omega$ meaning *to purify by the sprinkling or drinking sea-water*, any more than to mean *to intoxicate* by drinking wine. Palinurus was baptized into sleep by sprinkling his temples with Lethean dew.—*Æneid*, v, 855.

If this dreamer, having gone to the sea, had neither

plunged, nor dipped, nor sprinkled, nor drank its waters, nor, as Dr. Fuller suggests, "laid down upon the shore and let its billows roll over him," but had merely gone through the "mud-smearing" process of lustration, and was, thus, supposed to be free from defilement; Greek usage would give fullest sanction to his being called a *baptized* man.

If classic Greek pronounces that man who is *in a condition* of drunkenness to be a baptized man—or, *in a condition* of indebtedness, to be a baptized man—or, *in a condition* of intellectual imbecility, to be a baptized man—or, *in a condition* of obloquy, to be a baptized man—or, *in a condition* of grief, anger, or vehement desire, to be a baptized man—or *in a condition* of profound stupor, to be a baptized man—or, *in a condition* of suffering from misfortune, or from oppressive taxes, to be a baptized man—or, *in a condition* of mental perplexity, to be a baptized man—or, *in a condition* of disease, and under the influence of magical arts, to be a baptized man,—then, I say (although no instance may be found, either in the case before us, or in any other case "through all Greek literature," where a man restored by any competent influence to religious purity is said to be a baptized man, still), any one who chooses thus to apply the term (and to associate it with sprinkling as the act), will have, in so doing, the unanimous support of every classic Greek writer through a thousand years.

Take, for example, the following: "Οἱ ἐν Αἰγύπτῳ ἱερεις ἑαυτους περιρραινουσιν οὐ παντι ὑδατι, ἀλλ᾽ ἐκεινῳ ἐξ οὐ πεπιστευκασιν ὅτι ἀρα καὶ Ἶβις πεπωκεν."* "The priests in Egypt besprinkle themselves, not with any water, but with that of which they believe that Isis drank."—*Plutarch de Isid. et Osir.*, cap. 89. The term baptism is not applied to this transaction; but I affirm, that *a state of complete purification* induced by the sprinkling of Ibis water, is as legitimate and true a baptism, interpreted by classic Greek, as would be *a state*

---

* I follow Matthæi; *Exp. Bapt.*, p. 338. I have not found this precise language.

of complete covering of their bodies by their being sunk to the bottom of the Nile. The baptisms differ in their nature; but as to their legitimacy, under the severest interpretation, the former is as complete as the latter.

Sprinkling demands, not as of grace, but as of absolute right, the acknowledgment of its power to baptize.

A CLASS OF PERSONS—THOROUGHLY IMBUED.

Οὕτω καὶ ἡμεῖς παραβαπτίσται. So, also, we are Parabaptists (spuriously mersed). ARRIAN, ii, 9.

As this passage has some special interest and importance, I will give it more fully:

Τὸ πάθος τοῦ βεβαμμένου καὶ ἡρημένου τότε καὶ ἔστι τῳ ὄντι καὶ καλεῖται Ἰουδαῖος. οὕτω καὶ ἡμεῖς παραβαπτίσται, λόγῳ μὲν Ἰουδαῖοι, ἔργῳ δ'ἄλλοτι, ἀσυμπαθεῖς πρὸς τόν λόγον. μακρὰν ἀπὸ τοῦ χρῆσθαι τούτοις ἃ λέγομεν ἐφ' ὅις ὡς εἰδότες ἀυτα ἐπαιρόμεθα.

The caption to the chapter from which this extract is made is as follows:

"When we are unable to fulfil what the character of a man promises, we assume that of a philosopher." His theme is Character—True Manhood—False Assumption.

The translation and remarks of Prof. Stuart have been already given in connection with that part of the passage which relates to βάπτω. For convenience, I repeat what relates to the point before us: "Where we see any one acting with both parties, we are wont to say: He is no Jew, but plays the hypocrite. But when he takes on him the state and feelings of one who is washed or baptized, and has attached himself to the sect, then he is in truth and is called a Jew. But we are παραβαπτίσται, transgressors as to our baptism, or falsely baptized, if we are like a Jew in pretence and something else in reality."

Another translation: "But when he assumes the sentiments of one who hath been baptized and circumcised, then he both really is, and is called a Jew.' Thus we, falsifying our profession, are Jews in name, but in reality are something else. Our sentiments are inconsistent with our discourse; far from practising what we teach, and we pride ourselves in the knowledge of. Thus, while we are unable to fulfil what the character of a man promises, we assume, besides, so vast a weight as that of a philosopher. As if a person, incapable of lifting ten pounds, should endeavor to heave the same stone with Ajax."—*Elizabeth Carter. London*, 1758. "Parabaptistæ sumus, et non legitimé tincti."—*Politiani, Lugduni*, 1600. When speaking, heretofore, of "τὸ πάθυς τοῦ βεβαμμένου," I remarked that I had not found any writer who brought the secondary meaning of βάπτω to bear upon the passage. Since then, I am happy to say, I have met with one who does. In *Epicteti, &c., London*, 1670, *H. Wolfe*, we have this translation : "Cum autem affectum *illâ disciplinâ imbuti* sectamque professi adhibuerit, tum revera Judaius et est et nominatur."

All idea of any reference to Christian baptism, or Jewish baptism, or to the rite of circumcision, must, I think, be excluded, as incongruous, from the passage. I would read it thus: "When we see any one, now on one side, now on the other, we are used to say, he is not a Jew but a pretender. But when he adopts the sympathies of one imbued and convinced, then he is both in reality and is called a Jew. So, also, we are Parabaptists—mis-mersed—Jews in word, but something else in fact, un-sympathizing in heart with the utterances of our lips." (See Rom. 2 : 28, 29.)

1. The scope of a passage must largely control the interpretation of its parts. The passage has an exclusive regard to man's nature, and to genuine and spurious character. There is a severe exposure of the inconsistency exhibited between profession and practice. It is impossible, under these circumstances, that the elements of a profession should be made the chosen exponents of character. But this is done if a ritual baptism and a ritual circumcision are spoken of. Outward rites do not confer inward character. To adopt the character or sympathies of one ritually baptized, &c., is to adopt a nullity.

2. The phrase βεβαμμένου καὶ ἡρημένου may be interpreted in completest harmony with the scope of the passage. This has been, already, shown, and need not be repeated. To adopt "the sympathies of one imbued and convinced," is to adopt a real, and not a merely ritual character.

3. Παραβαπτισταὶ is capable of a like harmonious interpretation. Nothing is more unquestionable than that profound influence belongs to βαπτίζω, and is inseparable from all its forms. The form before us is met with, now, for the first time. It may occur, elsewhere, in classical writings; but, if so, I am not aware of it. In this infrequent occurrence, as well as in construction, it resembles ὅτι βάπται. The resemblance does not stop here. They both refer to classes of persons marked by decided character; βάπτης, through dyeing; βαπτίστης, through mersion. The former drops the element of color; the latter drops the form of intusposition. Parabaptist is very clearly expounded as one whose character is traceable no deeper than the utterances of the lip; while a Baptist, by implication, is one whose utterances are from the heart, or, as Antoninus says, "imbued with honesty *to the bottom*." A ritual water dipping is utterly out of place. Ὁ βάπτης was one tinctured with all that is vile; ὁ βαπτίστης is one thoroughly penetrated with the elements of character, honestly exhibited, whether good or bad.

We have, thus, in the progress of our classical inquiries, been brought face to face with *the Jew*, interpreters think with *Jewish baptism*.

The outer confine of the limits assigned to ourselves has been reached.

Sacred Baptism can have no possible influence over Classic Baptism; whatever influence the latter may have over the former. Every rational consideration demands that Classic Baptism should be discussed first in order, and be determined without any disturbing influence.

In an attempt to do this, the materials within my reach have, now, become exhausted. And here we rest.

GENERAL RESULTS.

In concluding this inquiry, and in gathering up results connected with it, it may be remarked:

1. Certain old and long-cherished errors have been abandoned.

(1.) That, *βάπτω and βαπτίζω are absolute equivalents*, is an error maintained through two centuries of controversy, but, at length, abandoned by all.

(2.) That, *βάπτω does not mean to dye*, is an error, now, left without a defender. It is instructive to remember that all cases of *dyeing* were once, controversially, treated as cases of *figure*, in which *dipping* was always present in fact or in imagination.

(3.) That, *βαπτίζω means to dip repeatedly*, is an error thoroughly exploded. Lexicons still give this meaning; but lexicographers must take a great deal on trust, or on a necessarily imperfect examination. Thoroughly developed usage is supreme.

2. Other errors remain to be corrected.

(1.) That, *βάπτω, primary, is sternly adherent to the modality of dipping, through all its usage*, is an error to be corrected. Why not accept to moisten, to wet, to wash, without modality, as well as to dye? These are the natural outgrowths of *dip*, as are to color, to stain, to gild, to glaze, to temper, to tincture, the legitimate language offspring of *dye*.

(2.) That, *βαπτίζω is but a reappearance of βάπτω "in a little longer coat,"* is an error. That any language should give birth to a word which was but a bald repetition of one already in existence, is a marvel which may be believed when proved. Besides, when the relationship between these words was settled, it was affirmed that βάπτω had but one, and that a modal, meaning; this is, now, abandoned, and an additional meaning, without modality, is admitted; surely, in view of so great a change, the relationship between these words calls for a review.

(3.) That, βαπτίζω *expresses a definite act of any kind*, is an error needing correction. The current of controversy has set toward the proof or disproof of certain acts,—*to dip, to plunge*, on the one side; *to sprinkle, to pour*, on the other. The controversy has proved to be both unsatisfactory and interminable. It would, still, continue to be so, if prolonged through three thousand years instead of three hundred. The idea that any form of act is justly involved in the controversy, is but a phantom of the imagination. There is no form of act inherent in βαπτίζω. It claims the agency of a band of servitors whose name is legion.

(4.) That, *any word expressive of condition can be self-limited, as to the form of the act effecting such condition*, is an error.

Βάπτω, secondary, demands for its object a dyed condition. It has no form of act of its own. It asks for no specific act. It accepts and cordially affiliates with dip, or drop, or press, or smear, or sprinkle, or pour, &c., &c.

Βαπτίζω demands for its object CONDITION: (1.) A change in its present condition, introducing it into a condition of *complete intusposition*. This word, like βάπτω (second), has no form of act of its own; it asks for none; it accepts indifferently of any, of all, competent to meet its demand. (2.) It demands a *complete change of condition*, physical, intellectual, moral, or ceremonial, *without intusposition*. And to meet this demand it accepts any agency, physical or spiritual, competent to the task. Hot iron made to pass *into a cold condition;* intoxicating wine made to pass *into an unintoxicating condition;* a defiled man made to pass *into a purified condition;* a sober man made to pass *into a drunken condition;* a wakeful man made to pass *into a dceply somnolent condition;* are all exemplifications of *baptism without intusposition* in fact, and without any evidence of intusposition by figure. The varied acts and agencies inducing these baptisms show that there is no limitation in these directions.

(5.) That, βαπτίζω *has any responsibility for the* FORM *of the act effecting primary baptism, or for the* MANNER *of applying the agency securing secondary baptism,* is an error. Dr. Carson says, " to dye (βάπτειν) by sprinkling is as legitimate as to dye by dipping." Because coloring matter, applied by sprinkling, effects a dyed condition, does βάπτω, therefore, mean to sprinkle, or has it anything to do with the mode of applying the color? To merse—βαπτίζειν—*to place in a condition of intusposition by sprinkling,* is as legitimate as to do so by sinking; but does βαπτίζω, therefore, mean to sprinkle, or has it any responsibility for the act by which the intusposition was effected? To merse—βαπτίζειν—*to bring into a new and completely changed condition, by sprinkling* (as, for example, bringing an impure man into a state of complete purity by sprinkling Ibis water), is as legitimate as any other conceivable method; but shall we tear asunder βαπτίζω and its condition, to ally it with the mode of applying the water, with which it has nothing to do? It is enough for any word to perform one duty well. When βαπτίζω has, with all fidelity, secured appropriate condition for its object, do not impose upon it the alien and impracticable duty of performing, also, the act by which that condition is effected.

3. USAGE, the accepted arbiter, has spoken freely, and, I think, has been reported faithfully, as teaching—

(1.) *Βάπτω,* TINGO, and DIP, are words, which, in their respective languages, represent, for the most part, the same identical ideas.

(2.) *Βαπτίζω,* MERGO, and MERSE, are words, which, in their respective languages, represent, for the most part, the same identical ideas.

(3.) These two classes of words differ from each other essentially. They are not interchanged, nor interchangeable ordinarily, much less identical.

(4.) *Βάπτω* and *Βαπτίζω* exhibit a perfect parallelism in their development.

1. *Βάπτω*; To DIP.
1. *Βαπτίζω*; To MERSE.

2. *Βάπτω*; To dip into any *coloring* liquid *for the sake of the effect;* To DYE.
2. *Βαπτίζω*; To merse into any liquid *for the sake of its influence;* To DROWN.

3. *Βάπτω*; To affect by the peculiar influence of coloring matter (*without the act of dipping*); e. g., *to sprinkle* blood; *to squeeze* a berry; *to bruise* by blows.
3. *Βαπτίζω*; To affect by any controlling influence (*without the condition of mersion*); e. g., *to sprinkle* poppy-juice; *to pour* water on hot iron; *to drink* intoxicating liquor.

The perfect parallelism of development thus exhibited, in these two words, goes far to show that the true interpretation of each has been secured.

(5.) Baptism is a myriad-sided word, adjusting itself to the most diverse cases.

Agamemnon was baptized; Bacchus was baptized; Cupid was baptized; Cleinias was baptized; Alexander was baptized; Panthia was baptized; Otho was baptized; Charicles was baptized; and a host of others were baptized, each differing from the other in the nature or the mode of their baptism, or both.

A blind man could more readily select any demanded color from the spectrum, or a child could more readily thread the Cretan labyrinth, than could "the seven wise men of Greece" declare the nature, or mode, of any given baptism by the naked help of βαπτίζω.

(6.) The master-key to the interpretation of βαπτίζω is CONDITION,—condition characterized by COMPLETENESS, with or without physical envelopment.

CONCLUSION.

Such are the results reached in an attempt to determine, from usage, the meaning of βαπτίζω, and the nature of Classic Baptism. No claim is made for absolute truth. Apologetic material is not lacking to extenuate the want of greater perfectness; but I care not to offer it. In the lack of service on the part of those more competent, I have done what I could. The method and the issue are cheerfully and deferentially submitted to all competent judges. Approval of every conception and definition I do not look for; a clear verdict of substantial truth, I do venture to expect. If in this expectation I shall not be disappointed, it is my purpose to pursue the inquiry "on this line" in relation to Jewish and Christian baptisms. But "one thing at a time" is a good rule. Under it, let all interested seek to give an answer, that shall be final, to the question, WHAT IS CLASSIC BAPTISM?

Over against the Baptist answers:

1. *Baptizing is dipping and dipping is baptizing.*
BAPTIST CONFESSION OF FAITH.

2. *To dip and nothing but dip through all Greek literature.*
ALEXANDER CARSON, LL.D., *Baptist Board of Publication.*

3. *To immerse, immerge, submerge, to dip, to plunge, to imbathe, to whelm.* T. J. CONANT, D.D., *Baptist Bible Union.*

I would place this answer:

WHATEVER IS CAPABLE OF THOROUGHLY CHANGING THE CHARACTER, STATE, OR CONDITION OF ANY OBJECT, IS CAPABLE OF BAPTIZING THAT OBJECT; AND BY SUCH CHANGE OF CHARACTER, STATE, OR CONDITION DOES, IN FACT, BAPTIZE IT.